THE IMPOTENT GIANT

Also by H. John Lyke
Walking on Air Without Stumbling
(with Jeanne Peterson)

THE IMPOTENT GIANT

How to Reclaim the Moral High Ground of America's Politics

H. John Lyke, PhD

iUniverse, Inc.
New York   Bloomington

THE IMPOTENT GIANT

How to Reclaim the Moral High Ground of America's Politics

iUniverse books may be ordered through booksellers or by contacting:

iUniverse
1663 Liberty Drive
Bloomington, IN 47403
www.iuniverse.com
1-800-Authors (1-800-288-4677)

ISBN: 978-0-595-46388-6 (pbk)
ISBN: 978-0-595-70664-8 (cloth)
ISBN: 978-0-595-90681-9 (ebk)

Printed in the United States of America

iUniverse rev. date: 10/21/2008

Excerpt from "Money Won't Buy You Happiness" reprinted with permission of Forbes.com, © 2007 Forbes.com

DEDICATION

This book is dedicated to all those Americans who want to return America to its former greatness, and in so doing, regain our high moral and political regard among nations.

CONTENTS

ACKNOWLEDGMENTS...ix

FOREWORD xi

PREFACE xiii

INTRODUCTION xxi

THE BIRTH OF A NATION...1

GIANTS, LILLIPUTIANS, AND YOU 7

A GOVERNMENT OF GLUTTONY....................................21

GEORGE W. BUSH: THE FORTY-THIRD PRESIDENT
    OF THE UNITED STATES 31

9/11: THE DATE GEORGE W. BUSH DEFINED HIS
    PRESIDENCY 43

BETTER LEADER, BETTER FUTURE 55

BECOMING A BETTER AMERICAN...................................75

THE FLAG AND THE PRESIDENCY: DIMINISHED
    ICONS..85

THE NEED TO COME TOGETHER AS A NATION........93

THE PROBLEM WITH EXTREMISM 103

PUBLIC OPINION AND THE PRESIDENCY...................121

THE BEST THINGS IN LIFE ARE FREE 139

INTEGRITY 151

WHAT IF ABE LINCOLN WERE ELECTED
    PRESIDENT IN THE YEAR 2000?................................167

WHAT DO WE AS A NATION VALUE? 179

HOW TO CURE OUR GIANT'S IMPOTENCE 199

WHERE DO WE GO FROM HERE? 215

INDEX 239

ACKNOWLEDGMENTS

I would indeed be remiss if I didn't express my deep appreciation for the love, care, and help my dear friend, Dr. Richard R. Waite, has given me since I moved to Colorado in 1967. I would never have written this book without his encouragement and belief in me.

It is safe to say that without Dick's understanding and acumen, I would not be where I am today, and—to quote Harry Stack Sullivan, noted psychiatrist of the twentieth century—I would have ended up an "inferior caricature of what I could have become."

Dick helped me unlock the mysteries of my mind, and in doing so, helped me appreciate who I am and what I believe is important in my life. That understanding provided me with the impetus to embark on and complete the momentous undertaking of writing this book.

Special thanks goes to my niece, Kim Augspurger, who provided the original artwork for the cover illustration.

In my book, I occasionally compare my personal ship of state with that of our nation. Well, if I was the captain of my ship of state, then for the purpose of this book, my editor, Jim Syring, was my navigator. His skills were excellent; he kept me on course throughout my voyage. Early on in our relationship, after I had sent him the lion's share of my manuscript, he observed that "a third of the book is filled with other people's quotes; I'm interested in hearing about your observations, not what others have to say."

I appreciated his implied message that my ideas were important, and that the only way to claim true ownership of my book would be to fill it with original thought.

The other thing I so appreciate is Jim's insistence that *The Impotent Giant* be a book I'd be proud to have written. He did that by believing in me and having the quiet confidence that I had the wherewithal to write a good book.

I so appreciate that he did not intercede and rescue me when the political waters got rough. By not interjecting his prose and thoughts into the writing, he made sure this was indeed my book.

The iUniverse team that I had the pleasure of working with not only lived up to what I would expect from my publisher but delivered much more. My thanks to Molly O'Bryan, Brittany Brauer, Michael Fiedler, Suzanne Lif, Jason Straw, Jenn Taylor and Jennifer Gilbert, who deserves special mention for her excellent work in the editing process.

The person most helpful and essential in completing this book is my friend Randy Pozniak. His contribution was invaluable. Randy provided me with some of the political information that forms the book's skeleton. From there, I was able to add meat to the bones by providing the psychological knowledge necessary to make a meaningful whole.

Whatever I asked Randy to do in the way of gathering information to help support a given thesis for the book, he did so willingly and forthrightly.

As I wrote this book, he offered both friendship and inspiration. In many ways, the book is as much his as mine.

FOREWORD

I am your average American. I work hard, I love my country, I pay my taxes … and most of the time, I feel ignored by the powers that run this country.

My friend H. John Lyke hears my concerns for this country and articulates them in *The Impotent Giant*. He seamlessly weaves his patriotic passions, his knowledge of history, his career in academia, his practice in psychotherapy, his intellectual curiosity, and his personal political journey into a study of what is wrong with this country's giant and what can be done to set our ship of state on the correct course to safely navigate the political waters of the twenty-first century.

This is a book for you and me—the concerned citizens of our great land who are alarmed about who and what the giant has become. Our giant has become obese, and John's book shows us how to improve its health with a diet of common sense and a regimen of patriotic exercise.

The ideas that John explores in this book and the recommendations he makes regarding how our leaders should behave will hopefully give us back the America that we have loved in the past—and that we know the country can and should be in the future.

Randy Pozniak

PREFACE

I'm a diplomate in clinical psychology (ABPP), which was awarded by the American Board of Professional Psychology. I received my PhD in psychology from Michigan State University and am a retired emeritus psychology professor. I spent over twenty-five years teaching at Metropolitan State College in Denver, Colorado. Throughout my employment there, I maintained a private practice as well. Part of that time, I served as a psychology consultant for the Tennyson Center for Children at the Colorado Christian Home, which is a residential treatment center.

Not long ago, in a quest to define the attributes that make a great leader, I read books on George Washington, Abraham Lincoln, and Benjamin Franklin. Just reading about their lives and their accomplishments made me feel proud to be an American. I was curious about why modern-day America failed to stir such a strong sense of pride within me. I decided to use my professional background in psychology to find out why I felt that way and to investigate what was right and what was wrong with our country and its leaders.

This book is the result of that arduous journey into the soul of America.

Sobering Realizations

When I began to look into all the little nooks and crannies of our great country, I didn't like what I saw. In fact, I became so distressed that I felt I just couldn't sit on my hands and do nothing. I felt compelled to write a book, and that's exactly what I did. That's how *The Impotent Giant* was born.

After we were attacked on 9/11, were we asked to sacrifice anything in order to pay back our enemies? No, we were told to go shopping, so we did. While a few young men and women made great sacrifices—including, in some cases, their lives—most of us were at the mall. Too many of us are uninterested in politics and in making America work. An improved nation can only come through a common effort, brought about by our united beliefs and actions.

I believe we need to treat each other with more civility—politicians and nonpoliticians alike. We need to restore to its former greatness the passion for and love of country that existed during the Revolutionary and Civil wars, as well as what existed during the Second World War. We need to recapture the common patriotic goals that were clearly present then, but which seem absent now. If this is not done, the freedoms that our forefathers struggled to create and protect will dwindle to nothing. Our country as we once knew it will no longer exist, replaced with anarchy, civil disorder, and discontent. Terrorism will have indeed won the war of ideas.

After reading about Washington and Lincoln, I compared them to the politicians of the twenty-first century. Unfortunately, I discovered that very few true statesmen work in politics today, unlike in the early days of our country.

Today, politicians and statesmen are like oil and water. A politician is only concerned with the present, while a statesman is concerned with not only the present generation's needs and well-being, but that of future generations as well. Currently, not all politicians are statesmen—in fact, fewer and fewer modern-day politicians can call themselves statesmen.

However, in rare instances, the best qualities of politics and statesmanship can reside in the same person. Washington was intricately involved with not only writing the Constitution, but also winning the Revolutionary War, so that future generations could live a life free of British domination. He and his fellow countrymen felt strongly enough that they were willing to die in order to ensure freedom. Lincoln succeeded in preserving the Union by winning the Civil War and was the prime mover in freeing the slaves so that future generations, regardless of race, color, or creed, could live in greater peace and tranquility.

Personal and Political Introspection

When I was younger, I had a very limited understanding of politics. I grew up aligning myself with the Republican Party. My whole family was conservative Republicans.

It was not until some years into adulthood that I decided being a Republican, let alone a conservative one, didn't fit me. As a result of psychotherapy, I eventually discovered that what I thought I had believed in no longer fit my new political persona. This change of heart came when, as a result of psychotherapy, I began to realize that I've lived a very fortunate and blessed life. This became even more clear when I compared my own good fortunes with those who were less fortunate than me.

That insight was only achieved after I had made enough progress in my own life to stop and take a look around. Before then, I was too self-absorbed and concerned with my own sense of worth and personal satisfaction to be worried about how others might be feeling.

This preoccupation with self is not unusual. We often spend a great deal of time contemplating our own dissatisfactions and failings. But Americans, just like any human beings on this earth, have more than themselves to worry about. Entire future generations depend on the decisions we make now—not just for ourselves, but for our country at large.

Psychotherapy allowed me to look at myself more realistically, and as a result, I saw the political landscape differently. I realized I had a greater duty to my country than I had felt before.

One of the very real by-products of therapy was a sense of empowerment. By that I mean I learned how to be a good caretaker of my life and a thoughtful steward of my country.

Empowerment is not an end goal in itself, but a means to an end. If feeling empowered were my goal, I would continually do things only for me. I would become self-absorbed. Only accomplishments pertaining to me would impress me; I would never look beyond myself for personal satisfaction. I believe this is the way our politicians are behaving. Their preoccupation with keeping themselves in office short-circuits any national concerns.

One of the basic theses of this book is that most politicians, including presidents, maintain their sense of power and influence by being selective in who they serve. For example, when they go out onto the campaign trail, their foremost thought is, *What must I do to get elected?* They're not necessarily going to appeal directly to the poor, the disadvantaged, or anybody else who they think cannot or will not support them, especially through financial contributions. Unlike dictatorships, the two-party system causes individual candidates to spend an inordinate amount of time trying to shore up their political base. Consequently, the portion of the public that exists outside of that base is ignored or disregarded. The needs of those who are less wealthy—and thus unable to financially contribute to a candidate's campaign—are ultimately overlooked. Year after year, election cycle after election cycle, the political needs and concerns of the poor remain unaddressed.

Unlike most modern presidents, Washington and Lincoln governed America more from the middle than the extremes. They wanted to unite the country, not divide it.

Politicians should serve all Americans, not just a select minority. If today's politicians and president were more reflective and introspective, they would ask themselves, "Is this a decision that will not only benefit me and my constituency, but also *all* Americans?" If our government operated under that mind-set, we as a nation would be more united and less divided than we are today.

Terrorism is anathema to this nation and is very divisive. Today, there are blue states and red states, conservative Republicans and liberal Democrats, and never the twain shall meet. Welcome to the Divided States of America. With the advent of terrorism, a whole new mind-set is required of our senators and representatives, to say nothing of our president. In order to combat terrorism, we need to adequately respond to national interests and concerns, and in that way build a sense of community with *all* Americans, not just with the political base who helped get our politicians elected in the first place. As a matter of fact, in order to hold terrorism to a minimum, we as a nation need to build a sense of unity not only with people in this country, but with all the nations of the world.

It's important to remain grounded when you're a politician. One of the reasons I chose to write *Giant* was that I felt that our political system does something to U.S. politicians, from the president on down, after they're elected. There are certainly exceptions, but generally speaking, our politicians lose their sense of who they are and the reason they hold that high office in the first place. They seem to become obsessed with the power and the money that comes with the job.

Introspection and reflection is a lifelong duty to self. If politicians would do what Socrates recommends, which is to reflect on their lives and engage in periodic self-examination, they could stay aware of why they chose to become politicians in the first place. Ideally, politicians run for office in order to represent all Americans—advocating for those who lack the resources to help themselves, fighting to protect the rights of citizens and uphold the Constitution, and making our country a better place. But somehow, those ideals dissipate once a politician is safely in power. At that point, he or she focuses on keeping that power, rather than using it to help others.

Political deceit will not cut it with the American people. In therapy, I learned that a lot of people really are only concerned about themselves and what they can get out of the system. A fair amount of such people end up in politics.

This kind of thinking will have to stop if we're going to survive as a nation.

Abraham Lincoln was a real American. He had an ability to talk to everyone—rich, poor, black, or white. He didn't care how anyone appeared. Nor did he care what they did or did not do for him. What remained central to his thinking was whether any given decision was right for all Americans, regardless of race, color, or creed. He spoke of love and caring for others. He was responsive to all peoples' needs. That is why he is considered by many as our greatest president. Why is there no politician of Lincoln's caliber today? Throughout the book, I will be using Lincoln and his administration as the gold standard for leadership.

Shrinking American Integrity

"All the world's a stage, and all the men and women merely players."
—William Shakespeare

As Shakespeare wrote, I too believe the whole world's a stage, and we are the actors. We also go through predictable stages.

I realize that at my age, my physical senses are weakening. But in the grand scheme of things, I steadfastly try to maintain, nourish, and preserve my sense of integrity. After all, what else will be fully functioning and intact at the end of life, if not one's integrity?

Politicians aren't the only ones shrinking their civic duty. Besides troops serving in Iraq, how many other Americans are willing to risk dying or being wounded to defend America?

If brave men and women in uniform are going to risk life and limb, the argument for that war should be clearly supported—not only by the president, but also Congress, as well as most of the American public. There is nothing more divisive than an unjustified war.

"The Greatest Generation"

Author and journalist Tom Brokaw wrote about "the greatest generation." His premise was that through self-sacrifice and courage, an entire generation of WWII vintage had distinguished itself as the greatest generation. While I believe that the generation he refers to was an exceptional one, I believe that the true greatest generation is yet to come. It will be the generation whose courage is measured by their level of compassion, tolerance, and empathy toward all peoples. It will be the generation that escapes the bounds of narcissism and sincerely strives for justice and liberty for all. It will be the generation that assumes its dutiful role as responsible stewards of the planet. It will be the generation that manages to achieve peace on earth. When the sum total of these conditions is met, we can declare them the greatest generation.

I am not naive to the point that I believe these conditions can be achieved anytime soon. I do feel strongly, however, that we need to begin our pursuit. We have come too far as a civilization to deny ourselves the chance of fulfilling these universal ideals. So let's start here. Our country is in need of a kick in the pants. Our country needs its people to make it great, to wrest back control of the government and insist that they represent our values and interests. Let's start here and demand that our government lead us down the path that will one day produce a future greatest generation.

INTRODUCTION

I've chosen *The Impotent Giant* as the title of this book to reflect the way our government (hence, our nation) appears to all who view it. This includes not only how the world at large sees us, but how we ourselves view our country. The reasons for our country's impotence will be discussed, and through the discussion, we will reacquaint ourselves with what it means to be an American.

I want it to be abundantly clear this book has nothing to do with being a Republican or a Democrat. However, it has everything to do with being an American. Don't worry—there's enough blame to go around, regardless of what party I'm discussing. As I said earlier, this insidious destruction of what has made this beloved country so great has occurred gradually, over many, many years. I want to attack the issues, not a specific party.

As you read this book, try to read it without thinking about whether it agrees with your personal political orientation, no matter what that is. That is particularly true if you embrace one of the extremes of the political spectrum. Otherwise, you may find yourself unwilling to read the parts of this book that run counter to your political beliefs. In a subsequent chapter, the reason for your thinking that way will be explained.

My objective is not to bash President Bush or Congress, but rather, to show how broken our system of government is. Although at times, it may seem that a little bashing is taking place, this criticism is designed to make a point or illustrate something. In order to criticize the system itself, I have to judge the officeholders' actions or inactions.

The president is discussed to a much greater degree than Congress because his actions or inactions are the most grievous and noteworthy.

At the end of this century, will the United States still be a world leader—or will we, like so many stumbling mammoth nations, become a fallen empire? Put another way, will the dreams and promises of Americans for their country become unattainable?

I feel it is vitally important for us, as a nation, to put aside our personal grievances and begin to work for the common good of all Americans. If we don't begin to do that, our great republic will not survive the challenges that lie ahead in the twenty-first century.

Crumbling Principles

The United States has forsaken what our Founding Fathers envisioned for us. The personality deficiencies of Richard Nixon, Bill Clinton, and George W. Bush made it impossible for them to execute faithfully the awesome responsibilities of the presidency. They deepened the divisions in America to such an extent that many of us have lost sight of the nation's basic values, rights, ideals, and aspirations.

In order to understand how America has gone astray, especially since 9/11, I invite you to examine its original values and principles as enunciated by Abraham Lincoln, considered by many as the greatest president of all time—and, in so doing, discover how those values can serve as a guide to get things back on track.

The book articulates the psychological factors that contribute to the failings of presidents. The book compares Lincoln's personal integrity with Nixon's clumsy, paranoid machinations and Clinton's abuse of the presidency with equivocal confessions of immorality. It contrasts Lincoln's steadfast resolve to win the Civil War with George W. Bush's bungled management of his ill-conceived invasion of Iraq.

Focusing on the disastrous course this nation has taken for the past thirty-five years, this book articulates what needs to be done to repair our ship of state—caulking the seams, mending the sails, and setting a new course toward leadership and respect in the world of nations.

Today, this country is so polarized that less than 35 percent of the American public approve of the way our president or Congress are handling the affairs of state.

To give you some idea of how fragmented this country is, if John Kerry had won the state of Ohio, he, rather than George W. Bush, would have been elected president. In terms of the popular vote, Bush's margin of victory was the smallest of any sitting president since Harry S. Truman in 1948.

After reading a number of books and papers on the subject of our government, its foreign policies, and the officials we have elected to run our country, I became aware that I was disenchanted with where our government has been heading ever since the early twentieth century. What I discovered was profoundly disturbing to me and needs to be rectified immediately if there's any chance that our great republic will indeed survive and be restored to its former status in the family of nations.

It is not a secret of history that great empires have risen to a position of supremacy and subsequently fallen to a level of irrelevance or disappeared entirely. With that thought in mind, I am prompted to recognize some of the traits our nation shares with empires of old, and to explore the policies, politics, and circumstances that have cued my awareness.

We must discard our present attitudes toward other nations. Our country must become an engaged partner in global concerns, rather than a narcissistic provocateur. Our current emphasis on military power and the overt willingness to employ it unilaterally and preemptively has undermined our nation's credibility as an altruistic society. We appear interested only in promoting our arrogant self-interests.

On the national front, it is imperative that we extinguish the preponderance of corruption that chokes our government and stifles the voice of mainstream Americans. We must, as a people, regain the idea that opportunity should be afforded all and ensure that those disenfranchised among us be raised to a level of self-reliance.

It is imperative that our current policies of unfettered, unrestrained, and unregulated capitalism be reined in to protect the backbone of our economic success: the middle class. Via lobbying leverage and political funding, large corporate and multinational conglomerates today enjoy a level of political influence not seen since the gilded age of the nineteenth century. When this kind of power runs afoul, politicians respond to the monied influences and not to the public at large. One consequence of such power is that jobs move overseas, which results in a loss of tax dollars necessary to run the country. It is crucial that we return to the day when laws were developed by legislators not beholden to deep-pocket entities, but rather, to the constituents those legislators have pledged to serve.

The recent rise in political influence of the religious right also needs to be restrained.

We need to recognize and embrace the plurality of beliefs and ideas that represents the strength of our union, rather than reverting to narrow ideologically or theologically driven views that represent a small portion of the populace.

A Passionate Message

It should be obvious that the current course we have charted as a nation causes me great concern and consternation. I am neither a "blame America first" pundit nor a contrarian without proposals. My sense of patriotism and civic responsibility compels me to criticize things as they are and submit proposals to chart a new path.

I feel I need to offer a personal note at this point. At times, my tone may appear a bit strident. The reason is because I am very passionate about this subject. If I appear a bit vociferous, please keep in mind it's a reflection of my concern that this country is moving in the wrong direction—and rapidly. My job is to convince you, first, that that is indeed the case. And second, that with your help, perhaps we can persuade the captain (president) and crew (Congress) that our ship of state must come about, trim sails, and set a new course in order to reach a port that represents what this country can and should stand for.

I can't do it alone. People like you must sound the alarm.

I am particularly concerned with what's happened to our political system in general, especially the office of the president of the United States, since the year 2000, when President George W. Bush entered the White House. I am not by nature a critical and negative person. It is with great reluctance on my part that this book will be critical of George W. Bush.

When I view any politician critically, I am looking at the man and how he views himself and his country. After looking critically at our current president, I will discuss what troubles me and why. I single out George W. Bush because I am particularly distressed about how he is so vigorously destroying what has made us feel so proud to be an American. If something isn't done to rectify the situation, we will face strife worldwide and economic uncertainty here at home.

One of the reasons I've written this book is to share with you what I consider to be some of the minimal required characteristics of politicians. I further plan to show how, on average, our current Congress and president fall far short of the mark.

If our politicians and president don't begin to understand why they were put into the office they hold in the first place, how are they going to run the country properly?

Whether I am discussing the president or Congress, it's my basic contention that if they all had steadfastly followed their moral compasses, this country would not have fallen out of grace in the eyes of our own citizens and the rest of the world.

To facilitate the comparison of one nation with another, I have invented mythological giants to represent all the countries in the world. The giant of each nation is composed of each of that country's citizenry. The reason I've created these giant creatures is to illustrate that the same psychological principles that apply in developing a mentally healthy human being can apply to building a healthy nation as well.

I hope to explain how our giant is sick when compared to other giants of the world. Therefore, it is no longer able to think straight in carrying out the people's business. As the book title suggests, I further hope to explain how our nation appears impotent when viewed by other countries.

I am very proud to be an American and always have been. I cherish and steadfastly defend the right to voice dissent regarding the policies and actions that do not represent the interests of the people or the ideals of our national philosophy. Consistent with that thinking, as Edward R. Morrow once said, "We must not confuse dissent with disloyalty."

Pride, patriotism, and dissent are prime movers of our democracy. None can be compromised if our country is to keep moving forward. The danger, however, lies in confusing pride with arrogance, patriotism with hubris, and dissent with disloyalty—or even treason. As with anything else in life, balance is key.

Katrina and Other Failings

Of late, the performance of our representation has been catastrophic to the well-being of our nation, our democratic roots, and our principles. There isn't much conversation today about the things that are going well, because ... well, frankly, not much is. However, some of our government's activities can still hearten the spirit, such as governmental involvement in public health care and education. Unfortunately, today, the headlines are dominated by what's gone wrong in this country. Such recent blunders as the Iraq war, torture as policy, and the denial of global warming are all embarrassing examples.

What makes things even more embarrassing is what happened— or didn't happen—after the Katrina disaster. Our government overreacted in Iraq and underreacted on Katrina. Because of the slow reaction time that FEMA showed New Orleans after the hurricane, the responsibility for many roles the state and federal government would have usually played had to be taken over by the local officials, overwhelming them. They had to assume such responsibilities as the feeding, sheltering, and long-term care of people—responsibilities normally provided by another governmental agency.

Many Americans are embarrassed, just as a parent is sometimes embarrassed by a child's behavior. The long-term solution is not to ignore the offending conduct, but to address it in a timely manner and administer corrective action.

A Call to Action

Our current circumstances have indeed shaken my faith in our great system of government, but they also have infused my patriotic fervor with the fortitude to speak out and promote corrective action. I feel this is what the Founding Fathers intended and expected of the citizenry when it was recognized that national policy and public thought were in opposition.

In sharing some of my own life with you, I hope you will be able to appreciate better the human condition, and by doing so, realize how broken our system of government is—and join me in fixing it.

THE BIRTH OF A NATION

I realize the title of this book is a bit funky, but it was chosen to get your attention. In the spirit of this metaphor, I'd like to spend some time in this section examining the ways in which America has grown into that impotent giant ever since it gained its independence from England, on November 20, 1782. That was when Great Britain acknowledged the United States' sovereignty.

On September 3, 1783, a treaty of peace was signed at Versailles, in France. And America was free.

Our Constitution developed during our country's gestation period, which began on July 4, 1776, when the Declaration of Independence was signed and ended when the Continental Congress gave birth to our nation in 1783.

Instead of growing to the size of a normal nation, our baby country kept growing way past the point where its growth spurt should have ended; today, the United States of America acts and thinks like a very large giant.

The problem is that we never took the infant, then child, then adult, then an average size giant, and now a humongous giant, for its annual checkup.

A Giant Problem

As is true with the other nations of the world, to be a giant of average size is to be expected, since it represents the collective selves

1

of the people who live in the country in which the giant was born. Obviously, because of its large size, any nation is going to be a little clumsy and disorganized when moving about.

However, to be a very large giant is another thing entirely. In America's case, part of the reason for its size is its diet. Our giant continued to grow above and beyond what was expected. Over the years, it simply was fed too much pork—the term for federal funding, jobs, or other favors distributed by politicians to gain political advantage. The giant's poor diet and its resulting obesity has made it difficult for the country to do the people's business with any degree of alacrity, because it is lethargic and no longer able to engage in critical thinking. This obesity has been caused by pork-barrel spending; the people who feed it regularly—people like the president, the politicians, and the lobbyists—throw a lot of pork its way.

Our giant nation no longer cares about responding to the needs of all Americans. The poor, handicapped, disadvantaged, or disenfranchised simply don't feed the giant and for that reason are ignored.

If the giant could subsist on the monies the special interest groups provide political parties and lobbyists, that would be one thing, but it lives off everybody, rich and not so rich alike, since it's the taxes that we all pay the government that keeps the giant happy and very well fed! You see, any governmental spending, whether it's pork barrel spending, defense spending, or any other kind of spending, adds to our giant's girth and heftiness, because he devours whatever comes his way with great delight.

Since it costs tremendous sums to keep special-interest programs like the military-industrial complex and Homeland Security afloat, little money is left over to fund the nation's health care, educational system, and special programs for the poor.

What our nation has done is become an overweight monster who terrorizes other smaller and less powerful giants (nations) by telling them what we as a nation feel is best for them. We tell them that democracy and freedom are what all nations want or should want for their people. What arrogance! No wonder many people here at home are now embarrassed by our foreign policy and the scorn it breeds.

Thomas Friedman, in his May 10, 2006, *New York Times* column, said, "In 2002 and 2003 everyone was talking about the American 'Hyper power,' said Eric Frey, editor of the Austrian daily *Der Standard*. [Frey goes on to say], 'No one these days is talking about overwhelming American power, and that has even added to the anti-Americanism. Because before you had resentment and respect, and now you have resentment and scorn.'"[1]

A Culture of Arrogance

Because of our nation's past track record of once being the most productive country in the world—and in many cases, regardless of what parameter was used, the envy of other nations regarding goods produced—America began to believe that it could do no wrong. Since, in the past, it had been at the forefront of industry and inventions, and because most countries paled when compared to what our relatively young nation had accomplished, why shouldn't we think that? I believe one of the most insulting things we do is to tell other countries how to conduct their internal affairs, but our giant seems oblivious to its misdeeds.

What has also added insult to injury throughout our nation's history was that because of what we've done for other countries, we feel justified in forcefully promoting our brand of government and system of free markets; after all, Father knows best. Besides, look at all the great things we've done for other giants in the world; we helped save them from being defeated in two world wars.

Our president and Congress believe that because we are the mightiest nation in the world, we can do no wrong, regardless of how we treat other nations. The longer this continues, the longer those politicians we depend on to safeguard our future will keep us in a world of hurt as a nation; the pain will only multiply over time. If we continue to deny the reality of our situation by believing we're the only nation that has the answers to real-world problems, the day of reckoning will eventually be upon us.

A dramatic—and in this case, a giant—makeover is in order. I think we have to put our giant on some type of regimen, so that it

---

[1] Thomas L. Friedman, "The Post-Post Cold War," *New York Times*, May 10, 2006. Used with permission of the *New York Times*.

is able to look at itself more realistically in relationship to the rest of the world.

Obviously, we can't roll back history and see what our giant looked like when it was an infant. However, history tells us that when it was a baby, it looked like any other nation's newborn giant.

What went wrong? Why does our country look so different today when compared to the way it looked when it was a toddler? Since our republic was established, what factors have played a role in corroding, bending, and in some cases breaking some of the basic tenets that our Founding Fathers put into the Constitution, Declaration of Independence, and the Bill of Rights? We are no longer a melting pot; we are now separate camps that do battle with one another, and the physical size of the country adds to that divisiveness.

We want to look further than that. For we also want to look at how our broken system of government has affected all aspects of each of our lives—the way we look at ourselves, the way we view each other, and the way we look at other nations of the world, as well as how other countries perceive us.

A Modern Fable

Let your mind wander for a moment. Let it drift back to never-never land, where all things are possible, and everybody believes in the tooth fairy.

Now that you are in the Land of Make Believe, just imagine that at some point in the recent past, the president and Congress were concerned about our giant's well-being. In order to get some measure of our country's physical and mental health, our Congress, with the president's blessing, decided to give our giant a physical and psychiatric evaluation.

There is no way we could measure with any degree of accuracy the true nature of any of the indices under investigation, whether they be physical or mental, because of the Tremendous, with a capital T, size, or mere Bulk, with a capital B, of the patient. The giant's magnitude would skew all of the findings.

For example, we couldn't get an accurate reading of any of the giant's physical measurements, like its height. The reason for that was because the giant was so tall that even an astronaut was unwilling to climb up to the top of its head, for fear he would run out of oxygen before he got the task completed.

You can certainly understand it would be virtually impossible to give our patient a mental-status exam. The psychiatrist would have no way of relating to or talking to the giant. She would not know whether the patient understood her. The giant might become violent because it's so primitive and stupid by its very nature. Such measurement simply wouldn't be worth the gamble.

So … as you can see, making a guesstimate was the only way to go. Of course, that too was understandable, because sometimes that was how our government had to operate when they had to attach a specific figure to some of the projects included in the Department of Defense budget. The cost of some of these supposedly must-have items had gotten so mammoth that sometimes we could only guesstimate at the budget for some things. Well, when you compound the problem a thousandfold, how would anyone expect to get an accurate reading of a greatly oversized giant? Nobody has enough fingers and toes to get that one right!

As you might imagine, the price tag to do all that went into the trillions of dollars.

When our giant had its first and only physical since its birth, it had to be weighed. Well, as you might imagine, because of its size, a normal scale would be crushed if the giant just put one foot on it. So America, like it has done so many times before in its history when a problem occurred, fixed it.

If we were able to measure America's weight, what we would come to realize is that America is bloated with corruption.

What we needed to do is invent a special scale that would accommodate our giant's needs. Because it was absolutely impossible to measure the full weight of the giant all at once, it had to be done on a piecemeal basis—an arm here, and a leg there, that kind of a procedure. Well, you can just imagine how difficult that in itself would be to do, but we must. A clear measurement of America's problems will help us better understand how to get back on track.

GIANTS, LILLIPUTIANS, AND YOU

Our nation and the other national giants of the world represent each country's government, made up of the politicians' collective selves. The more divorced our government becomes from its citizenry, the people that the politician is there to serve, the larger and more obstreperous our giant becomes.

Because all national giants of the world represent each country's governmental officials, every living person in that nation is viewed by their giant as being like the Lilliputians in *Gulliver's Travels*. That being the case, it behooves you to understand what your giant, or your nation, really thinks of you.

The giant concept is based on the fable *Gulliver's Travels*, published in 1726 and still in print today. Through satire and ridicule, the author of *Gulliver's Travels* criticizes civilization's faults. Lemuel Gulliver, a ship's surgeon, tells the story of his shipwreck on the island of Lilliput. Here, the Lilliputian people are six inches rather than six feet tall; therefore, to them, Gulliver appears as a giant. Through the book, Swift traces Gulliver's travels throughout the world in an attempt to mock the English political and religious debates and thinking of the time.

Our government should represent our collective souls, or our individual spirits or beliefs. Therefore, if our nation does something to offend our sense of self, or our belief in the way we think it should behave, we have all the right in the world to get upset. In fact, if the transgression is serious enough, you might get very upset. Unfortunately, for most of us, that's where it ends. We might say to ourselves, "I'm just one of three hundred million people in this country. What influence do I have over the system? The answer to that question is zero. So why should I try to do anything?" Each of us feels even smaller than a Lilliputian.

On the surface, the "how could I possibly have any impact?" question is a good one. However, when you dig a little deeper, you come up with a very compelling reason to act: you've got your own moral compass that needs to be considered and responded to. I'm sure you don't want to feel you govern your daily activities and thoughts based on what your government feels is the thing to do.

The Will of the People

Back in 1776, just before the outbreak of the Revolutionary War, the colonists were quite up front regarding how they felt about going to war with Great Britain. Their dedication to their cause, despite what the ruling government wanted, changed the course of history. Individuals do matter, even when their opinions don't line up with those of the government.

In more modern times, such as during World War II, much more than just a simple majority was for supporting the war. There were few Nazi sympathizers living in America. President Franklin D. Roosevelt reinforced the country's loyalty to America's cause through his Fireside Chats, which were a series of radio addresses. In those speeches, he discussed the vital issues of the day he felt the American people should be aware of. Roosevelt realized that he had to keep his American public behind his war effort, and the best way to do that was to instill a sense of national patriotism within the country at large.

Unfortunately, President Bush never followed up his attack on Iraq by keeping us up to date with his thoughts of what he planned to do after the invasion to keep the peace in Iraq—if he had a plan at all. Nor was he willing to share with us the progress we have made since the war began.

In the Revolutionary War, the Civil War, and World War II, the American public knew why their government was conducting the war, and there was little question in anyone's mind where everyone stood in supporting or not supporting the war. But as in the Vietnam War, the onset of the second Iraq war is an example of war becoming politicized. In an effort to attain political support for that war, deceit and deception were used. Instead of having a number of members of Congress from both sides of the aisle debate the merits and demerits of preemptively invading Iraq, it was decided by a handful of neoconservatives. Yes, ultimately, the president received the support of Congress, but it was only attained after the so-called facts for going to war were presented through pretense and trickery. So it was just another case where our government has hijacked our giant and the collective will of the majority, and instead of doing the work of the people, caused our giant to misbehave, to our nation's detriment.

Today, it is now generally accepted that the Iraq war was a failed policy. Democrats and Republicans concurred with that thinking. The Iraq failure is just the tip of the iceberg. What our country has become has caused me much anxiety and consternation. What I see is not pretty. If we don't quickly and forthrightly change course, we will indeed hit that iceberg.

What is so tragic about the Iraq war fiasco is that we can no longer depend on our president and Congress to make foreign policy decisions that will reflect the best interest of this country. Not that they have consistently made good decisions in the past, as evidenced by the Vietnam War misadventure; however, in comparison to other wars, the disastrous Iraq conflict is an especially bitter pill to have to swallow. No loss of life or limb is justified in an ill-advised war. The cost to our country's treasury has been astronomical and has put this country in serious debt for years to come.

Irreparable Damage

When former Secretary of State Powell was part of the president's cabinet, he cautioned President Bush on invading Iraq by stating the pottery-store rule, which is, "If you break it, you own it." Unfortunately, because of the havoc and turmoil that has occurred in Iraq since we invaded that country, there may never be enough Scotch tape available to repair the broken pottery that is Iraq.

To me, that's more than tragic—it's an absolute outrage. How can our government do that to another country? How can we live with ourselves as a nation? What are we going to say to the men and women who fought so valiantly in Iraq, to say nothing about those who have lost sons, daughters, husbands, wives, and loved ones because they believed in our government and trusted it not to lead them astray? Doesn't our government have any conscience whatsoever? Where's our soul? Our credibility as a nation has diminished considerably, because we never are going to be able to finish the job to either ours or the Iraqis' satisfaction. The reason for that is because it was a failed policy to begin with. What we've done is just create more chaos, death, and destruction than would have existed if Sadaam Hussein had been left in power—and all for the sake of democracy. Give me a break.

The bipartisan Iraq Study Group, a federal committee formed in 2006, reported the situation as being "grave and deteriorating." What the committee urged was that our ship of state needed to chart a new course as soon as possible in order to avoid a major civil war.

I realize that hindsight is always 20/20, but nevertheless, an important decision like attacking a sovereign nation such as Iraq, with all of the unfortunate unattended consequences, requires our president to fully analyze the situation first before going forward. There is too much at stake in regard to the safety and well-being of this nation for him or her to do otherwise.

Diminished Pride

Irrespective of our nation's Iraq war misadventure, and prior to that war, Americans felt they were willing to have their president represent worldwide what we personally valued as a nation. However, since President George W. Bush's election, a number of Americans are not willing to proudly say he is our president. This is because he seems so inept at running the affairs of state. He appears to not use his cabinet and advisors in a way that enhances the image of our country—not only in our own eyes, but in the eyes of other nations as well.

He acts as if he's not sure of who he is and what he's about. He seems to be continually trying to prove to himself and the citizenry that he is capable of being president of the United States, and that, as a result of being president, by definition, he knows what's best for the country. As a result, he appears to try to single-handedly run the government. It's obvious that he wants the American people to know he is the "decider," and that he alone makes the ultimate decisions—even though the judgment of the "decider" no longer reflects the will of the American public, since over two-thirds of them disapprove of our remaining in Iraq war. To a psychologist, that seemingly stubborn behavior in the face of popular opposition suggests he wants to prove he's right. This is possibly done because of deep-seated feelings of inferiority and self-doubt, for he is truly wondering if he's up to the task of adequately running the country.

Unfortunately, up to now, that is exactly the impression he's conveyed, all of which helps explain why our giant appears so impotent, not only in the eyes of the world, but in the terrorists' eyes as well.

We as a nation must continually question the policies enacted by our government. Even prior to George W. Bush being elected president, this should have been our standard operating procedure. Unfortunately, over time, the general voter has become complacent, and as a result, the politicians court only those who can keep them in office.

Financial Strife

The Americans who keep the politicians in office are in turn the beneficiaries of the government largess. The Bush tax cuts in 2001 and 2003 are good examples. Even though the first massive tax cut was made in the month of July, just a few months prior to 9/11, he refused to rescind it in order to help fund the needed appropriations to fight the war on terrorism, including the Iraq War.

Obviously, it appears that money to line the pockets of the well-heeled is more important to President Bush than reducing the massive debt, funding homeland security, fighting the war in Afghanistan, and fighting the war in Iraq.

Since its onset, the Iraq war alone has cost us over $300 billion—and the debt is still rising. That money could be used to respond to the needs and suffering of those who are less fortunate and who are struggling just to eke out a living. Many Americans are struggling to make it financially. As a result, they have to decide whether to continue to eat a balanced diet as they're entitled to do just because they're Americans, or forfeit that right in favor of responding to their medical needs. Some have to cut down on both their food and medical requirements, and thereby risk their basic survival. As long as our government allows these deplorable conditions to exist for people we call Americans, our system needs fixing.

I feel this way because if our country, the United States of America, is truly one of the richest countries on the planet, then none of its citizens should ever have to decide between putting food on the table or having necessary medicine available. Shouldn't it mean something to be a citizen of these United States? If this is supposed to be the greatest country on earth, shouldn't we act more magnanimously toward those who are unable to make it on their own because of circumstances completely out of their control? Even those who have made bad personal choices should be offered our assistance; certainly, if they have children, the children should not be victimized and should have the opportunity to live a life different than that of their parents. Every citizen should be entitled to adequate housing, adequate health care, and adequate nourishment.

In the best of circumstances, all countries would like to provide all of these basic services to their citizens. We have the financial wherewithal to do just that, so we need to rethink how we use our funds. It is the age-old economic quandary: guns or butter?

Priorities Reexamined

The advent of terrorism in this country has triggered a need for America to reassess what we as a country value. It's the randomness of the act that is so unsettling. Each of our lives stand a chance of being snuffed out, just like that. Eventually—perhaps sooner rather than later—the terrorist attack striking our country could be much more devastating than the last one that was experienced.

It's tempting to relax and not question anything that goes on in our government, feeling that the president and Congress are several cuts above the Americans they were elected to serve—because, after all, we voted them into those high offices. Consequently, they must know better than us what's best for our country. That being so, we might erroneously conclude, we don't need to become involved in the affairs of state. That is indeed a very dangerous position to take, because we then risk the possibility that ultimately our rights as Americans will eventually be taken away from us.

When our government enacts a policy you can't live with, you can't just sit around and do nothing. Rather, you have to do all that you can to change the system—even though, more likely than not, you know that you alone won't be able to do much in the way of effecting a change. Nevertheless, you owe it to yourself and your nation to be true to who you are and what you believe in by doing something. After all, that's what life's about: honoring where you're coming from and respecting your sense of integrity, or what you value as a human being.

It would have been easy for the colonists to overlook the abuses committed by their mother country, England. They could have overlooked the tax Britain placed on their imported tea that resulted in taxation without representation in England. But they were unwilling to do that, resulting in the Boston Tea Party. That event, plus others, precipitated the Revolutionary War.

Similarly, it would have been easy for Abraham Lincoln to compromise his sense of self and what he thought was right by placating the Southern states in hopes of averting a Civil War. But that was not in his character.

It would be easy for me not to write this book and do many other things that are of a more pressing nature; however, I have chosen to do this, because I feel it's my patriotic duty to do everything in my power to stop the senseless bloodshed the war in Iraq has evoked.

Writing this book makes me feel good—the same kind of feeling that you experience when you do something to ease the pain and sorrow that someone else is experiencing. You do it because it makes you feel good that you were able to help another soul in that way.

We must continue to cry out and protest when we see our elected officials abuse our system of government in such a way that offends our sense of morality, both on an individual and national level. Considering many of the events that have taken place since George W. Bush became president, there is a lot to outrage us.

Imperfect Past, Imperfect Future

We as a nation must learn from our past mistakes. Only then can we continue to be proud of who we are as a nation. I realize that no nation is perfect, but because we are a democracy, we the people must constantly remind our government officials that we expect them to learn from our past mistakes, so that we can continue our rich heritage of being a great nation—not only in our eyes, but in other nations' eyes as well.

In the name of the country, our politicians have committed many great wrongs, some unforgivable in nature.

Our New World conquest was one of those wrongs. We drove the Native Americans off their land, either killing them or putting them on reservations.

In the past, we romanticized territorial conquests. As a child, I went to the movies to see cowboys and the calvary vanquish the Native Americans. It never dawned on me that I was being entertained by a story of genocide.

Even today, a few politicians are trying to influence other nations by calling what we do "spreading democracy and freedom," when what we really want to do is maintain and extend our global reach to satisfy our own needs and interests.

It was only after our Lincoln wrote the Emancipation Proclamation that slavery in this country was eliminated. Nevertheless, even today, in some way or another, African Americans face discrimination daily, and the illegal Latino immigrant has become the twenty-first-century slave as a result of current immigration and labor policies.

These days, high-tech weapons make the state of the world even less stable and manageable. It is an exercise in futility to attempt to adequately police the world and prevent thousands, if not millions, of people from dying as a result of the use of a nuclear device, or any other weapon of mass destruction. This was true before the advent of terrorism, and now the threat has multiplied a hundredfold.

It was much easier to keep our eye on what other giants of the world were doing before we had to monitor what each individual nation's Lilliputian was doing as well—particularly when the Lilliputian is a terrorist who is willing to give up his or her life for what each believes is a cause worthy of dying for.

A New Kind of War

Terrorism needs to be attacked at its core. It is largely recognized that the roots of terrorism are political in nature and not a symptom of ignorance, poverty, or hopelessness. The perpetrators of the 9/11 attacks were largely well-educated, middle-class individuals determined to strike at what they saw as a corrupt Western materialism that they perceive to be the greatest threat to the dignity of their faith and the security of their lands.

Terrorism is a response to a perceived sense of humiliation and disappointment.

International terrorists' bond is their common enemy, the West. No matter their country of origin, they unite in their jihad against the powerful West, which is viewed as the enabler and/or the source of corruption of their own repressive governments.

It is in the hearts and minds of the world's disgruntled Lilliputians that the battle needs to be fought. I wouldn't be so naive to suggest engaging the terrorists directly. Rather, I would suggest that we preemptively and diplomatically engage the potential terrorist, starting with a thorough and comprehensive review of our Middle East policies, before the terrorism recruiting stations overflow with recruits. Our primary weapon against terrorism is ideas, not bullets.

Accurately identifying the roots of terrorism is the first step. The reason the Iraq war is so grievous is because we started it. Iraq did not have a relationship with Bin Laden or Al Qaeda; consequently, it was not even remotely responsible for 9/11. All the other reasons for preemptively waging war with Iraq have turned out to be bogus.

In an article titled *Fight the Roots of Terrorism*, published on September 21, 2001, in Common Dreams News Center, author

15

Steve Niva, who teaches international politics and Middle Eastern studies at Evergreen State College, said that we must first avoid the temptation to use massive military power in response to horrific attacks like 9/11. Instead, we should begin to understand the mind-set of the perpetrators of the attack and roots of anti-American sentiments in the Middle East.

Niva mentioned that we shouldn't completely focus our attention on Osama Bin Laden as the sole mastermind of the attacks, even though the media often reports that to be so. He said that since about 1995, attacks that were not directly related to Bin Laden took place at U.S. facilities around the world. That is not to say that Bin Laden doesn't aid various splinter groups and factions with logistic and financial support (because, as Niva says, he does).

Niva also stated that Bin Laden's network has no permanent location. "It appears to be a kaleidoscopic overlay of cells and links that span the globe from camps on the Afghan-Pakistan borderlands to immigrant ghettoes in Europe and the U.S." [2]

It's important to recognize what has just been stated, because it shows how complex and difficult it is to fight terrorism using conventional methods, such as massive military power.

Niva further states that there are a variety of reasons why the hatred of the United States may have less to do with being Islamic and more to do with the political factors, such as believing the Muslims have received the "brunt of international violence over the last decade" as witnessed by the "genocide against Bosnian Muslims, the Russian war in Chechnya, the conflict between India and Pakistan over Kashmir, the Israeli occupation of Palestinian lands, and the UN sanctions against Iraq." Niva states that in all these instances, "U.S. policies either tacitly condone the violence or actively support it."

According to Niva, the conclusion to be drawn from all of this is that even though we may kill or capture Bin Laden and a number of his followers, the far-flung militants will still be alive and well and will continue to carry out further terrorist attacks with greater zeal because of the death of Bin Laden. If "massive American military might is brought to bear on a Muslim nation, especially one that kills

---

[2] Steven Niva, "Fight the Roots of Terrorism." Web site: http://www. commondreams.org/views01/0921-06.htm, September 21, 2001.

innocent civilians in the process, this is precisely the type of action these militants hope will create the conditions for unifying greater numbers of Muslims against the United States." Niva concluded by saying, "It would confirm their view that the U.S. is an arrogant superpower that cares little about Muslim lives." [3]

Frankly, it's difficult to argue with Niva's logic. What we in the United States must realize is that the image we project around the world can be just as lethal as bullets in destroying the goodwill and empathy other nations feel toward the United States. If we fail to eliminate the root causes of terrorism, for every terrorist we capture or eliminate, dozens more will show up and be willing to attempt to repeat another 9/11 scenario.

Niva feels that terrorism should be prosecuted as a crime, not retaliated against as an act of war. "Massive international law enforcement effort" combined with a "political strategy designed to isolate and undermine these militant networks" is what's necessary. He urges that the United States use "all its resources to compel international cooperation to ensure that the perpetrators have no place to hide." [4]

Niva suggests that identifying Bin Laden and his gang of criminals will help isolate them and others who violate international law and will make it extremely difficult for countries to harbor them in the future. Because the terrorist networks are so dispersed, Niva feels that "only international cooperation will work to root them out. American declarations of war inhibit rather than promote this cooperation." [5]

The number of allied nations that strongly disagreed with our giant's preemptive declaration of war on Iraq was evidence enough that war with Iraq should have never been contemplated, let alone carried out. This second Iraq War will go down in American history as one of the greatest foreign-policy blunders this country has ever incurred.

In order to avoid a recurrence of such a blunder, Niva suggests, "In words and deeds, the U.S. must clearly make a distinction between Islam as a religion and violent extremism." He also suggests we

---

[3] Ibid.
[4] Ibid.
[5] Ibid.

reexamine our policies in the Middle East. Niva believes that we must appreciate that many Arabs and Muslims harbor "deep and legitimate grievances with U.S. policies, but do not support violence."[6]

Niva urges the United States to "condemn the serious human rights abuses committed by its allies with the same force as it condemns other regimes in the region ..." One of the conditions of U.S. aid should be conditioned on the progress made to open up "closed political systems."[7]

Niva also urges support of a "legitimate Palestinian aspiration for an independent state alongside a secure Israel."[8]

Niva concluded his article by stating that "Such an approach is not a concession to terrorism, but a more realistic and effective response that is closer to the values that the United States claims to uphold."[9]

According to the bipartisan Iraq Study Group—and consistent with what Niva stated—the key to reestablishing peace in the Middle East is to resolve the Israeli-Palestinian question. There will always be discord in that region of the world, as long as the territorial dispute between the Israelis and the Palestinians continue. The advisory panel's report suggested that efforts to find a solution between Israel and Palestine could have a conciliatory effect on the Iraq situation. The report emphasized the need for peace between those two countries, because the moderate Arabs are very concerned about that region of the world. In order for peace to be recognized in the Middle East, peaceful coexistence between Israel and Palestine needs to be established. Then it is hoped the more moderate Arabs will appeal to the sensibilities of their extreme Arab brethren to use greater moderation in dealing with the West. According to Lee Hamilton, cochairman of the Iraq Study Group, we will lose the war on terrorism if we don't have the moderate Arabs on our side.

Our giant's tendency to engage militarily because it feels good and we're good at it only inflames already festering resentment.

In order to preserve our nation and what our country stands for, which are our ideals, we must recognize the need to use other means

[6] Ibid.

[7] Ibid.

[8] Ibid.

[9] Ibid.

besides war to settle conflict and strife among nations. Regardless of how advanced our future weaponry becomes, tools of war will never supplant words and ideas in resolving differences. Using the primitive means of war to settle differences—resulting in the winner taking all and the vanquished being forced to live under a regime that is philosophically repugnant—resolves nothing.

I'm not a pacifist. I served my time in the Army Medical Service Corps in Korea. Nevertheless, the argument that our vital interests are in jeopardy, and therefore we need to go to war to protect them, is no longer valid. We're fast approaching the time when waging full-scale war against another nation should be considered out of the question because of the devastation caused by weapons of mass destruction. With North Korea having nuclear weapons and Iran eventually getting them, and other countries ultimately having either the weaponry or the means to produce such weapons, we need to foster relationships with all nations who are willing to embrace peace. That means we must begin to repair the serious damage our giant has inflicted on other nations.

Going to war to protect our major vital interest in the region, which is oil, has caused us greater harm without making our vital interest any more secure. The thinking went something like this: if we could also establish a democracy in that part of the world, that would help us establish a foothold, which would better guarantee our vital interest was assured. However, we jumped the gun on that one, because we didn't do our homework. If we had, we would have realized that democracy may not be possible to establish in that part of the world.

A number of authorities on Islam and its culture argue that it's foolhardy to assume that all Islamic countries desire to become democracies. These nations believe that their religion, or theocracy, is part of their cultural identity. It has been that way for centuries, and it is for that reason they're not about to abandon that part of their culture for a system of government that doesn't fit them.

Echoing what has just been said, Robert Merry, in his book *Sands of Empire*, stated that not all Islamic nations choose to become democracies. He says that for many Islamic states, their religion, or theocracy, is part of their cultural identity. It has been that way for centuries, and for that reason, they're not about to abandon that part of their culture for democracy. In discussing the prospects of the United States waging war with Iraq, Merry stated that two of our allies argued that we should take the route of "moderation":

> The moderation advocated by France and Germany was based on three rationales: that there was insufficient evidence that the threat posed by Saddam was imminent; that the goal of building democracy was going to be infinitely more difficult, long, and bloody than anticipated; and that the resulting occupation would enflame anti-Western passions throughout Islam. The French and Germans were right on all three points.[10]

Considering that war has proven itself a lousy way to settle differences throughout the course of time, you'd think by now we'd realize that doesn't resolve anything. The winner takes all—where's the justice in that? Compromise is the only way to go if we want to survive as a species. It is no longer a matter of honor for honor's sake. The stakes are too high, and the cost in human resources and treasure are too great to warrant military action just to protect our vital interest. If our country is deliberately attacked or attack appears imminent, then military action may be warranted. Otherwise, it is not.

I realize that we the people cannot influence our government directly; we need to work through our senators and representatives to do that. Presently, an imperial president doesn't want to listen to us, as witnessed by our continued occupation of Iraq, even when the clear majority of Americans wish it would stop.

In order to stop being apathetic and allowing ourselves to ignore what our president and government are doing, we must become more actively involved as individuals. In doing that, you will no longer feel like a helpless pawn in the system. Rather, you will feel proud of yourself, because you are following your conscience and doing what you think is right.to make your nation a better country in which to live.

---

[10] Robert W. Merry, *Sands of Empire: Missionary Zeal, American Foreign Policy, and the Hazards of Global Ambition,* 246. Reprinted with the permission of Simon and Schuster Adult Publishing Group. © 2005 by Robert Merry.

A GOVERNMENT OF GLUTTONY

Why has our giant gotten so fat and unwieldy?

What has contributed to our national budget—hence, our giant's waistline—is all the pork it eats. Whereas American teenagers of today tend to gravitate to McDonald's hamburgers as their favored food, our giant has loved pork ever since lobbying groups introduced pork-barrel spending to it.

Our giant has consumed so many goodies from the pork barrel that its girth makes it barely recognizable as its old self. Because our giant is so bloated, his great size has caused destruction and havoc in the real world.

The number of pork burgers change from one year to the next, but the general trend continues in the same direction: up. No wonder our giant has such a weight problem. Congress has never seen a helping of pork it didn't like.

In 2003, some of the pork-barrel entries that our giant might have feasted upon were such things as

- $50,000 for a tattoo-removal project in San Luis Obispo
- $2 million for the Center on Obesity
- $270,000 to combat goth culture in Blue Springs, Missouri

In 2004, the Omnibus Appropriations bill had the following pet pork projects listed among the thousands stuffed into the $375 billion bill:

- $1.8 million for exotic pet disease research in California
- $50 million for an indoor rain forest in Coralville, Iowa
- $450,000 for the Johnny Appleseed Heritage Center in Ohio
- $100,000 for the State Historical Society of Iowa for developing the World Food Prize
- $175,000 for the painting of a mural on a flood wall in a Missouri city
- $90,000 for fruit-fly research in Montpelier, Vermont
- $225,000 for the restoration of an opera house in Traverse City, Michigan
- $250,000 for the Alaska Aviation Heritage Museum
- $200,000 for the construction and renovation of a shopping center in Guadalupe, Arkansas
- $325,000 for the construction of a swimming pool in Salinas, California
- $100,000 for the renovation of the Coca-Cola building in Macon, Georgia
- $238,000 for the National Wild Turkey Federation
- $200,000 for recreational improvements in North Pole, Alaska
- $100,000 for the restoration of the Jefferson County Court House clock tower in Washington state
- $220,000 for the Blueberry Hill Farm in Maine
- $2 million for the First Tee Program, which teaches young people to play golf
- $40 million for the construction of a cargo terminal in the port of Philadelphia to support "high-speed military sealift and other military purposes" vessels—which, as Senator John McCain noted, "do not even exist, nor are they being championed by the military."

We better not let our giant read this list. By the time it got halfway down, it would be slobbering all over the place.

Bridge to Nowhere

One of the biggest pork-barrel spending boondoggles was what has come to be known as the bridge to nowhere. The $223 million, quarter-mile span would connect the port town of Ketchikan, Alaska, to an airport on the neighboring Gravina Island. A ferry currently links the two.

In the *Denver Post/Rocky Mountain News* Parade section on November 4, 2005, reporter David Wallechinsky described the $315 million bridge project, $223 million of which had already been approved by Congress. The proposed bridge would replace a five-minute ferry ride. Did this bridge connect two major metropolitan areas? Not exactly … unless you consider the town of Ketchikan, Alaska, pop. 8,200, to be a major metropolitan area. The destination on the other end of the bridge is even less urban, despite its possession of an airport; the island of Gravina is home only to fifty people.

"In the wake of the recent hurricane calamities," Wallechhinsky wrote, "many Americans are wondering how our government can spend $6.8 billion a year ($2.5 million a day) and still not have enough for disaster preparedness, such as reinforcing New Orleans' levees and efficiently evacuating Houston and other cities." He pointed to pork-barrel projects like the bridge to nowhere as the main problem: "Every year, members of Congress try to gain funding for as many projects as possible in his or her district." Wallechhinsky observed that the project eventual cost of the bridge, $315 million, amounted to more than $23,000 per citizen of Ketchikan.

Some locals supported the bridge; Wallechhinsky quoted one assemblyman, Dave Kiffer, as saying, "The general feeling here is that if someone else is paying for it, sure, why not?" But the reporter noted that "One young man—who requested anonymity, fearing retribution from his pro-bridge boss—told me of his recent visit to the lower 48 states: Every time he drove over a pothole or got stuck in traffic, he said he thought about The Bridge and figured the money could be better used elsewhere."[11]

It's obvious that this appropriation was inappropriate and should never have been requested.

---

[11] David Wallechinsky, "A Visit to the Bridge to Nowhere," *Parade Magazine*, November 6, 2005. Reprinted with permission of Parade Publications.

It is indeed unfortunate that the general feeling in Ketchikan was, "if someone else is paying for it, sure, why not?" That attitude is simply symptomatic of our nation as a whole. As long as they think the other guy is paying for the project, people aren't that concerned. They may stand to benefit from the spending in their district, but they're also paying for the pork being cooked in other areas of the country.

In terms of the monetary distribution of pork projects, some states pay more, some less, but pork is pork. Some get it well done, and others get it rare.

The bridge-to-nowhere project was eventually rejected by the Senate only because of the adverse publicity surrounding it. That rejection is a shining example of how government can be forced to act when the people care and get involved.

But more must be done. Pork-barrel spending continues to rise. Citizens Against Government Waste, CAGW, has stated that in the year 1995, the number of earmarked projects was 1,439, and the cost for those pig activities was $10.1 billion. By the end of the year 2005, that figure had risen to $27.3 billion and funded 13,997 projects. No wonder our giant's midsection keeps expanding at such a prodigious rate!

Indefensible Defense Spending

What in part has led to our giant's bulk is not only being able to pig out on pork burgers, but also the tremendous amount of money we spend on defense. The United States spends more on defense than all the other countries of the world combined. The budget for defense for 2006 was more than $441 billion and did not include money for Iraq and Afghanistan. President Bush planned to ask Congress for an additional $50 billion to $70 billion to pay for the wars in Iraq and Afghanistan.

To put the cost of the Iraq war in its proper perspective, it is estimated the U.S. government spends about $4.5 billion a month on the conflict in Iraq, or $100,000 per minute. Remember, this is for financing a war that need not have taken place.

If you look at the war strictly from a dollars-and-cents standpoint, it doesn't look like you're getting the bang for the buck that you should be getting, particularly when you consider what it also costs us in terms of lives lost.

Frankly, I think your odds would be better if you went to Las Vegas to gamble your money away at the crap tables.

Competing in the arms race is a no-win situation. If we and other nations continue to compete in the arms race without each of our giants having some kind of regard or respect for one another, ultimately the world as we know it will no longer be. Some rogue nation or radical group could trigger a worldwide holocaust through the employment of some weapon of mass destruction, such as an atomic device. And if that happens, for many, poof, that's it, there ain't no more.

Wouldn't our money be better spent on projects that improve humanity, rather than destroy it? There is absolutely no legitimate reason to continue to participate in the arms race; we already have enough weaponry to destroy the world as it is. Building more weapons will not fulfill our nation's goals. Russia and the United States have nuclear arsenals large enough to destroy life on most of the planet, yet the proliferation continues. When is this madness going to end?

A Self-Perpetuating Problem

Our nation's approach to defense reminds me of how I used to think before I realized I needed therapy. I felt like a dog chasing its tail, for I would unwittingly continue to repeat behavior that was self-defeating—so defeating that I would over and over again end up where I had begun, never ever getting off dead center. This senseless activity prevented me from getting on with the business of life—which was living life to the fullest.

That's what has happened with the arms race. Not only does the size of our military budget add to our unsustainable debt posture, but it also sets up a circular situation where the more security we buy through military spending, the more threatening we become to other nations. They in turn form alliances to resist. As a consequence, this further threatens our feelings of security, thus closing the ever-expanding circle. Our current policies reinforce this theory.

It is obvious that our participation in this charade simply increases the world's sense of insecurity and fear of ultimate annihilation.

Clearly, the accumulation of nuclear weapons for superiority's sake needs to end immediately.

North Korea and Iran are showing the United States and the rest of the world how the threat and actual development of nuclear weaponry can be used as bargaining chips for the acquisition of goods and services, as well as a possible source of revenue desperately needed in those countries.

Such brinkmanship also puts such countries on the world stage, where they receive attention in a way that would not otherwise be shown. It's too bad the reinforcement is negative and not positive, where their attention-seeking behavior would be rewarded for the purpose of peaceful pursuits rather than for bellicose reasons.

A case in point: the current posturing by Iran regarding their activation of programs to enrich uranium for a supposedly peaceful nuclear-energy program reinforces this notion that it is seeking attention and sees what it is doing as a bargaining chip, as well as possibly a revenue producer. Iran has certainly gotten the world's attention.

The debilitating costs of perpetuating militarism and weapons proliferation are both moral and fiscal.

We should not reject the utopian idea that we can break this pattern of escalation and diminish the threats that weapons proliferation poses to all nations. To that end, we need to first recognize our own failed policies and embrace our global leadership responsibilities by restructuring those policies to shape a path toward cooperation, disarmament, and mutual security among every nation of the world.

In 1795, James Madison, in *Political Observations*, said of war,

> Of all the enemies to public liberty war is, perhaps, the most to be dreaded because it comprises and develops the germ of every other. War is the parent of armies; from these proceed debts and taxes ... known instruments for bringing the many under the domination of the few.... No nation could preserve its freedom in the midst of continual warfare.

Our once-beloved giant, our nation, was respected and listened to by other giants of the world. Today, those other giants no longer respect what we do or say, because they know our country is only interested in promoting its own interests, rather than genuinely being concerned about other nations' needs and concerns.

You'd think that considering the amount of money and human resources we've put into Iraq, we'd have more to show for it. And to think that all this was done in the name of freedom and democracy, so that we can nurture Iraq to adulthood so that it can grow up to be just like us. But I don't believe that was our true motive.

Capitalism in Disguise

It is important for us to understand that our giant's self-image is not necessarily the image that is projected abroad. The giant tends to try to flatter himself by claiming to be a moral crusader—spreading the ideals of freedom, liberty, and democracy across the globe. Our government preaches the gospel of human rights, quality of life, and fairness in trade and commerce. But while these talking points play well to the captive audience within our shores, the perception abroad is quite different.

Especially of late, unfortunately, the lumbering giant has exposed itself to the international community as grossly self-absorbed. Our ambitious effort to democratize selective regions of the world—those with the most oil—is perceived by many countries as a self-serving ploy to ensure that we have a supply of that precious commodity.

Some see our efforts not as liberation through the exportation of democracy, but rather an extension of self-interested capitalism.

Until I started to write this book and researched what made this country tick, I thought all of the good fortunes that have been bestowed upon this nation were due to democracy. It wasn't until I studied the subject in greater detail that I realized it is capitalism, not democracy alone, that has allowed this country to become the richest nation in the world.

When our president says he wishes to further democracy and freedom in the world, this is disingenuous. The true goal is to further capitalism. Though democracy is founded on the principle that the majority rules, and the people's issues deserve a response; in actuality, that's not what happens at all. Capitalism is based on satisfying the individual's needs and appetites; democracy provides the capitalist with a platform for that economic system to thrive.

Our capitalistic pursuit of dependable energy sources has led to the dubious policy of attempting to impose democracy where it may not fit.

Noted author and veteran political journalist Robert W. Merry, in his book *Sands of Empire*, explains that when the West intervenes in conflicts or attempts to shape the politics of those regions, it is often ignorant of the significance of a particular region's history and culture. Dismissing such information can lead to disastrous unintended consequences. He writes,

> The historical and cultural ignorance that guided America in the Balkans led to unfortunate results far removed from what had been predicted by those policies' architects. But the stakes were low for America and the outcome of limited consequence. The stakes in the war with Islam are enormous, and policies guided by similar historical and cultural ignorance could lead to disaster.

After stressing that America's leaders lack the necessary knowledge about the sentiments and goals surrounding Islamic culture, Merry refers to our democratization efforts in Iraq as "probably the worst approach to a cultural clash that could be devised at such a stage of hostilities."[12]

Merry comments on the dangers of undertaking "a new kind of war" to spread "Western-style democracy" without regard for history and culture when he writes, "Captivated by the Cold War mentality of his top advisers and intoxicated with the idea of spreading Western-style democracy throughout the lands of Arabia, Bush embraced a post-9/11 foreign policy destined from the beginning to lead his country toward calamity."[13]

Merry contemplates our future in light of our current shallow approach to foreign policy when he writes, "Culture remains the single most potent factor in history and geopolitics, and with the end of the Cold war the forces of culture were unleashed with a vengeance

---

[12] Robert W. Merry, *Sands of Empire: Missionary Zeal, American Foreign Policy, and the Hazards of Global Ambition*, 175–76. Reprinted with the permission of Simon and Schuster Adult Publishing Group. © 2005 by Robert Merry.

[13] Ibid., p. 195.

upon the globe. This is the reality of the twenty-first century, and it is a reality that demands from the West a steady, careful, measured approach to diplomacy and war."

In contemplating future American foreign policy, Merry warns,

> The war with Islam is so complex, so dangerous, so multifarious that missteps could have dire consequences. In such a war, unprecedented in modern history, probably the most destabilizing approach would be a combination of Theodore Roosevelt's Will to Power imperialism and Woodrow Wilson's missionary idealism. And yet this is precisely the dual policy that emerged from the George W. Bush administration after 9/11. Whether America can extricate itself from the consequences of that dual policy remains one of the most important foreign policy questions facing the country today.[14]

Merry's observations only highlight America's need to change its course, before those "dire consequences" become a reality.

Not everyone is convinced that America's democratization efforts are out of line. Because of our government's arrogance and egocentric posture, many Americans feel other countries should automatically not only accept, but also appreciate the invitation we've extended to them to join us and become another member of the democratic family of nations.

The implied message our government gives to those countries that don't embrace democracy is that their way of governing themselves is clearly inferior, and that their citizenry should rise up and cast off the shackles and oppression that prevent them from thriving. We must ask ourselves why many of the Muslim nations and other countries fail to respond to America's infinite wisdom. Could it simply be that not all countries are psychologically and culturally predisposed to our form of government? There is ample evidence to suggest that is indeed the case.

Besides, how in the world can our nation, given its own often-turbulent brief history, expect that our rules of governance can and should be applied universally?

---

[14] Ibid., p. 192.

Moral Obligations

When a nation such as the United States, because of its military and economic might, is considered to be the most powerful country in the world, it needs to be careful to do what's morally right, rather than pursue a course which furthers the ambitions and interests of the United States at the expense of other nations' general welfare and concerns.

In order to make prudent international decisions, our government must first understand and appreciate the cultural heritage and predispositions of other nations before intruding into their internal affairs. If we feel our involvement is morally justified and the other country welcomes our taking part in their internal affairs, then we can proceed. We must always remember that we enter the host nation's world as their guest, so we don't want to wear out our welcome.

The Iraq government didn't invite us to help them rid themselves of Saddam Hussein; no willing host opened the door for us. And who can blame the Iraq government for its lack of hospitality? Our motives for invading that country were less than pure. Many political pundits, along with many ordinary U.S. citizens, seriously questioned that the motive for our nation to preemptively invade Iraq was to establish freedom and democracy in that country.

Our cultural ignorance and misplaced motives have prompted Iraq to view us as occupiers rather than guests, in the same way Nazi Germany was viewed by the French when they occupied that country during the Second World War. The Iraq invasion will go down in history as one of the most disastrous foreign policy misadventures in our country's history.

It seems evident that a fresh approach to foreign policy needs to be developed and practiced if it is to represent the core values of our great nation and its peoples. I think our giant has temporarily gone astray, but fear not; all is not lost, as long as our giant reflects on its experiences and applies the lessons learned in its youth.

GEORGE W. BUSH: THE FORTY-THIRD PRESIDENT OF THE UNITED STATES

When the subject of our president is introduced in conversation, frequently one or more people say they can't stand watching and listening to him on television. When he's not reading a script, he often acts anything but presidential. Many tell me that they don't feel he's too bright. Is that the image we want our president and the leader of the free world to project to the rest of the world? I think not.

What verbal and nonverbal cues did the public miss that might have made them reject George Walker Bush as a presidential candidate?

The politician's tools of the trade are words,whether spoken or written.

I believe that our sixteenth president, Abraham Lincoln, was the greatest verbal communicator in our country's presidential history. Although Lincoln never liked speaking extemporaneously, he excelled in giving speeches that were carefully crafted and delivered flawlessly; he was an excellent speaker and storyteller.

According to Donald Phillips in his book *Lincoln on Leadership*, Lincoln clearly knew the power of language in communicating to his audience. Frequently, he would not only practice giving his speech before delivering it, but he would read out loud anything else that might interest him. When he was a young lawyer, this practice would annoy his law partner, William Herndon, who said,

> Mr. Lincoln's habits, methods of reading law, politics, poetry, etc., were to come into the office, pick up a book, newspaper, etc., and to sprawl himself out on the sofa, chair, etc., and read aloud much to my annoyance. I have asked him often why he did so, and his invariable reply was: "I catch the idea by two senses. But when I read aloud I hear what is read, and I see it, and hence two sense get it and I remember it better, if I do not understand it better."[15]

Phillips states,

> Though Abraham Lincoln was an outstanding writer and public speaker, he was even more adept at the art of conversation. He could talk to anyone, brilliant scientist, wily politician, visiting head of state, or simple backwoods farmer. He had a terrific sense of humor and often sprinkled his conversations with witty stories and humorous anecdotes that he used as persuasive tools. He has come to be regarded as the only president of the United States who was a true humorist in the tradition of Mark Twain or Will Rogers.[16]

Phillips tells of Lincoln explaining to a friend why he often related stories in the course of normal conversations. "They say I tell a great many stories. I reckon I do; but I have learned from long experience that plain people, take them as they run, are more easily influenced through the medium of a broad and humorous illustration than in any other way ..."[17]

Disturbing Differences

When it comes to extemporaneous speaking and verbal communication, how does Bush rate in comparison to one of the greatest leaders in our nation's history?

---

[15] Donald Phillips II, *Lincoln on Leadership*, 152. With permission of Warner Books. © 2004 by Donald Phillips II.

[16] Ibid., 155.

[17] Ibid., 155.

On February 4, 2005, President Bush gave a speech at the Tampa Convention Center in Tampa, Florida. This was billed as one of his "town hall" meetings arranged to drum up support for proposed changes to the Social Security system.

After the speech, a woman in attendance queried the president about the efficacy of proposed changes to the Social Security system he had advocated in his prepared speech. To her inquiry, he said,

> Because the—all which is on the table begins to address the big cost drivers. For example, how benefits are calculated, for example, is on the table, whether or not benefits rise based upon wage increases or price increases. There's a series of parts of the formula that are being considered. And when you couple that, those different cost drivers, affecting those—changing those with personal accounts, the idea is to get what has been promised more likely to be—or closer delivered to what has been promised. Does that make any sense to you? It's kind of muddled. Look, there's a series of things that cause the—like, for example, benefits are calculated based upon the increase of wages, as opposed to the increase of prices. Some have suggested that we calculate—the benefits will rise based upon inflation, as opposed to wage increases. There is a reform that would help solve the red if that were put into effect. In other words, how fast benefits grow, how fast the promised benefits grow, if those—if that growth is affected, it will help on the red. Okay, better? I'll keep working on it. [Laughter][18]

Word Salads

Frankly, if I was still a practicing clinical psychologist, and didn't know the president of the United States had made those extemporaneous remarks, if I were told what I read was a verbatim transcript of a patient who was hospitalized for schizophrenia, I would believe it. Technically speaking, the speech appears to be a word salad—a cluster of words that make no sense to the outside observer, but would have some delusional significance to the patient who uttered them.

---

[18] White House Transcript, http://www.snopes.com/politics/bush/muddled. asp.

I know that President Bush is not psychotic. I know that he must be reasonably smart, since he graduated from Yale and Harvard Business School. So why, at times, does he behave in such a bizarre way when he tries to speak extemporaneously?

Whenever he is expected to speak with or without limited notes or doesn't have a prepared speech to refer to, we never know what will be uttered from his mouth. These humiliating moments are not an infrequent momentary lapse of memory or judgment. They occur with some degree of regularity.

Examples of these moments are as follows:

"I'm honored to shake the hand of a brave Iraqi citizen who had his hand cut off by Saddam Hussein."—Washington DC, May 25, 2004

> "If the Iranians were to have a nuclear weapon they could proliferate."—Washington DC, March 21, 2006

> "I've reminded the prime minister—the American people, Mr. Prime Minister, over the past months that it was not always a given that the United States and America would have a close relationship."—Washington DC, June 29, 2006

> "You know, when I campaigned here in 2000, I said, I want to be a war president. No president wants to be a war president, but I am one."—Des Moines, Iowa, October 26, 2006

> "I think—tide turning—see, as I remember—I was raised in the desert, but tides kind of—it's easy to see a tide turn—did I say those words?"—Washington DC, June 14, 2006

An occasional verbal gaffe from anybody who has to speak before the public is most understandable. But the number of malapropisms President Bush has uttered on a regular basis is embarrassing.

Based on what I have observed, I believe our president has a problem with processing information.

Some authorities in the field of psychology surmise that President George W. Bush is suffering from an Attention Deficit Hyperactivity Disorder (ADHD), and I would concur. Although he has not been formally diagnosed as having that malady, ample behavioral indices strongly suggest he may have ADHD.

The Case for ADHD

A number of people are able to mask their ADHD sufficiently so that they're able to reach adulthood without their ADHD being detected. It doesn't mean they're able to remain unscathed as a result of having that disease. What it does mean is that they're able to just get by in their efforts to adjust to this disorder.

What is unfortunate is that by not coming to terms with having such an ailment, and trying to hide the disease from others, the person makes excuses for his or her perceived handicap. ADHD then becomes like a sore that continues to fester and trouble the person to a degree that is mentally unhealthy. This is what I believe is happening with our president.

Does having ADHD disqualify someone from running for president? Considering the distinct possibility that George W. Bush suffers from ADHD, is becoming the president of the United States the right course to follow? If he does not get adequate treatment to curb the ill effects accompanying the disorder, the answer to that question is a resounding no.

President Bush expends a lot of psychic energy trying to defend and cover up his alleged ADHD. Rather than acknowledge he has problems sitting still and containing his anxieties, that he has a short attention span, that he doesn't like to read, that he finds it difficult to come to a logical conclusion when following several complex ideas, and that he may also be dyslexic, he makes jokes about these kinds of classical ADHD symptoms by engaging in clownish, inappropriate behavior. Not only does he do that as president of the United States, but he has also had a history of being a less-than-serious student in grade school and college as well.

Those with ADHD problems often mask their anxieties by acting out and displaying inappropriate, juvenile behavior. President Bush has always been thought of as a cutup throughout his academic life, regardless of whether we're talking about grade school, high school, or college. It makes no difference. The old saying "once a kid, always a kid" certainly applies to our president.

Because President Bush has never truly grown up, he has carried the symptoms related to his ADHD to the present. Sometimes, depending upon the amount of stress he's experiencing, the only way he can manage his anxiety is by allowing his impulsive behavior to express itself. That's known as managing your behavior at someone else's expense.

On July 19, 2006, Maureen Dowd wrote a *New York Times* op-ed column titled "Animal House Summit."[19] In it, she reports the shenanigans President Bush engaged in while he attended the Big Eight Economic Summit hosted by President Putin. She wrote,

> Reporters who covered W.'s 2000 campaign often wondered whether the Bush scion would give up acting the fool if he got to be the king.
>
> Would he stop playing peek-a-boo with his pre-meal moist towels during airplane interviews? Would he quit scrunching up his face and wiggling his eyebrows at memorial services? Would he replace inanity with gravity?
>
> "In many regards, the Bush I knew did not seem to be built for what lay ahead," wrote Frank Bruni, the Times writer who covered W.'s ascent, in his book *Ambling Into History*. "The Bush I knew was part scamp and part bumbler, a timeless fraternity boy and heedless cutup, a weekday gym rat and weekend napster, an adult with an inner child that often brimmed to the surface or burst through."
>
> The open-microphone incident at the G-8 lunch in St. Petersburg on Monday illustrated once more that W. never made any effort to adapt. The president has enshrined his immaturity and insularity, turning every environment he inhabits—no matter how decorous or serious—into a comfortable frat house.

Dowd went on to highlight some of the president's inappropriate, impulsive behaviors, such as offering impromptu shoulder rubs or talking with his mouth full. "He can make even a global summit

---

[19] Maureen Dowd, "Animal House Summit," *New York Times*, July 19, 2006. Used with permission of the *New York Times*.

meeting seem like a kegger," Dowd observed. She reported that the president said he hadn't prepared any closing remarks and seemed impatient when listening to other leaders talk for an extended period of time.

Dowd noted that Bush spoke urgently about going home, even though a spokesman later said he had nothing scheduled on the evening of his return. "The world may be blowing up, and the president may have a rare opportunity to jaw-jaw about bang-bang with his peers," Dowd observed drily, "But that pales in comparison with his burning desire to return to his feather pillow and gym back at the White House."

In her article, Dowd noted some of the clownish behavior I described earlier:

> He treated Tony "As It Were" Blair like the servant in "The Remains of the Day," blowing off his offer to help with the Israel-Lebanon crisis, and changing the subject from substance to fluff at one point, noting about his 60th-birthday Burberry gift: "Thanks for the sweater. Awfully thoughtful of you." Then he razzed the British prime minister, who was hovering and wheedling like an abused wife: "I know you picked it out yourself."

Finally, Dowd made this observation: "He seems to have no clue that his own headlong, heedless actions in the Middle East have contributed to the deepening chaos there, and to Iran's growing influence and America's diminished leverage." Clearly, our careless giant is in danger of tripping over its own boorish feet and falling hard.

Knowing that President Bush may be suffering from untreated ADHD, it's not surprising that the acting-out behavior he displayed from grade school through college is still occurring. The president finds it difficult not being the center of attention and being in complete control of the situation in the way that he'd like to be.

There is a certain diplomatic protocol that needs to be observed when meeting with other heads of state, and I'm sure that giving shoulder massages isn't part of the etiquette—even if it is Angela Merkel, the chancellor of Germany, as it was in this case. When President Bush gave her an uninvited shoulder rub, she was clearly not amused. Judging from the expression she showed on the videotape, she was mortified and embarrassed that someone would have the audacity to surprise her in that way. Here, our president, who is supposed to be an expert on nonverbal communication—and can tell by looking in a person's eyes whether he has a soul or not—doesn't seem to know that one of the first tenets in nonverbal communication is that you don't invade another person's life space without their permission. And certainly not from the rear! Who knows what that might connote?

I would imagine that if I were to confront the president and ask him what in the world was he thinking, he might say, "Oh, I was only joshing. That was just a friendly gesture that I might do with any friend." It wasn't that at all. His ADHD was beginning to act up, and he acted impulsively, because he was tired and anxious to get home.

These are just a few of the observable behaviors that may very well have changed the public's mind about Bush's suitability for the presidency, had the voting public seen some examples prior to his election.

The president has been able to mask his potential disability quite successfully by being a jokester, denigrating his role as commander in chief by frequently failing to show the seriousness of purpose that you'd expect from a president, poking fun at himself for mispronouncing words or any other error of language he may commit.

Even if we ignore the president's bouts of nonsensical public speaking, body language is considered more revealing than what is said. There is more to communication than what we hear. Important nonverbal cues include facial expressions, gestures, posture, personal appearance, and other cues too numerous to mention here.

In examining nonverbal cues, we realize that our president looks anything but confident when he goes before the American public. In many ways, he looks uncomfortable whenever he has to speak extemporaneously. He may do a lot of eye rolling, wiggling, blinking, foot jiggling, and shifting of his weight whenever he's expected to think on his feet.

President Bush consistently appears out of his element whenever he has to appear before the American public and act presidential. Sometimes, his verbal and nonverbal discomfort becomes so embarrassing that it's difficult to watch and listen to him address his audience.

Other Presidents Compared

Other presidents were more aware of their nonverbal communications.

There were times when Lincoln was aware of the impact his nonverbal communication had on others. During moments when he felt down, he was conscious of the importance of shaking off his despondency, since that was not the kind of public image he wanted to project.

Lincoln had all the right in the world to be publicly despondent. He had two sons who died before their time; Ann Rutledge, one of his early loves, died at a very early age; and he had a melancholy personality, which gave him a kind of license to be depressed whenever such a feeling came over him. Nevertheless, he recognized how important it was to have an uplifting and positive demeanor whenever he appeared in public. Abraham Lincoln's persona was the roadway to his soul. It always mirrored not only his thoughts, but his actions as well.

Lincoln was able to use his geniality, joke-telling ability, and good humor to mask his underlying melancholy, as evidenced by what author Donald Phillips relates in his book *Lincoln on Leadership*:

> Carl Schutz, a Republican contemporary of Lincoln, and later a Union general, recounted his first meeting with the future president:

> "All at once, after the train had left a way-station, I observed a great commotion among my fellow-passengers, many of whom jumped from their seats and pressed eagerly around a tall man who had just entered the car. They addressed him in the most familiar style. 'Hello Abe! How are you?' and so on. And he responded in the same manner: 'Good-evening Ben! How are you, Joe? Glad to see you, Dick!' and there was much laughter at some things he said, which, in the confusion of voices, I could not understand.

'Why,' exclaimed my companion, the committeeman, 'there's Lincoln himself!' He pressed through the crowd and introduced me to Abraham Lincoln, whom I then saw for the first time ... He received me with an off-hand cordiality, like an old acquaintance ... and we sat down together. In a somewhat high-pitched but pleasant voice ... [he] talked in so simple and familiar a strain, and his manner and homely phrase were so absolutely free from any semblance of self-consciousness or pretension of superiority, that I soon felt as if I had known him all my life, and we had very long been close friends."[20]

President Franklin Delano Roosevelt was also conscious of the importance of projecting a positive and virile image whenever he spoke before the public. As a result, like Lincoln, who became adept at hiding his despondency from the masses, Roosevelt also became adept at hiding his infantile paralysis (poliomyelitis) from public scrutiny. Even though he was confined to using a wheelchair, he was seen at many public gatherings appearing able to stand or sit in an ordinary chair, where his steel leg and arm braces remained out of public view. I, like many others, didn't realize Roosevelt had polio until many years after his death.

The old saying "actions speak louder than words" is certainly true in the world of politics, isn't it? Take, for example, John Edwards, one of a number of presidential hopefuls in the 2008 presidential elections, who recently received a four-hundred-dollar haircut. When I saw him on TV receiving it, I couldn't help think what bad publicity that haircut would generate. Here he claims he is for the common, mainstream, ordinary American electorate, but he receives a four-hundred-dollar haircut! Wow, something doesn't compute. There's a disconnect somewhere. "Seeing is believing" is certainly true, isn't it? John Edwards can talk a good game, but it's what he does that is all so much more powerful in demonstrating what is really at the heart of what he believes. After all, it's what is in a person's soul that people resonate with, because that is what's good and loved by others.

People in political life need to be good communicators. Our best presidents have been masters of these skills. While people will accept

---

[20] Donald Phillips II, *Lincoln on Leadership*, 156–57. With permission of Warner Books. © 2004 by Donald Phillips II.

sometimes clownish or even boorish behavior in local politicians, on the national and world stage, we want and should demand the highest level of communication skills.

Voters need to critically judge the values and policies the candidate espouses, as well as how he or she articulates those thoughts in presenting his or her case.

9/11: THE DATE GEORGE W. BUSH DEFINED HIS PRESIDENCY

9/11 marked the moment when George W. Bush identified why he was elected president of the United States. It was to fight terrorism. Prior to the terrorist attack on this country, the president was focused on two things: his tax cut, designed to be a supply-side boon to the ailing economy, and education, the issue on which his record in Texas was strongest.

I have no quarrel with the president's wish to devote most of his energies to fighting terrorism; however, what I do question are the tactics he chose to accomplish that mission.

"On September 11, 2001," the 9/11 Commission reported,

> America was viciously attacked by nineteen men affiliated with Osama Bin Laden and Al-Qaeda terrorists. These men simultaneously hijacked four U.S. domestic Commercial airliners. Two were crashed into the World Trade Center in Manhattan, New York City—one into each of the two tallest towers, about 18 minutes apart—shortly after which both towers collapsed. The third aircraft crashed into the U.S. Department of Defense headquarters, the Pentagon, in Arlington County, Virginia. The fourth plane crashed into a rural field in Somerset County, Pennsylvania, 80 miles east of

Pittsburgh, following passenger resistance. The official count records 2986 deaths in the attacks.

The 9/11 Commission reported that these attackers

> turned the hijacked planes into the largest suicide bombs in history—in one of the most lethal acts ever carried out in the United States. The September 11th attacks are among the most significant events to have occurred so far in the 21st century in terms of the profound economic, social, political, cultural, and military effects that followed in the United States and many other parts of the world.

The fact that the twin towers' destruction was captured on television simply added to the magnitude and horror of some of the events that occurred on 9/11; such happenings would cause anyone who witnessed the destruction to sit up and take notice. I couldn't believe this was happening in America.

Right after 9/11, our allies were all on our side. They were clearly empathetic and sympathetic toward our plight and willing to help us fight the war on terrorism. Today, after the Iraq mistake, it's a different story. Now, many of those same allies are against us. In fact, most of the nations of the world are very angry and deeply embarrassed at what we've said and done since we took our eye off the target and switched from our pursuit of Bin Laden in Afghanistan to fighting a war in Iraq.

Though there was a fissure between the two major parties before the 9/11 era, the divide has become much greater than before the terrorist attack. We have yet to learn how to live with terrorism. It's like some forms of cancer: if we can't prevent them from happening, at least we can contain them and in that way learn to live with them. Before we can effectively deal with terrorism, we have to look at the problem less emotionally, and more rationally.

A Formidable Opponent

No amount of military might is going to stamp out terrorism once and for all. The belief that might makes right, and that as long as we appear strong and invincible, we are in the driver's seat and have nothing to fear, represents the kind of thinking that has gone the way of the dinosaur. Massive amounts of troops and shock-and-awe firepower might have been the way to go in the Second World War, but it has outlived its effectiveness in today's age and therefore belongs to a bygone era. It should be put in our history books right next to where the dinosaurs reside.

Remember, our government cannot possibly protect this country from a terrorist attack 100 percent of the time. Therefore, another attack will happen—hopefully later rather than sooner, but it will occur. We as a nation must prepare ourselves for that eventuality. Massive denial will not cut it. We must begin to take a square look at our current reality. Just thinking of what we will do on an individual level to combat terrorism is not a viable strategy. Not only is it terribly selfish, but it also is ineffective. What is required is a community effort—an effort involving looking beyond our individual and selfish concerns, but rather at the needs of the community as a whole. "What we can do for others in distress?" should be our mantra here, in the twenty-first century.

United We Stood

Since the president knew Bin Laden was behind the 9/11 attacks, and since he knew the Taliban training facility was in Afghanistan, his attacking Afghanistan by aggressively bombing the terrorists was the logical thing to do. He had America's backing when he chose to take that action; America was still an undivided nation.

Prior to our declaring war on Iraq, many authorities claimed the United States couldn't simultaneously fight a war in Afghanistan and win in Iraq. Nevertheless, the president ignored such fears and doggedly persevered in believing that both wars could be fought and won.

If others question the wisdom of carrying out two wars at once, why did the president decide to ignore their advice? He felt that the wars on both fronts would cause the people of those countries to revolt and demand democracy. He was wrong.

The more pertinent question that needs to be asked is, "What system flaws contributed to President Bush's ability to do this?" The reason we have three branches of government—the executive, legislative, and judicial—is to offer safeguards so that none of the governmental branches will overstep their bounds and assume more power than they should. All three branches serve as checks and balances to one another. However, when one branch either abdicates their responsibilities or overreaches their jurisdiction, then the system breaks down.

It's the responsibility of the citizens to be knowledgeable enough to recognize any breach of the balance of power and to correct it through the power of their vote.

Cultural Ignorance

On September 24, 2006, David Brooks, an op-ed columnist for the *New York Times*, wrote a column titled "Closing of a Nation," which concerned President Bush's supposedly visionary plan to transform Iraq. Brooks's observations about Iraq show us that Bush must have known very little about the culture he was dealing with, or he would never have chosen to attempt to democratize it in the first place.

"Iraq is the most xenophobic, sexist and reactionary society on earth," Brooks said. To illustrate Iraq's cultural resistance to an outside presence, he cited a study by World Values Survey involving more than two thousand adults from Iraq. After noting that years of war and strife have left the Iraqi people in survival mode, Brooks quoted the World Values researchers as saying that Iraqis "reject foreigners to a degree that is virtually unknown in other societies throughout the world, including more than a dozen predominantly Islamic countries."

The study described in the article revealed that ninety percent of Iraqi Arabs rejected the idea of a foreign neighbor, compared to nine percent of Americans. "Iraqi Arabs almost universally reject Americans, Britons and the French," Brooks added.

So Iraqis aren't interested in a foreign presence. This doesn't mean they won't embrace democratic ideas within their own culture once the foreigners have retreated a little, right? Wrong. Iraqis aren't just unusually resistant to foreigners, according to the survey. They are also resistant to female leaders, the separation of church and state, and notions of independence over obedience. In raising children,

Brooks observed, "they emphasized 'obedience' and 'religious faith' more than any of the 80 other societies that have been studied."

Brooks's conclusion had damning implications for the Iraq war: "if you're going to do nation-building, you have to understand the values of the people you're going to build a nation with."[21]

Perhaps President Bush could have used that advice before charging forward with an Iraq war. Or perhaps a more suited political leader would have done his homework and drawn such conclusions for himself.

It is largely agreed by most analysts discussing the issue that democracy is indeed possible in predominantly Muslim countries, with the caveat that any democracy that emerges must reflect and fit the culture and traditions of that region. This logical analysis brings with it the notion that the type of democracy that ultimately emerges may not be to the liking of, or in the interests of, Western influence. Democracy is generally reflective of the will of the people, and in the Muslim world, this would mean a democracy heavily influenced by the Islamic tradition. In other words, President Bush's plan to institute some fast-acting Americanized ideal of democracy was doomed to failure from the beginning.

In the Muslim world, the desire for democracy is layered with the desire to maintain Islamic traditions and laws. With the establishment of democracy in those Islamist nations that will accept such a doctrine, the risk of such an adoption is almost palatable. What happens if the type of democracy established reflects interests that other democratic nations find difficult to accept? Those countries that are rich in Islamic theology, laws, and traditions can easily evolve into a belief system that runs quite contrary to what we in the United States would find acceptable.

Another major consideration in the development of democracy in the Muslim world is the duration of time allowed for the development process. It is often noted that Western-style democracy has endured and enjoyed a long duration of development and refinement. One of the questions raised in introducing democracy to the Muslim world is how the world can expect the nations of Islam to embrace democratic

---

[21] David Brooks, "Closing of a Nation," NYT.com, September 24, 2006. Used with permission of the *New York Times*.

governance in such a compressed time frame. Sure, to the Americans watching this war from home, it might seem as if ages have passed since President Bush's declaration of victory over Iraq in 2003. This makes sense, as the subsequent years of that conflict have been both expensive and deadly to Americans. But was it ever realistic to expect otherwise? When we consider the data on Iraqi culture, it seems that President Bush's plan to quickly shock and awe the Iraqi people into democracy was unworkable from the start.

War was never the answer. The best weapon we have to promote our brand of democracy for other nations to adopt, whether Islamic or not, is the ability to view the populace with affection, appreciating them as human beings trying to peacefully coexist with us and other nations of the world. It is important to remember that while democracy is possible and even desired in the Muslim world, it can't be imposed or expected to be a clone of the Western version.

As it is likely to be recognized by these nations' populations that it is in their best interests, democracy in some form is destined to emerge in the Arab Muslim nations. When it will happen and what shape it will take remains to be seen. Will it be friendly to Western governments and agreeable among its neighbors? Will the West honor and recognize that which emerges as legitimate? Will its framework allow for an Arab-Israeli solution? Will human rights and the will of the people be served? Time, and only time, will tell whether our giant can learn to tread more lightly and speak more softly before it's too late.

At the end of 2006, former Secretary of State Colin Powell broke his long public silence on his objections to the president's insistence to continue to stay the course in Iraq, feeling that because we are losing and because what's happening in Iraq is a civil war, we should begin to withdraw our troops by the middle of 2007.

The president rejected part of the conclusions stated by the Iraq Study Group and his former Secretary of Defense's recommendations to set parameters for a phased withdrawal beginning in 2007. Instead, he continued to insist the violence in Iraq did not represent a civil war. This was done after considering various options for a new military strategy—among them a surge of 15,000 to 30,000 troops added to the current 140,000 in Iraq, to secure Baghdad and to accelerate the training of Iraqi forces. The president ultimately made the decision to add 20,000 additional troops.

The president chose to reject what Senator. John McCain and others had proposed, which was a redirection of the U.S. military away from the insurgency to focus mainly on hunting Al-Qaeda terrorists, a proposal which our nation's top military leaders had earlier made to the president.

After listening to the pros and cons of a given issue, there are times when the president must go it alone, even if the majority doesn't agree. JFK's handling of the Cuban missile crisis is a good example. There are other times when it's clearly required that the president not only listens to others, even if he disagrees with the consensus, but also implements the decision, for the good of the country.

Congress is not any more immune to criticism than the president. Percentagewise, the American approval rating for the president is in the low thirties. When Congress itself is polled, even fewer think our country is going in the right direction; the percentage is in the high twenties. One of the reasons why Congress's approval rating is so low is because of the great division between the Democratic and Republican parties. Instead of reaching across the aisle and trying to come to a consensus of what would be best for our country to do, they engage in political bickering to such an extent that no consensus is forthcoming.

Of course, the loser in all of this is the American public, because nothing gets done. That's why our Congress ends up being described as a do-nothing Congress.

Just because democracy works for us doesn't mean it's a form of government every country wishes to embrace. That's why it's so difficult to watch our government continue to pursue a failed policy. It is disturbing enough to see billions of dollars a week being expended in that country when many have already concluded we have lost the war. However, what is even more disconcerting is the number of young Americans whose lives are lost fighting a "war we must win," as President Bush described it. Is it fair for those brave American men and women to continue to fight and risk their lives for a war the politicians realize we've already lost? I think not.

In a policy brief titled "Fighting Terrorism: Lessons from the Cold War," Anatol Lieven, a senior associate at the Carnegie Endowment for International Peace, summarized a broad strategy to successfully combat terrorism. He wrote, "Like the Cold war, the war against terrorism will be a very long struggle in which ideological, political, and socioeconomic campaigns will be as important as military campaigns. To achieve any kind of long-term success, the United States must combat not only the terrorist groups themselves, but the wider movements that give them support and shelter."[22]

Lieven highlights the deficiency of regional expertise in our military, intelligence community, and planning bureaucracy. He argues that a thorough understanding of the enemy—its political, cultural, religious, and nationalistic attitudes—is the first step in winning the war of ideas. He blames ignorance and prejudice for many American blunders and says, "This has got to stop. A U.S. planner who cannot tell the difference between a Shia and a Sunni or a Sufi and a Wahabi should be encouraged to exercise his or her planning skills in a different field."[23]

Lieven goes on to make his case for the limited use of U.S. military might in the fight against terrorism, noting the counterproductive consequences of waging war in our traditional manner. He writes,

> A key lesson of the Cold War is that neither the use nor even the deployment of U.S. forces necessarily needs to be extensive....
>
> The full support of the authorities and ordinary people in the Muslim states for the struggle against terrorism is absolutely essential, most of all in the fields of intelligence and policing, as it was in many countries in the struggle against communist subversion during the Cold War.[24]

Unfortunately, what Lieven says we should not do is exactly what we did in Iraq. We are all painfully aware that we won the Iraq war but were unable to keep the peace. There is little question in anyone's

---

[22] Anatol Lieven, "Fighting Terrorism: Lessons from the Cold War." Published on www.carnegieendowment.org. Used with permission of the New America Foundation, www.newamerica.net.

[23] Ibid.

[24] Ibid.

mind that we will have to leave Iraq, like we did Vietnam, before we are able to complete our mission. This is because President Bush and Congress failed to accurately assess what we were up against prior to waging war. We let our own arrogance and belief that we knew what was best for Iraq determine our policy.

Leading by Example

If we can't win the war on terrorism with bombs and guns, what's the answer?

Since the war on terrorism has to do with winning the hearts and minds of those who are prone to adopting terrorist beliefs, we must be proactive and demonstrate there are other ways of dealing with disillusionment and frustration than by engaging in senseless murder and mayhem. Being active, anticipating problems, and providing solutions to potential troubles is the only way we're going to defeat the terrorists. Since they're willing to die for what they believe in, we must counter their belief system by giving them hope and a sense of a future where our way of life shows more promise to them and would be preferred over what they believe to be true.

To do that, we must lead by example, and we can do that by being more responsive to the needs of people in this country. Instead of being self-absorbed and concerned only for our own personal welfare, we must begin to genuinely respond to the needs and welfare of others and to show how the monies put into guns and bullets— approximately 500 billion as of 2008—could be better used to show others and our community how money could be used as a means to an end rather than to an end in itself.

The best way that we, as American citizens, can uphold and strengthen our way of life is by becoming actively involved in the democratic system by voting, protesting, and lobbying for those laws and policies that we believe in.

Hopefully, the moderate Muslim who is part of that community will begin to see the merits of our way of life and will rein in the Islamic extremist by actively preventing them from engaging in destructive and devastating behavior. Ultimately, if our war on terrorism is to be successful, the moderate Muslim must be a major player in making it happen.

Leading with Partnership

Islamic terrorism has changed how we look at war. These terrorists are willing to use whatever means necessary to eliminate all the "infidels" in the world (except those in their own culture, of course). They are willing to die to accomplish that goal. Life means nothing to them. As days turn to weeks, and weeks turn to months, and months turn to years, the possibility increases that eventually they will get their hands on weapons of mass destruction. If that ever happens, considering their willingness to die for their cause, it is possible that millions of people may be killed.

In an ideal future, our respect for life and humanity should prevent us from killing a like number of people to even the score. If we were to retaliate for the mass destruction that a few terrorists caused, many innocent lives would be at risk, because it is extremely difficult to identify the terrorist from the non-insurgent. We would have to be indiscriminate in taking lives. Because today's style of warfare follows no reasonable rules of engagement, many innocent people would die. Therefore, conventional war is no longer a viable option.

We must engage in dialogue—not only with nations that are our friends, but those who are our enemies. We must not put preconditions on whether we will talk to our adversaries. By that I mean we should not make grand pronouncements about how evil and wicked our adversaries are, before or even after our peace talks. We should not announce our intentions of what we expect to obtain from the meetings before they begin. We should keep as open a mind as possible before and during the meeting, and we should be willing to compromise.

I am not for a moment suggesting we negotiate with the terrorists. What I am suggesting is that the funds that are normally used to increase our nuclear arsenal and the usual kinds of weapons and heavy equipment that comes out of the military-industrial complex be redirected to fund projects related to the twenty-first-century war on terrorism. After all, we already have enough nuclear bombs to eliminate whole cities and contaminate and make uninhabitable miles and miles of land. In fact, we have enough nuclear material to destroy the world, so why add to an already bloated stockpile?

It's safe to say that we must work with moderate Muslims to convince their radical brothers and sisters to stop the insanity of killing innocent people for the sake of Allah. They, and they alone, will be the ones needed to convince the insurgents of the error of their ways. Without their help, terrorism will not be contained. Containment is all that we can hope for, as terrorism will never be completely defeated.

Though we need the moderate Muslim's help in order to be successful in battling terrorism, we also need the world community of nations.

We must expend our monies and energy in working with one another in this country and with the community of world nations to fight terrorism. If there is ever a time when the friendly nations of the world need to get together and work for a common cause, it is now. We should not let our differences, whether they be free trade, human-rights issues, or a host of other concerns, set up barriers that prevent us from getting together to discuss how to deal with the common enemy that is terrorism. As a community of nations, we need to speak with one voice. Up to now, we haven't done a very good job of listening to our allies, such as France and Germany. We must put aside our petty differences and stop believing that our way is the only way to do things. We should start having summits to discuss terrorism, just as we've had economic summits in the past. Through those kinds of discussions, we can develop a worldwide strategy to deal with the terrorism threat.

The stakes are too great. If we don't learn to live with all nations on this marvelous planet of ours, we will soon all perish, regardless of how righteous and noble our causes might be. America or any other nation cannot afford to have another major war. Each time a war occurs, there's a greater possibility of all-out holocaust.

We can no longer think that what's good for America is also good for the world. That is not only a statement that is filled with arrogance and self-importance, but it is flatly wrong. We must begin to see the value in all countries, friend and foe alike. We must no longer summarily refuse to work with countries like Iran and Syria because they happen to hold ideals different than our own. Even though the values of their leaders may be diametrically opposite ours, we must learn to coexist with them. Our basic survival depends upon it.

The essentials of future war will not be technology, wealth, or industrial capacity. The key components in the future will be commitment, patience, and a steadfastness born of belief in the fight. Short of obliterating the countries that house terrorists, the United States will be unable to defeat its opponents quickly. Military leaders trained to think that all they need for victory is to fight a climatic battle and then return home triumphant will find themselves as obsolete as Stone Age weapons.

The important element of future war will be time. Because the enemy does fight for a cause and not under the flag of a country, it will be impossible to achieve a formal surrender. Extra-national terrorist groups will not surrender. They will have to be eliminated individually. This will take time ... and our enemies have that in great supply.

We, like the family of nations, will never be able to defeat terrorism to the point where it no longer remains a menace in each of our lives. The best we can do is to learn to live with it, so that terrorism doesn't become all-consuming and threatening to the point where we and other nations are unable to function even reasonably well in our everyday lives. Perhaps if America can learn to lead by example and with partnership, we can succeed in greatly reducing the global toll of terrorism.

BETTER LEADER, BETTER FUTURE

Though at times it may seem that way, this is not a book designed to bash President Bush. I've outlined some of his mistakes. Now it's time to more closely examine what we want in a future leader. What can we learn from our past? What traits should we encourage in future presidents?

Glaring Inconsistencies

When President Bush went to the United Nations to seek support for the Iraq war, he said Sadaam Hussein was a tyrant who had weapons of mass destruction and had to be removed. He said Sadaam Hussein was working on a nuclear device which should be available in but a few years, and he said Saddam Hussein was involved with the 9/11 attacks. None of those supposed certainties that George W. Bush uttered proved to be true.

So here we have a president charging a dictator with acts he did not commit. Yes, Sadaam was a brutal dictator, but so were several other rulers, who also massacred thousands of their people, but no one removed any of them.

In fact, our government has a long history of backing freedom- and liberty-hating governments if it served our strategic or economic interests.

One moment, America is befriending dictators who commit atrocious deeds. The next moment, America is starting wars with dictators over events that never happened. Ethically speaking, America's relations with dictators have never made much sense.

In an editorial titled "With Friends Like These,"[25] the *Washington Post*'s editorial staff examined a meeting between Secretary of State Condoleezza Rice and President of Equatorial Guinea (Africa's third largest oil producer), Teodoro Obiang Nguema.

This oil-rich country is fostering a cooperative relationship with the United States and its oil firms. But, as the *Post*'s staff editorial writers point out, this relationship may not mesh with our government's freedom and liberty rhetoric.

> But oil has done little to help Equatorial Guinea's 540,000 people, some 400,000 of whom suffer from malnutrition. Those who are hungry know better than to complain.
>
> According to State Department reports, the president's goons have urinated on prisoners, sliced their ears and smeared them with oil to attract stinging ants.
>
> So it is uncontroversial to observe that Mr. Obiang is no friend to his people. But he is a "good friend" of the United States, at least according to Secretary of State Condoleezza Rice, who met with him last week in Washington. "I'm very pleased to welcome the president," Ms. Rice told reporters after the meeting. "Thank you very much for your presence here."

The article went on to note that when it comes to political and civil liberties, only seven countries rate worse than Equatorial Guinea. Why, then, was the Bush administration "throwing bouquets to odious dictators," as the article phrased it? Though the administration's reasoning was never explained, the article hypothesizes that Obiang's favorable relationship with U.S. oil firms might have had something to do with it.

---

[25] The Washington Post Editorial Staff, "With Friends Like These," *Washington Post*, © 2006, http://www.washingtonpost.com/wp-dyn/content/article/2006/04/17/AR2006041701368.html. Reprinted with permission.

Gone should be the days where we court favor with brutal dictators because it serves our vital interests. Being duplicitous with any nation by telling them what we think they want to hear, rather than what we honestly believe to be so, should stop immediately. Honest diplomacy needs to replace dishonest rhetoric.

If American voters choose carefully, perhaps future leaders will base their decisions on diplomacy and ethics, not on which dictator has something profitable to offer them today.

A Team Mentality

When playing football or any team sport, it's important to be loyal to the coach and the team, because, after all, it's a team sport. By definition, you, as a player, must not just think of your own interests and desires to be viewed as the star of the team because you make the most touchdowns, baskets, home runs, or what have you. Rather, you're expected to be loyal to the team's goals, which means to work as a unit and, through teamwork, put more points on the board than your opposition.

When President Bush demanded unquestioned faith from his followers regarding his military decisions, he wasn't operating according to America's best interests, but his own.

Because there is ample evidence to suggest President Bush may be suffering from Attention Deficit Hyperactivity Disorder and therefore finds it difficult to contain his anxieties for an extended period of time, he's inclined to make decisions quickly. Since this is so, meetings and their length are held to a minimum. Because debate is of short duration, and assuming each member of his administration is eager to have the president adopt his or her recommendations, it's easy to understand how each will try to slant their arguments by telling the commander in chief what he wants to hear, rather than what really needs to be said. I'm sure President Bush telegraphs what he wants to hear through the questions he asks as well as through the body language he transmits. If that is so, obviously any information the president receives is biased and distorted from the get-go.

In the future, we should choose a president who considers America's best interests—and is also willing to stand under scrutiny and remain accountable. A president who truly believes in democracy is not going to insist that Congress and the Supreme Court remain unquestioningly loyal. Such a president would never expect automatic and wholehearted support without examination. In a similar vein, a worthy president should not fill his or her administration with sycophants who will automatically agree with every decision.

Thomas L. Friedman wrote an op-ed piece in the *New York Times* on May 17, 2006, titled "Saying No to Bush's Yes Men,"[26] that scathingly took the president to task on preferring to choose people who are loyal to the administration over those who are right for the job. Whereas in times past, Friedman has been inclined not to talk so harshly about the errors the president has made in conducting the people's business, that was not the case in this article.

He opens by saying,

> President Bush has slipped in one recent poll to a 29 percent approval rating. Frankly, I can't believe that.

> I mean, really, ask yourself: How could there still be 29 percent of the people who approve of this presidency?

> Personally, I think the president can reshuffle his cabinet all he wants, but his poll ratings are not going to substantially recover—ever.

Friedman observed that while wartime conditions had slowed and perhaps temporarily clouded America's judgment, "a lot of Americans in recent months have simply lost confidence in this administration's competence and honesty."

Friedman takes issue with the very concern that prompted me to write this book, criticizing the administration's prioritization of politics over America's best interests.

President Bush's pandering cabinet can easily be perceived as a symptom of such political motivations. "If you had worked for so long to be president," Friedman asks, "wouldn't you want to staff your administration with the very best people you could find, especially in national security and especially in the area of intelligence, which has been the source of so much controversy—from Sept. 11 to Iraq? Wouldn't that be your instinct?"

---

[26] Thomas L. Friedman, "Saying No To Bush's Yes Men," *New York Times*, May 17, 2006. Used with permission of the *New York Times*.

In particular, Friedman criticized CIA nominations like those of Porter Goss and Kyle "Dusty" Foggo, both of whom boasted plenty of loyalty to the president, but neither of whom offered much in the way of expertise. After calling Goss a "complete partisan hack," Friedman later goes on to observe, "Foggo is not an expert on Iran or Iraq or Russia, but rather on Perrier, Poland Spring and Fiji water. That is the guy the Bush team chose as its chief operating officer at the CIA."

Both men later resigned, but not before wasting a year of America's time. Besides, those appointments are just one symptom of a greater ailment, as Friedman observes:

> In his excellent book on the Iraq war, *The Assassins' Gate*, George Packer tells the story of how some of the State Department's best Iraq experts were barred from going to Iraq immediately after the invasion—because they didn't pass Dick Cheney's or Don Rumsfeld's ideology tests. And that is the core of the matter: The Bush team believes in loyalty over expertise. When ideology always trumps reality, loyalty always trumps expertise.

As long as the president insists on loyalty over expertise in order to monopolize on the spotlight, the public approval rating won't improve. As Friedman says,

> The idea that the president's poll numbers would go up if he replaced his Treasury secretary is ludicrous. Replacing him would be like replacing one ghost with another.
>
> I understand that loyalty is important, but what good is it to have loyal crewmembers when the ship is sinking? So they can sing your praises on the way down to the ocean floor? I just don't understand how a president whose whole legacy depends on getting national security and intelligence right would have tolerated anything but the very best in those areas. What in the world was he thinking?[27]

It's obvious Friedman believes politics or ideology has taken over the government. In other words, instead of the president choosing the best person for the job, so that the American public will be the

---

[27] Thomas L. Friedman, "Saying No To Bush's Yes Men," *New York Times*, May 17, 2006. Used with permission of the *New York Times*.

beneficiaries of such a choice, his only job qualification is who will be the most loyal. The degree to which President Bush values loyalty over expertise clearly suggests that he feels very insecure in his job.

The president should share his decision-making powers with others. In contrast to President Lincoln's wish to have men around him who were willing to debate policy, and who held views different than his own, Mr. Bush made it quite clear that he didn't wish to have any of his administration second-guess or challenge any of his decisions once they were made.

Political Moderation

What is also very troublesome is the president's decisions appear to be driven primarily by his political and moral ideology; what drives him is based on his own inner core political beliefs, devoid of what the nonpolitical Americans value and embrace. That's why his decisions have such a rigid moralistic tone to them, which leads his thinking to be either all black or all white. There's no gray area to be considered. This in itself is very dangerous, because the world is not built on absolutes. When one begins to think there's only one way to view the world, and that way is, in this case, furthest right (it could be furthest left) from the political center, extremism rears its ugly head. When that occurs, watch out, because that way of thinking breeds radicalism and intolerance, which is reflected in low tolerance for people who think differently than you do. In this instance, intolerance may be shown through unwillingness to support stem-cell research, same-sex unions, or the theory of evolution. In the case of the Republican Party, what it does urge is for the extremist to embrace the far-right extreme religious view and other right-wing political ideology.

If that thinking permeates the politician's soul, which it has done in President Bush's case, then his idiosyncratic, very personal view of how to look at and deal with all of life's issues becomes very predictable, for all of life is viewed through his self-righteous eyes.

To the degree that President Bush's moral, church-related issues become integrated into all his political thought and discussion, this kind of thinking can't help but violate the First Amendment, which is to keep separate issues related to the church with that related to the state. This is yet another danger of political extremism based on inflexible personal beliefs, rather than a more moderate, thought-out approach designed to reflect the collective needs of the American people. How could future leaders contrast with these political flaws? In order to envision a more ideal future, we need only look to the past. As our examination of valuable presidential traits continues, we find an excellent example in President Lincoln.

Encouragement of Diversity

Whereas President Bush was looking for loyalty, support, and commonality in thought, Lincoln was looking for just the opposite, which was diversity in thought and view. Since he wanted people in his cabinet who represented the people at large, and because he wanted to be able to look at all sides of the issue before coming to a decision, he chose a cabinet with that thought in mind. What he ended up doing was to appoint the three men who were his chief rivals for the Republican nomination for president, and whom Lincoln had defeated. So, as you might imagine, even though they all accepted Lincoln's invitation to join his cabinet, they were anything but happy campers at the onset of their appointments. Nevertheless, Lincoln was able to tame the savage beasts by utilizing their strengths and assets before making policy decisions.

By the end of Lincoln's presidency, he was loved and admired by not only all of his cabinet members but many of his so-called enemies, for he was a man of great character and principle and was never willing to compromise his sense of integrity for political gain or advantage.

Confidence

As a respected leader and incredible public speaker, it's obvious that President Lincoln had great confidence in his ability to serve as president of the United States. In contrast, I wonder if President Bush feels the same degree of confidence that Lincoln felt when he became president. Based on what already has been said, it doesn't appear to be so.

Lincoln's confidence stemmed from the overcoming of many obstacles on his way to the presidency. Lincoln did not come from a background of privilege. Unlike President Bush, Lincoln had to struggle his entire life to prove himself. It is only through struggle and failure that a sense of confidence can be achieved.

Lincoln's confidence as a leader prompted respect, not coddling. President Bush's level of confidence—or lack thereof—has invoked a very different reaction. Even though Brent Scowcroft was adamantly opposed to President Bush Jr. going to war with Iraq, he didn't want to be vociferous about his objections. Since Scowcroft had served on George Sr.'s cabinet and was a close friend of his, he wanted to keep his objections low-key, so as not to give the impression that President Bush's father was watching his every move. In that sense, he didn't want the George W. to lose confidence and question his ability to run the country.

What is amazing is that both Scowcroft and Bush Senior felt they needed to protect George Jr.'s self-confidence. We're talking about the man who occupies the highest office in the land. We're not talking about an adolescent who just started a new job, having never worked a day in his life before. We're talking about our president and the leader of the free world! Confidence is key in any leader. If voters are wise, they'll choose a poised public speaker who is secure enough to share the limelight and hear dissenting opinions. Only a confident leader can take on the vast responsibility of the presidency without resorting to hasty decisions out of intimidation or insecurity. Like Lincoln, a confident leader will share the limelight, remain open to dissenting views, and carry out his or her duties honorably.

Respect for the Separation of Church and State

Our Founding Fathers enacted the First Amendment to prevent precisely what President Bush has done, which is to allow the church and God's teachings to be a primary determinant in conducting the affairs of state. He has mixed apples with oranges. Not that God or the American public is either one of those two fruits, and not to be sacrilegious by using that analogy, but I do feel that affairs of state, the people's business, needs to be considered quite separate and distinct from the president's personal religious beliefs. If that doesn't happen, how then are we able to know what reasoning went into our president's decisions? Did he decide on faith or on sound empirical evidence?

It's conceivable that President Bush unconsciously has turned to God to give him the confidence to make secular, far-reaching, life-or-death decisions. Since displacement is an ego defense mechanism, therefore unconsciously determined; it is a convenient means of temporarily shifting the decision-making responsibility to a higher power, and in that way, avoiding feeling the responsibility for any ill effects of enacting such a policy. This mechanism is of particular value when life-or-death issues are involved. If it turns out that he has made an earth-shaking error of judgment, such as peremptorily declaring war on Iraq, it is not his fault. After all, he was only following God's will.

It's obvious to anyone who has observed our president in action that he's a very religious man. It is also clear that he practices his religion on a daily basis. That in itself is not what I object to. What I do take issue with is President Bush allowing his personal religious views to frequently seep into his daily political discourse, where he allows such thinking to unduly influence his political and governmental policy decisions.

This practice undermines the First Amendment and the very foundations of our democratic country.

Thomas Jefferson wrote a letter to Edward Livingston on July 10, 1822. In it, he said, "Every new and successful example, therefore, of a perfect separation between the ecclesiastical and civil matters, is of importance; and I have no doubt that every new example will succeed, as every past one has done, in showing that religion and Government will both exist in greater purity the less they are mixed together."

To the degree that President Bush has allowed his private religious thought to seep into matters of state, he is violating Thomas Jefferson's dictum.

There has been much written about the influence of God in our president's life. George W. identifies the deciding moment in his presidency as being when the terrorist attacked our country in 9/11. He has also been asked about the impact his father has played in his life—more specifically, his presidency. His answer does not suggest a great deal of influence. They were not very close. What I've read indicates that since he became president, George W. Bush has not allowed his father's presidential experience to influence him in any significant way.

There is a strong suggestion that he feels he has a personal relationship with God, and that God is helping him make policy decisions to such an extent that it's difficult to know where God's influence ends and his begins. I am personally not comfortable with the thought of any deity deciding what my nation should do. As a citizen, that's my job.

Some have made interesting comparisons of the thought processes of President Bush to those of his archenemy, Osama Bin Laden. They note the same rigidity of ideology, the righteousness and certainty of their cause, the simplistic labeling of good and evil, an uncompromising stance toward solutions, and an overwhelming sense of divine empowerment and obligation.

The driven, obsessive, and messianic quality in the president's thinking about terrorism helps us understand why he appears so preoccupied with the whole subject. It also helps us to better appreciate why he never appears ahead of the curve when dealing with the people's business. To do all of the people's business more efficiently and with greater alacrity, President Bush needs to more expeditiously deal with the matters at hand, while still maintaining a thoughtful attitude.

It is too bad that here, in America, an open discussion and debate is rarely held in a public forum so that the extreme views of any religious teaching, be it Muslim fundamentalism or Evangelical conservatism, could be better understood by the public at large. By having such a dialogue, we, as Americans, could better understand the dangers and pitfalls of any excessive religious point of view that may influence matters of state—and in doing so, understand why it's important to separate those issues related to the church from those related to the state.

Perhaps getting involved at the community level through town meetings, where the public is able to air their religious differences, would be a first step to rectify the situation.

Action can be taken in the voting booth as well. Future leaders should be elected for their willingness and ability to uphold the values that America was built upon. Voters should ensure that any potential president has the same reverence for our personal freedoms and rights as our forefathers and first presidents did.

Highly Developed Cognitive Abilities

Our president does not appear to be a very thoughtful man.

Because the president openly acknowledges that he's not a great reader, he has a member of his staff read much of what he receives. The reader, in turn, summarizes this correspondence for the president. That being the case, our president openly acknowledges he relies heavily on his instincts, or his gut, when making important decisions.

Just as President Bush attempts to ease decisions by letting God do the heavy lifting, he avoids any mental heavy lifting himself by not reading or engaging in any personal fact finding.

Rather than value cognition, investigation, and reading (all of which involve critical thinking) and using those tools to arrive at a logical, intellectual conclusion, our president's favored tool to accomplish this process is the use of his "instincts," as he delights in calling his gut feelings.

Since President Bush relies heavily on gut feelings, it's easy to understand why he finds it difficult not to appear defensive when questions are raised about the many problems that have occurred during his presidency.

His defensive posture is warranted, because he has made a number of poor decisions, such as waging the Iraq war, lowering taxes in the first place (and, after lowering them, allowing them to stand, even though our national debt is astronomical), not responding in a timely manner to the Katrina disaster, not doing anything constructive to slow the advance of global warming ... the list goes on and on. Essentially, President Bush's defensiveness occurs because he has acted when action shouldn't have taken place, or he has failed to act when some kind of action was required.

A good leader must display excellent cognitive abilities. Intellectualism, philosophy, and critical thought are essential to making the incredibly complex decisions that the leader of our nation will face every day. No one's gut can be expected to handle that kind of reasoning; our future presidents should display mental faculties far beyond those that President Bush has demonstrated.

Enduring Dedication to America's Best Interests

In George Bush Sr.'s book *All the Best, George Bush: My Life in Letters and Other Writings,* he talked about why he chose not to go into Iraq and capture Saddam Hussein. He didn't want to do that because he knew, which his son discovered later, that it would be easy to win the war, but difficult to keep the peace.

I don't know if President Bush read his father's book or not. But considering how his father was so adamant in not wanting to go into Baghdad and capture Hussein, upon learning that his son was seriously contemplating it, I would think he might have had some discussions with George Jr. about the wisdom of his choice. If George Sr. did that, why was he unable to convince his son that it was unwise to do just what he ended up doing—namely, starting the second Iraq war?

On the other hand, if George Sr. never discussed his concerns with his son, shame on him.

Presidents are like parents: once a president or parent, always a president or parent. This means that after they leave office, they must understand that they continue to assume that role and need to speak out when speaking out is required. Parents don't cease to be caring and concerned about their children's safety and welfare once the children reach their majority. They continue to play the maternal and paternal role throughout their lives.

Upon leaving office, there is ample evidence to indicate George Sr. made a conscious decision to stay clear of advising or offering suggestions on how future presidents should conduct their affairs of state. He has not commented publicly on the Clinton White House and has refrained from saying anything about how his son is handling being president.

The senior President Bush is not doing himself or the country any favors by thinking his presidential responsibilities end the millisecond the new president takes the oath of office. At that time, he doesn't suddenly look at his watch and say, "Well, it's time to go, I'm out of here!" No, not by a long shot. Even after a president leaves office and returns to being a regular citizen, he should continue to serve as a resource to the country. Not that all presidents do that, but they should. What they can give the country in the way of advice and counsel is invaluable. At the time George Sr. left office as president, only forty others led the country before him. They represent a cadre of men who can provide not only future presidents, but also the nation, with invaluable wisdom and advice.

Voters should look for a patriotic, loyal president who considers America's freedoms and best interests a lifelong priority. A desire to avoid conflict with family and friends should not get in the way of what is best for an entire country, and a good leader will know that.

A Passion for Ethics and Integrity

"There is also an artificial aristocracy founded on wealth and birth, without either virtue or talents ... the artificial aristocracy is a mischievous ingredient in government, and provisions should be made to prevent its ascendancy." —Thomas Jefferson

What Jefferson says is so true. Wealth and birth alone do not a president make. What a president needs to have done is to have resolved all of the conflicts he or she has had growing up, so that such a person is not burdened down by unfinished issues and concerns. Because if that is the case, some of the important decisions as they apply to being president will never be adequately made, resulting in a presidency that falls far short of what America wants and expects. The reason for that is because the unresolved conflicts between parent and child (now president), remain in the unconscious and are therefore not accessible for conscious examination and control. What happens then is that unwittingly, the president acts out his conflicts in a way that appears immature and inappropriate, thus bringing shame, embarrassment, or mortification to the White House and anyone who may be witness to or aware of such behavior.

If we include Washington, Lincoln, F. D. Roosevelt, Truman, Eisenhower, Kennedy, and George H. W. Bush as successful, what do we see? Each man, in his own way, had matured into an individual who was no longer caught up in immature struggles with his parents. Each had matured, overcoming difficulties, hardships, life-threatening situations, and the like: Washington's defeats as an officer in the king's army; FDR's polio; Eisenhower, JFK, and George Herbert Walker Bush's wartime experiences; Lincoln's hard and difficult struggles in his early years and his failures as a politician; Truman's WWI experiences and his failures in business, and so on. What they all had in common is that they had all separated from their birth families and became individuals in their own right, something President George W. Bush has never done.

We can also learn from our failures, as an electorate, by looking at the characteristics of those who failed us as presidents—men such as Nixon, who brought the country to the brink of disaster by trashing the presidency, and Clinton, who dishonored the presidency and left the door open for anybody who talked about "morality" to become president. Nixon clearly was an immature, spiteful, semi-paranoid, grumpy preadolescent; he had no principles that would have mitigated his overwhelming desire to win at all costs, leading to the destruction of his presidency. And Clinton, like Nixon, did not make the kind of identifications that would have given him some guiding principles. Those principles, had they existed, would have helped him listen more to the brain in his head than the one in his crotch. Clinton not only disgraced the image of the presidency, but also sacrificed the integrity of the office for momentary sexual pleasure. Without principles, Clinton failed to make the most of his gifted intelligence and his charismatic ability to lead people.

Because this whole subject tends to be so abstract that it's difficult to understand what I mean when I talk about past successful presidencies, I have chosen a relatively recent president from each of the major parties to use as an example of men who were successful presidents, and why:

With respect to the Republican President Dwight D. Eisenhower: he saw the need and country's wish to end the stalemated Korean conflict, and he ended it. He also saw the need for the postwar country to settle down and get growing with the impetus of new jobs, a resurgent economy, and a wonderful GI bill that enabled thousands to move beyond a high-school education and (at least) move to the middle class. So he didn't push for any big changes. But on the basis of his personally acquired principles, he cautioned against the dominance of the military-industrial complex, a caution that went against his party's (Republican) interests in making money for the corporations.

He was a man of principle, as was his predecessor, President Harry Truman, and the country responded to both of them with calm and a sense of decency and respect for the institutions provided for in the Constitution.

With respect to the Democratic President John F. Kennedy: he correctly identified his generation's and the following generation's yearning for a better world and provided avenues for their expression, as in the Peace Corps. And he eloquently captured the country's yearning for unity and dedication to the best in humankind. And most of all, in the Cuban missile crisis, he used his skills and knowledge of Russian leaders and diplomacy to provide a way out short of nuclear disaster while quietly stonewalling the militaristic urges of generals like Curtis LeMay, who wanted to nuke every country in their path.

One common theme that exists with presidents who were considered good civil servants is that they had principles (stemming from good and firm introjections), and therefore integrity. Poor presidents haven't made those kinds of good introjections (witness Clinton, Nixon, and President George W. Bush), and therefore lack integrity. But remember, it is the electorate that needs to learn from their mistakes in electing losers. Lousy presidents never learn from their mistakes. They just continue to lie and deny and blame others.

I keep thinking of JFK in the midst of the missile crisis, knowing that his first obligation was to keep his country intact. Knowing that nuclear war would be disastrous, he was extremely reluctant to give credence to the wishes and designs of the warmongering generals. On the other hand, we have Nixon stonewalling Congress, Clinton denying that he had "sex with that woman," and President Bush arguing that Iran threatened WWIII with its quest for nuclear capabilities.

Since presidents don't grow up in a vacuum, and because their parents are the key influence in helping them become all that they can become in their life, we need to look at how that comes to pass.

One of the basic responsibilities that all parents have toward their kids is to serve as their children's reality as they grow up. Incidentally, that is the same essential duty that all psychotherapists have with their client population—to be their clients' reality while helping them work on their problem in therapy.

When children are young and innocent, it's the parents' responsibility to understand each of their children's personalities sufficiently so that they can help them make the most of their interests, intellect, aptitudes, and moral and emotional development.

When they reach their majority, or at any age where they're viewed as being able to adequately run their own lives, that's when the unsolicited advice and guidance stops. However, it's still the parents' responsibility to advise their son or daughter when they jeopardize others or their own sense of well-being.

Once a parent, always a parent. Parents' responsibilities toward their children's welfare do not end when the children reach their majority. One of the continuing responsibilities parents have is to look after their children and, if necessary, offer them advice, even if it's unsolicited. This is particularly true if it looks like they're going to hurt themselves or others because of the kinds of choices they may make. The only criteria that determines whether the parents say something or not is how serious the consequences of a particular ill-advised decision will be.

Assuming George W. Bush's possible ADHD remained untreated, his parents should have served as his reality when he contemplated running for president and told George W. that his ADHD and/or dyslexia, if left untreated, disqualified him from running for the highest office in the land.

Because President Bush has never truly grown up, he has carried the symptoms related to his ADHD to the present.

Obviously, any president needs to know who he or she is and what he or she believes. If they don't have a sense of personal history of who the most influential people in their lives have been and what the personal struggles were that they've had to overcome, they will not appreciate the strength of their own character and therefore will not have the self-confidence necessary to handle the job. Simply put, all presidential candidates must appreciate their personal life journeys.

Discipline, Independence, and Perspective

Empowerment and confidence are not achieved through entitlement. One deep concern I have about President Bush is that he comes from a privileged background. As a result, he has never really had to struggle with life to get where he's gotten today. George W.'s swagger, phony machismo, and so-called toughness are all without foundation. As a child or an adolescent, he never went through the often painful demands of reality that promote grounded adult self-assurance, an internally cohesive belief in one's own strength, and knowing through experience the long-term benefits of resolve and other hard-won attitudes.

When things are not resolved, one's unconscious takes control. It's no accident that President Bush ended up with the old masters of the gruff and bluff Washington game, Donald Rumsfeld and Richard Cheney. Unconsciously, he realized he needed them. He must have given a real sigh of relief when they agreed to be part of his cabinet. He could now lean on them when leaning was necessary. Based on President Bush's track record to date, he is a leaner par excellence. If leaning were an Olympic event, he would win hands down.

When you don't know your own mind, you rely on others to decide. President Bush neither had the experience nor the necessary self-confidence to make his own decisions. As a consequence, he accepted Rumsfeld and Cheney's ideas and justified "his" decisions on the basis of the words their spin doctors provided. He didn't publicly (or, I believe, privately) disagree with either the then Secretary of Defense Rumsfeld nor Vice President Cheney, which in itself is rather curious.

By knowing and understanding some of the psychological dynamics that come to play in any candidate's personal life, you, the voter, can do a better job assessing his or her qualities to become president of the United States. Such an understanding can only be gained by reading and listening to political pundits and others regarding prospective presidential candidates.

If you don't do that kind of analysis, but instead just accept that because the candidate comes from privilege and money, that is reason alone to qualify him or her to be president, then you're not learning from past mistakes, and eventually, history will indeed again repeat itself. Both in terms of our country's treasure and human resources, we can ill afford to allow that to continue to occur.

Let the Past Guide Our Future

In order to avoid the mistakes of the past, we need to pay attention to the words of past leaders. Too often we fail to do that.

> "Every gun that is made, every warship launched, every rocket fired signifies in the final sense, a theft from those who hunger and are not fed, those who are cold and are not clothed. This world in arms is not spending money alone. It is spending the sweat of its laborers, the genius of its scientists, the hopes of its children. This is not a way of life at all in any true sense. Under the clouds of war, it is humanity hanging on a cross of iron."

Dwight D. Eisenhower

> "There never was a good war or a bad peace."

Benjamin Franklin

> "In the councils of government, we must guard against the acquisition of unwarranted influence, whether sought or unsought, by the industrial-military complex. The potential for the disastrous rise of misplaced power exists and will persist."

Dwight D. Eisenhower

> "I have known war as few men now living know it. Its very destructiveness on both friend and foe has rendered it useless as a means of settling international disputes."

General Douglas MacArthur

"Wars can be prevented just as surely as they can be provoked, and we who fail to prevent them must share the guilt for the dead."

General Omar N. Bradley

"The world has achieved brilliance without wisdom, power without conscience. Ours is a world of nuclear giants and ethical infants ... we know more about war than we know about peace, more about killing than we know about living. We have grasped the mystery of the atom and rejected the Sermon on the Mount."

General Omar N. Bradley

"History teaches us that war begins when governments believe the price of aggression is cheap."

Ronald Reagan

"To announce that there must be no criticism of the president, or that we are to stand by the president, right or wrong, is not only unpatriotic and servile, but it is morally treasonable to the American public."

Theodore Roosevelt

"When I take action, I'm not going to fire a two-million-dollar missile at a ten-dollar empty tent and hit a camel in the butt. It's going to be decisive."

President George W. Bush

BECOMING A BETTER
AMERICAN

AMERICA, THE BEAUTIFUL

O beautiful for spacious skies, for amber waves of grain,
For purple mountain majesties, above the fruited plain!
America! America! God shed his grace on thee
And crown thy good with brotherhood, from sea to
shining sea.

Most of us are familiar with the opening lines of "America, the Beautiful," but few of us are familiar with some of the other thoughts conveyed in that song.

A thoroughfare of freedom beat, across the wilderness!
America! America! God mend thine every flaw,
Confirm thy soul in self-control, thy liberty in law!…
When once and twice, for man's avail, men
lavished precious life!
America! America! God shed his grace on thee
Till selfish gain no longer stain, the banner of the free!

Many of the thoughts behind those words have lost their meaning and value in today's America. This is of particular concern to me because the very essence of what is embodied in those words—which is what America was once all about—is rapidly disappearing over the horizon.

"America, the Beautiful" describes precious values and beautiful, majestic landscapes. Today, how we view these things is truly an instance of beauty being in the eye of the beholder. Our perception of beauty is dependent on our needs and desires. What may be beautiful in one setting may not be in another. To take it one step further, what may appear beautiful to you may not appear that way to others; it all depends upon your frame of reference. Frame of reference even effects how we view our president. It all depends on whether he meets your needs. It's a very personal thing.

For example, if your greatest desire in life is to accumulate as much wealth as possible, then President Bush is your man! The fact that he cut taxes during his first term as president would make you feel pretty good. The fact that he did it again makes you feel even better. In fact, you'd probably feel he's a great president, and America is indeed beautiful.

On the other hand, if you had a son or daughter who was killed or maimed for life fighting in Iraq, and if you were against the war, chances are you would no longer feel America was beautiful. You may very well feel it to be quite ugly. So, if you are an American, is President Bush meeting your individual needs? That will determine how you view America.

But traditionally, America's beauty has not been about the individual experience, but the collective one. How long has it been since most American voters concerned themselves with their duty to their nation, rather than the other way around?

Let's take a look at the state of patriotism, both past and present. What individual ideals are coloring your perception of your country? What kinds of needs is our president helping you meet—and at what expense to the rest of America? Is President Bush's goal of a Middle East that is a clone of American democracy worth the expenditure of our country's human resources and treasure, and does his goal satisfy any of our needs?

The luster and shine that is embodied in the song "America, the Beautiful" has been badly tarnished by environmental abuses, governmental corruption, and special-interest lobbying. This has transformed our society from one of giving and caring for others to one that often chants, "Screw you. I got mine."

A Changed Physical and Political Landscape

America is not as physically beautiful as it once was. Many of its once-pristine rivers and lakes are now polluted. Its purple mountain majesties are now dotted with McMansions.

Because America has evolved into such a materialistic society, our values have changed from treasuring ideas to acquiring things. Rather than relying on our own inner resources to create ideas and solve problems, today's generation is more interested in being consumers of others' creations. Somehow, many of us believe that material possessions and money will make us happy. We believe that more of anything equates to happiness. Well, how wrong we are!

Many wealthy people are spiritually impoverished. They don't use their wealth for the betterment of humankind. If they do, they give merely a pittance.

Those who are spiritually bankrupt lack a belief system that might sustain them during periods of need or distress. Some try to fill their spiritual void with material goods—much as an emotionally deprived child or adult tries to fill his or her emotional void by overeating. When such inappropriate compensation occurs, such deprived people never discover how their sense of self is related to a supreme power. If they did, their spiritual belief would have filled their emptiness, and they would have put their acquisition of wealth into its proper perspective—believing that there is much more to life than accumulating wealth for wealth's sake. Believing instead that affluence should be viewed as a means to an end—that end being to help the poor and disadvantaged in our society.

In this day and age, nobody is concerned about the other guy anymore. We have become self-centered as a society. Where's that neighborhood spirit that was so prevalent in years gone by? So many people today are only interested in serving themselves. They are not interested in helping others by responding to human need and the necessities of those less fortunate than themselves.

Many of us live very insulated and compartmentalized lives. We think that since we have social-service agencies, mental-health workers, psychiatrists, psychologists, and social workers to tend to the needy, why should we be involved? Since the advent of terrorism, it's survival of the fittest, every man for himself. It's a dog-eat-dog kind of world out there.

A Short-Lived Reprieve

After 9/11, a momentary hope surfaced that perhaps we had returned to a more patriotic attitude. Shortly after that fateful day, people packed the churches, and there was a run on the purchase of American flags around the country.

It was as if America had returned to an earlier time in our history. I felt like a real patriot —just like I would have imagined the colonists felt during the Revolutionary War. Just as the patriots of that period worked toward a common goal of defeating the British, I too wanted to show the world my 1776 spirit. I wasn't going to cower and be intimidated by terrorists who were trying to destroy our way of life.

Unfortunately, that sense of 9/11 patriotism was short-lived. It didn't take long before many of the American flags in front of homes and on cars disappeared, and we quickly returned to our pre-9/11 life style. Today, many people live their lives as if 9/11 never happened.

We wouldn't even know there was a war out there if it wasn't for the news media to constantly remind us that, yes, we are indeed at war.

So, what happened? You certainly can reflect on how earlier generations were raised and contrast that with how kids are raised today. The influx of various cultures along with current child-rearing styles in the classroom results on less emphasis in teaching children what it really means to be an American.

Past Patriotism and Future Hopes

Having a sense of patriotism is no longer part of the American scene in the way it was during World War II. I'm old enough to remember what it was like. I didn't have to ask anyone alive then what his or her feelings were about being an American. I knew the answer from the way other people acted and from what my dad told me. He told my two brothers, and me, that this was the greatest country in the world. He was too old to serve in the war. However, he said that he would be willing to die for this country in order to protect and preserve the freedoms that are spelled out in the American Constitution—our country's bible.

Like Dad, many other people of that generation were proud Americans who were devoted to loving, supporting, and defending their country. They were dedicated to that cause. The acid test of devotion to one's country for anyone who had lived during those times was the willingness to defend one's country with one's life. That was the ultimate sacrifice that most were willing to make—and many did make. Today, only a few are called on to make that sacrifice.

During WWII, the people of our nation showed their support for the country by making sacrifices to support the war effort. These sacrifices included gas and food rationing and the recruitment of women into the workforce to replace the men serving in the military.

Everyone was on gas rationing. There was a rubber shortage. There were food stamps and ration books. The Second World War saw all luxuries and many necessities disappear from local shops in order that the armed forces were well supplied.

Because of the manpower shortage during the war, governmental, industrial, and civic organizations used patriotism to recruit women to serve our nation on the home front. Women left home to work in shipyards, steel mills, foundries, warehouses, offices, hospitals, and day-care centers. While they welded and riveted, most still maintained their traditional duties as mothers and homemakers.

What personal sacrifices are we making to support the military? Let's compare that earlier period of history with the kinds of personal sacrifices we are making in this country to support the troops in Afghanistan and Iraq. We have made none.

The only people making sacrifices are the men and women in the armed forces who are fighting in a foreign land.

How can the troops overseas be successful in battling terrorism when ordinary American citizens lack patriotism or don't seem to support the troops? The soldiers need the support of America's hearts and minds.

The reintroduction of the military draft would help restore a sense of patriotism in this country, or it would at least force the country to take sides for or against the war. Once again, the ramifications of war would be felt across society, not just by a select segment of our population.

That old saying, "United we stand, divided we fall," certainly applies to our country today. That saying is not just another cliché. If we don't begin to pull together, to think collectively about what we need to do as a nation, we will not contain terrorism. It will defeat us. It may not defeat us militarily, but it will indeed defeat us—economically, politically, morally, and spiritually.

It's our president's job to show the American people what needs to be done to support the war effort. He must foster a sense of patriotism; otherwise, we will lose this major war we are fighting with the terrorists.

Patriotism is so important because if you feel patriotic, you are willing to forgo your own selfish desires and ambitions for the good of the country.

The president's legacy will depend upon whether he has been able to make a divided nation whole again.

Clearly, the president feels this war with Iraq is a war we must win.

On August 22, 2005, in Salt Lake City, President Bush gave a speech to the Veterans of Foreign Wars. He stated, "Like the great struggles of the twentieth century, the war on terror demands every element of our national power."

Since our president has said that the war we are in with the terrorists is a war we must and will win, obviously, he feels the stakes are as high as they were during the Second World War, another war we felt we must win.

If this is true, why does our government tell us to continue our lives as we have done in the past? We're not supposed to alter our lifestyles one bit. We've been told to continue to shop and do all the other things we've been doing, even though the "war on terror" demands "every element of our national power."

The only thing our government has urged us to do differently from the pre-terrorist days is to be "vigilant." We are supposed to report any suspicious activity to the authorities. That's all we're called to do. Give me a break!

During the Second World War, every American's lifestyle was altered. All were expected to make sacrifices to support the war effort. One way we can instill a sense of patriotism and help make this country become whole again is by having the American citizenry make specific sacrifices to help support the troops over seas.

With the exception of the flag-draped coffins that are delivered to cities and towns across the country, I know the kind of war we're fighting today is not comparable to the war we fought during the Second World War. The enemy does not wear a distinctive uniform, and he does not come from a specific country that we can strike back at. It is a global ideology that has declared war on us. Nevertheless, in order to instill a feeling that we as Americans are in this terrorism battle together, specific sacrifices need to be made. Two sacrifices that might be employed would be gas rationing and increasing the federal income tax to help pay for the war effort. Just as was done in the Second World War, war bonds might be another useful means of fostering patriotism.

I did not support the Iraq war, and I don't support the occupation. I believe the whole Iraq episode destroyed any sense of patriotism that the country had mustered. It caused us to lose track of the main objective, which was to root out the terrorists who attacked our homeland. The fighting our troops are engaged in has become an unreal, distant activity to which most Americans have no connection. Also, unlike WWII, the Iraq war requires no investment or sacrifice of any kind by most of us.

If the majority of the American public would be willing to sacrifice their lives for their country, the president would know he has the country's support. Not just the military, but all of America as well. Aside from the military, the question I need to pose for myself, as well as for the rest of America, is this: are any of us willing to put our lives on the line to help preserve our way of life? I think if we were to answer that question as one voice, collectively, the answer would be no. Our president has never set the stage for us to think any other way.

Americans need to return to emphasizing patriotism in a leader. A good presidential candidate will understand the value of patriotism and be adept at fostering it. For example, if President Bush were more dedicated to fostering patriotism, he would often address the nation in order to discuss various issues related to his war on terrorism, much like what President Franklin Delano Roosevelt did before and during the Second World War when he gave his famous Fireside Chats from the White House.

On May 26, 1940, prior to this nation entering into the Second World War, FDR said in his Fireside Chat,

> But as this program proceeds there are several things we must continue to watch and safeguard, things which are just as important to the sound defense of a nation as physical armament itself. While our navy and our airplanes and our guns and our ships may be our first line of defense, it is still clear that way down at the bottom, underlying them all, giving them their strength, sustenance and power, are the spirit and morale of a free people.... The development of our defense program makes it essential that each and every one of us, men and women, feel that we have some contribution to make toward the security of our country.

Through these periodic Fireside Chats, Roosevelt nurtured and maintained a sense of patriotism during WWII.

If, in his own version of the Fireside Chats, President Bush periodically spoke to the nation about what's needed from Americans in order to win the battle over terrorism, he, like FDR, could instill a sense of patriotism in many of us.

Of course, fostering patriotism isn't solely the responsibility of the president. Because this is not a unified country in the way America was during WWII, and because the Republicans and Democrats are so divided (in part because of the Iraq war, but for other reasons as well), it is difficult at this juncture for President Bush to capture the hearts and minds of the American public. No one wants war, but when it becomes a necessity, the people must unite in order to bring about victory.

The reason the president appeared unduly defensive regarding his policy of winning the war in Iraq was because he knew he entered the war under false pretenses, and he knew that he didn't have America's full support to continue the conflict. Because a majority of the American public was against continuing the war effort, he was between a rock and a hard place.

Congress is in an untenable position as well. No politician ever wants to have to make a decision where he angers more than just a handful of his constituency, for the voter is the congressperson's lifeblood. Bush doesn't have to worry; he can't run for president again. President Bush should now focus his energy on winning the hearts and minds of Americans and on healing the great divide within our own country. I'm sure President Bush believes that he is doing what's right for the country, and that this accomplishment will be reflected by his legacy. However, by pandering to his conservative political base, he may misunderstand what his priorities should be, and such missteps may tarnish his legacy.

President Abraham Lincoln knew what his priorities were. Do you think President Lincoln was interested in his legacy or in pleasing his political base when he fought the Civil War? No. He was interested in preserving the Union, even though the price of doing so cost over 970,000 casualties, including approximately 560,300 deaths—a loss of more American lives than any other conflict in United States history.

Lincoln understood his priorities. Conversely, right after 9/11, too much of President Bush's energy was expended on pleasing special-interest groups and his political base. Instead, he should have more carefully thought through his options for a war on terror. Whatever course he chose to follow, it should have been consistent with his primary goal of repairing this country's divisions, so that he could make America whole again.

If America hopes to change its course, a shift back to its patriotic roots is necessary. Voters can do their part by electing a president who values unity and patriotism in a way that we haven't seen in a long time. Modern leaders are generally more interested in political gain than patriotism. By examining the stronger character of patriots like Roosevelt and Lincoln, we can rediscover the traits we need in our future leaders.

THE FLAG AND
THE PRESIDENCY:
DIMINISHED ICONS

In measuring the state of American patriotism, it's helpful to examine the public's attitude toward two icons that once were revered as the embodiment of the American spirit: the American flag and the American presidency.

The American flag represents all that's good in this country and is the most important symbol in the nation. It expresses patriotism and love of country. The flag also stands for the hope, beliefs, and accomplishments of our nation.

But our American flag is not being shown the same kind of reverence today as it has been given in past years.

When I was a fourth-grader, every morning at 8:45 AM, one student would raise the flag, with assistance from another student. It was a great honor to be selected. We would always know who was chosen, because his or her name would appear on the blackboard. This was done the afternoon of the previous day, before school was out, at 3:30 PM.

It was very important not to allow the flag to hit the ground whenever we put it up or took it down. We handled it very respectfully, as though it had a personality of its own. After all, it was the American flag. The Second World War was being fought at the time. I can remember the principal flag-raiser or assistant would tell the other, "Now, don't let it touch the ground!" After taking it down, it had to be folded to make a triangle with the field of stars on top.

When I was growing up, our government didn't have to worry about the American flag being desecrated. Today, there is much more civil unrest in this country, which reflects great divisions of opinions of how our country should be run. Slowly, the American reverence for the American flag has faded as our government became more and more politicized and divided. For some, the flag was used as a kind of whipping boy. All of the protesters' dislikes of governmental policy were taken out on the American flag. Burning it is a popular and dramatic form of abuse.

A Political Distraction

In 1968, in response to the burning of the American flag in protest demonstrations against the Vietnam War—which we have, not coincidentally, compared to the Iraq war—the first federal Flag Protection Act was passed by Congress. Over time, forty-eight of the fifty states also enacted similar flag protection laws as well. All of these statutes were overturned by the United States Supreme Court by a 5–4 vote. The slim margin overturning the statues determined they were unconstitutional because they restricted public expression—a violation of our First Amendment right of free speech.

Congress quickly passed a new Flag Protection Act, which was also struck down by the Supreme Court the following year by the same 5–4 majority. Again, the Court felt the desecration of the flag constituted a form of expression, protected by our First Amendment right of free speech.

Because the Supreme Court decisions were very controversial, Congress considered the only remaining legal avenue to enact flag-protection statutes—a constitutional amendment. Each Congress since 1989 has considered creating a flag-desecration amendment.

Even though at this time in history, flag burning is legal, it is periodically debated, year after year. Obviously, the issue is being used as a political football, much to the detriment to our country.

This is yet another instance of elected leaders playing politics rather than focusing on the real issue.

What would be achieved if the desecration of the flag were considered to be an illegal act? How is the amendment going to be enforced? And at what cost to the country? If a law or amendment is made, the powers that be need to be able to enforce what has been legislated and amended to the Constitution, and I don't believe it's enforceable with any consistency and regularity. Even if we could enforce bans on flag burning, is that really the best use of our resources? As so often happens in modern politics, more important issues—ones that affect actual people, not just rectangles of fabric—are being drowned out with political grandstanding.

Rather than wasting their time on such an issue, I suggest the president and Congress look beyond the actual pictorial perception of the desecration of the flag and try to empathize with the protesters—and in that way, better understand what disturbs them about the government.

If Abraham Lincoln would have been the president today, he would have viewed the desecration of the American flag as being symptomatic of an underlying problem. Since he viewed controversy as part of the political process, he would have attacked disagreement head-on. He would have listened intently to the opposition and, depending upon what the concern was, might have explained why he could or could not accommodate the protester's distress.

Because President Lincoln had a marvelous capacity to empathize with others, he would have utilized this ability to identify with the protester's concern. Then, through his compassionate understanding, he could help temper the demonstrator's vituperative spirit.

Just as you can't put a price tag on good health, you can't put a price tag on your love of country.

To put it simply, love is priceless. If you have it, you're on top of the world. If you don't, you may feel out of sorts with yourself and with life.

When we talk about love of country and flag, we're responding to those qualities that make us uniquely American. Those characteristics make us proud to be a citizen of these United States. A good leader is going to work to foster that love of country and open a dialogue with displeased citizens, rather than forbidding their protests or punishing them for burning a flag.

More Than Just a Job

The American flag isn't the only icon that once symbolized our way of life.

In the more distant past, the president was viewed by many as representing the epitome of what this country stood for. That was certainly the average American's thinking until the fantasy of becoming the president of the United States was no longer an attractive dream.

Much earlier in history, most Americans viewed the presidency with a degree of awe and respect. Many viewed the president as being bigger than life. That's most understandable, considering the tremendous responsibility our country's leader is expected to shoulder.

Because the president occupies the highest office in the land, and since he is the leader of the free world, he has a responsibility to act presidential, which means being above reproach morally, intellectually, and emotionally. Anyone falling short of the mark in any of those three areas should not run for president, regardless of whether they feel they are electable.

Since no person interested in running for that high office thinks of those issues, nor would their ego permit them to think of themselves that way, it becomes a moot concern. Nevertheless, it should be mentioned, because as of late, the presidents of recent years have fallen far short of the mark in at least one of the aforementioned areas.

President Bush is not alone in showing a lack of presidential class in holding the highest office in the land. The name of William Jefferson Clinton immediately comes to mind. His sexual escapades in the Oval Office were a national disgrace.

On August 8, 1974, President Richard Nixon was forced to resign because of his involvement in the Watergate cover-up. As the investigation got closer to the White House, Nixon instructed his men to cover up the crime. Under the threat of impeachment, and as a result of possibly being charged with conspiracy, obstruction of justice, and destruction of evidence, Nixon resigned. He was the first sitting president ever to resign his presidential office.

Many pundits and historians blame Nixon for the lack of respect for the office of the president.

When compared to Nixon's moral indiscretion, there was no constitutional crisis involved in what Clinton did. Nevertheless, Clinton's moral indiscretion was in many ways much more dramatic and shocking.

President Lyndon Johnson held an informal press conference twelve days after he had undergone a major operation. He pulled up his shirt and exposed his unsightly twelve-inch scar for the entire world to see. Apparently, Johnson felt chagrined at what he had done, because several days later, he said, "I didn't mean to be crude when I showed my incision the other day."

The other incident that demonstrates Johnson's uncouth behavior was when he picked up his pet beagle by the ears to show the dog to the press corps. He had to apologize to the animal-rights organizations for that action.

I'm sure you can understand that the behavior Clinton and Nixon exhibited was unbecoming to a president. However, you might feel Johnson's behavior was not offensive enough to warrant admonishment. I would think otherwise.

By virtue of occupying the highest office in the land, whoever is chosen to be president of the United States must constantly appreciate the image that is projected. Metaphorically speaking, it is sad that the bloom is gone from the rose, and that the respect and admiration for that high office of president of the United States is smudged, if not permanently damaged. It will take years—perhaps decades—to reestablish the office to its former greatness.

To be able to do that, each American citizen must have a sufficient understanding of American history. If whatever indiscretions he or she observed in the past—in not only our presidents, but also any one of our politicians—do not support the standard he or she feels a politician should meet, then he or she should not support and vote for that kind of candidate in the future. If we don't reflect on past political histories and ferret out what it is we like or dislike in a prospective candidate, then history is bound to repeat itself—the good, bad, and the ugly.

Ronald Reagan was always aware of what his presence meant to others and the kind of image he needed to portray while he was president. He was so cognizant of that image, and he felt so much reverence for the office that he always wore a coat and tie when working in the Oval Office.

As an ordinary citizen, if you reflect on how you feel about that esteemed place of work, you know that you want whoever occupies that seat of power to actualize all of the thoughts and feelings we have come to expect of a president. All of us want to feel proud that our presidents do an admirable job representing America not only to us, but to the world at large.

Less Than Equipped

Unfortunately, George W. Bush does not project an image that we can all feel proud of. He appears anything but presidential. He doesn't seem to feel within himself the quiet confidence that all presidents should project. Even with all the questions Lincoln must have had concerning his ability to make the Union whole again, he anguished about it in private; publicly, through his words and actions, he exhibited confidence and a belief not only in himself, but also that eventually the North and the South would be reunited.

Unfortunately, President Bush doesn't project the kind of inner peace that causes others to believe that whatever decisions he makes will ultimately turn out to be what is best for this nation and other nations as well.

On the surface, President George W. Bush does not appear to be intellectually equipped to be president. I say "on the surface" because, after all, he did graduate from Yale University and Harvard Business School. Therefore, intellectually, he should be able to handle the rigors that come with the job of being president of the United States. However, his persona betrays his intellectual acumen. When left to his own devices, when he deviates from his normal routine and speaks extemporaneously, he projects an image that is anything but flattering. As we have discussed, speaking extemporaneously is not his forte, and his verbal missteps are an embarrassment not only to our nation, but to the world as well.

Because of past and present events, love of country or flag is not as strong as it once was. Perhaps such feelings can only be reconstituted through what our president says and does. He must lead by example. He must communicate what it is about this country that makes us proud. He must rise above petty politics and discuss what needs to be done to rectify the many injustices he sees existing in this nation. He must no longer respond to the clamor of special-interest groups and his political base, but rather, begin to respond to the needs of the less fortunate, poor, and disadvantaged people of our country.

He must help this country refocus on the true meaning of what America stands for. It has nothing to do with how much money you have in the bank, how many houses you own, or how many cars you have in the driveway.

To be an American is to be responsive to human need. There are too many broken people in these United States. They're broken in spirit. They're broken by spending most of their waking hours trying to make enough money to support a family. They're broken because both partners are working so much that they are too tired to be intimate and loving toward one another. We must first heal our own broken spirits, and then we will be able to take on the task of regenerating a love of flag and country.

THE NEED TO COME TOGETHER AS A NATION

I feel the time has come for each of us to dig deep into our individual souls and answer the question, "What does being an American mean to me?" You may need to be ready to answer the question sooner than you think, because the day will come when the question will be asked. I hope each of us has a ready answer when that day arrives, because someday, we're going to have to respond with the answer from within the very depths of our being, rather than simply reflexively reacting to domestic and world events as they unfold.

That day will be when the terrorists attack us with such force that millions of us die in one fell swoop. Those of us still living will have to decide if we're only going to look after our own selfish interests or if we are going to extend ourselves to others by responding to their needs as well.

Because I don't believe the government has a thoughtful plan for dealing with a severe terrorist attack, a good number of us would be at a loss regarding how to respond. I don't believe they have a plan because I haven't heard of any; have you? Where will our government be when that attack happens? Since a devastating attack can occur at any time, how is our government going to respond in a way that expeditiously keeps panic, injury, and loss of life to a minimum?

Back in the 1700s, wasn't this nation originally formed to serve the people? At least that's what our Constitution said, and what the colonists fought hard to preserve and protect.

Since we can't wait for the do-nothing government to act, we must take it upon ourselves to decide what's best for the country. Then, through community involvement, we must come to a consensus as to how our nation should proceed.

We as a nation have lost touch with what being an American is all about. We have moved away from caring for one another. Today, a perfect stranger's need is routinely ignored. It has gotten to the point where we treasure only ourselves, our families, or maybe our friends.

This lack of empathy exists because of the priorities our president and many members of Congress have placed on our nation. Instead of being concerned about all Americans, our president and government are concerned with only responding to the needs of the wealthy, their political party, and special-interest groups—in other words, everyone who put them in office in the first place.

Because this is so, our government must pass legislation that will dramatically limit the amount of money allowed to be donated to any politician, whether he or she is running for president or Congress. That would also be true for those individual candidates who are running for office but have large amounts of money to spend on their campaign. By doing that, it would put candidates on a level playing field, because in order to be elected, they will have to appeal to all of the electorate, not just to the monied few who have deep pockets.

We, as voters, through our own lobbying efforts, can demand this be done.

Before I studied this whole subject of America and what it means to be an American, I didn't realize the extent to which we as a nation are not caring for one another the way we should. In fact, it's not a high priority for many people. It's not on many people's to-do lists. Point of fact, it shouldn't be on anyone's list per se, but rather, an internalized response. People should want to care for others, regardless of their economic circumstances or station in life. God's grand design was for us to be caring toward all of life, be it plant or animal.

The fact that our government was so slow to respond to those people who suffered from the devastating aftereffects of Katrina causes me to wonder how this can happen in America. I was astonished to see how long it took for stranded people to be rescued.

That just doesn't happen in America! Well, I guess it does after all.

What does it take for our public officials to step up to the plate and take care of America's business—and in so doing, respond to all of America, not just to the minority interests that provide the politicians with the financial wherewithal to get them elected in the first place?

Obviously, politicians need to think more about the American public and less about themselves. Instead of immediately thinking how they can get reelected after entering their office door for the first time, they need to take off their political suits and put on suits that represent all Americans. They can then use their public images to determine their actions. By doing that, they'll be responding to the needs of all Americans, not just those who got them elected.

Because of the advent of terrorism in this country, if there ever were a time when we have to test the moral and political fiber of our great nation, it is now. We must stop our political bickering and look beyond ourselves, focusing on what's good for our community and our country at large, rather than solely concerning ourselves with our own selfish interests and petty concerns.

Reflections on a Nation

I would like to share some thoughts and reflections about how I see our country presently and what needs to be done to help us better manage our anxieties and concerns during this most troublesome time in American history.

Ever since 9/11, the American public, the president, his administration, and Congress have all lost our perspective. As a result, much fear, anxiety, and apprehension is experienced by all Americans.

This is a time of reflection and coming together as a nation to decide how best to deal with the angst that terrorism brings to us and our community. Rather than doing that, our nation, through the news media, is repeatedly exposed to issues such as stem-cell research, abortion rights, tax cuts, religion in the schools, and many other peripheral issues, while terrorism remains the one concern that plagues our country. Of course, in addition to all of that, we're continually reminded that neither the Republicans nor the Democrats have a plan to successfully deal with the war in Iraq. And, if that's not enough, sex scandals and corruption of all kinds continue to compete for print space and airtime.

The repeated exposure of all those topics divides this country. Unification, not polarization, is necessary to mend the psychological wounds that we as a nation have endured since 9/11. In order to successfully deal with terrorism in the twenty-first century, we need to begin to speak with one voice. And the one voice needs to come from the very top of government on down. Yes, our president needs to come out, front and center, and level with the American public about what we as a nation need to do to regain our balance and belief in our country.

In order to restore our nation's pride and belief in itself, it's clear that strong leadership is important today. On August 13, 2006, Dr. Christine Johnson, president of the Community College of Denver, wrote an article in the *Denver Post* titled "A Call for Leadership." In it, she says,

> America is at a crossroads. Our country faces numerous critical challenges. Whether it is winning the war on terrorism, or restoring respect and good will on the international front, finding solutions to reduce our national debt or improving the performance of all American students in public and higher education to win the global talent race or solving the immigration problem, our national character is being tested.

> The great American hero, Rev. Martin Luther King, inspired us with his words:

> "The ultimate measure of a man is not where he stands in moments of comfort and convenience, but where he stands at times of challenge and controversy."

> As Americans, we can choose to attack and belittle one another or choose to help and uplift; we can choose our

words to build up or tear down, heal or hurt, denigrate or edify. The choice is ours.[28]

As Dr. Johnson implies, if there has ever been a need for strong direction from all people in government, it's today. That includes not only our president, but all national and state governmental officials as well.

America is more than just a presidency or a flag or a government. As American voters, we need to take our decision-making responsibilities seriously as we examine what being a citizen of this country means to us. Integrity is the lubricant—the oil, if you please—that makes the political process work smoothly and unimpeded. Nurturing, treasuring, and building on your sense of integrity, whether you're a civil servant or an ordinary citizen, is the key to living a happy and successful life.

Up to now, this country has been able to rely on our military power to assure our nation's safety. This is no longer the case. There's not a circumstance or a state of affairs that, if followed, would completely eliminate terrorism in this country. We, as Americans, are not used to thinking that way. One of the things that has made this country a great nation is that when we had a problem, we figured out a solution. It was our inventiveness as a nation that has helped us become the great power we are today. However, when it comes to terrorism, we must modify our thinking.

Unlike other problems we've encountered, where we were able to ultimately provide a solution that eliminated the problem or at least helped us better live with it, terrorism is not an issue with an end point. We will never be able to say definitively that we have defeated terrorism. In that sense, the threat of that kind of violence is now a permanent part of our political backdrop; as a result, we, as Americans, have to adjust our thinking accordingly. That doesn't mean we have to feel that terrorism has defeated us because we haven't eliminated it, but rather, we must accept reality for what it is. That's because fighting terrorism is interminable. There will always be another terrorist to take the place of the one we capture or destroy. Even if we win the war of ideas, and even if the terrorists exist only on

---

[28] Christine Johnson, "A Call for Leadership," *The Denver Post*, August 13, 2006. Used with permission of the author.

this country's fringes, terrorism will continue to be part of America's landscape. So we'll never be able to lower our guard, relax, and return to the pre-9/11 days.

Because there doesn't seem to be a permanent solution to the problem where we can stamp out terrorism once and for all, it's hard for American voters to even know how to start to deal with the dilemma. But deal we must. Otherwise, we all will continue to feel impotent, scared, and unable to cope. Certainly, because of the changing times, with the introduction of terrorism on our shores, our country will never feel as strong, able, and potent as we once felt, because we know how vulnerable we as a nation are and will be from now on.

The fact that a handful of terrorists have the potential to take the lives of millions of our citizens is too horrible to contemplate. We can never be completely safe. We will never be able to adequately protect our borders so terrorists will not be able to breach them. If an enterprising fanatic really wants to get into this country, he or she will find a way to do so. There is absolutely no way to stop them. The terrorist may be unsuccessful the first go-around, but finally will succeed—or the person who takes his or her place will eventually make a successful entry. As our president has said many times, "The terrorist need be right only once; we have to be right a hundred percent of the time." Because we are a democracy and not a police state, the porous nature of our borders will always remain.

Our government must stop making policies that will provide only a temporary solution to a permanent problem. Terrorism is like an open sore that continues to become more and more infected as the days turn into weeks, and weeks turn into months, and months turn into years. Since that fateful day, we have only been putting Band-Aids on an angry and painful wound that continues to become more and more infected over time.

We must stop repeating the mantra, "Fighting terrorism over there in Iraq keeps us from having to fight terrorism here." What is implied is that there is a one-to-one relationship between fighting the war in Iraq and keeping the terrorists from landing on our soil. That is false and misleading advertising. It's simply a political gimmick. It provides us with a phony sense of security. It is President Bush's attempt to again try to convince us that there was another reason for starting the ill-conceived and unjustified war in Iraq. Since it's plausible, but not the real reason for the president's preemptive Iraq war, it's known as rationalization. Like denial, which he has massively used since the Iraq invasion, rationalization is another ego defense mechanism.

All of these mechanisms are used to protect our president's and our own senses of self-worth. It is a stopgap measure to help us not feel bad for making the wrong decision. It's like putting blinders on a presidential decision that we, as a nation, don't want to look at. We don't want to have to consciously feel the pain of having to admit the Iraq war was an ill-conceived policy from the get-go. But the decision to go to war with Iraq was made by our president, and as a result, the consequences are still visible to our nation and the world. No amount of Band-Aids could cover up that big of a wound.

Just because we haven't had another terrorist attack since 9/11 doesn't mean that we are safer today or that we are winning the war against the terrorists. There is ample evidence to suggest that the terrorists are winning. It's conceivable that the terrorists have us just where they want us. When you consider the price we've had to pay in treasure and lives lost or wounded, the balance sheet is hardly balanced. It looks pretty lopsided to me. The fact that we've spent billions and billions of dollars, to say nothing of the lives lost or wounded, makes it clear that the Iraq war is bankrupting this nation in a way that we can ill afford. This isn't just the president's problem, or the Senate's problem, or the House's problem. This is America's problem. This is our problem. What are American voters going to do about it? How can we reach out to one another and unite to find answers?

Since terrorism hit our shores, and since we all know there is strength in numbers, in order to get a handle on the fear and anxiety that came with the attack, I urge all of us to begin to share our thoughts and anxieties with one another in general conversation. To start with, it's somewhat comforting to know there are others who think like you. Besides, talking is good for the soul—not only your own, but everybody else's as well. One of the best ways to alleviate anxiety is to talk about what's bothering you. We need to share our thinking with others. That not only includes our anxieties about terrorism, but also our religious and political beliefs as well. Right now, religion and politics are verboten subjects to discuss with anyone but our closest friends—and then, perhaps, with some hesitation. We were able to get away with not doing that in the past, but since the advent of terrorism, and because our nation is so divided, we must begin to hear and appreciate points of view different than our own. It doesn't mean we have to agree with what's said. There's a difference between agreeing and understanding.

We need to apply the same principles that work when we listen to a child explain why he or she is afraid of the dark. Even though we may feel their fears are without merit, we listen to what they say. By doing so, we make them feel better, because they know that others understand what they are feeling. They don't necessarily want you to fix the problem; they just want you to understand, to empathize with their situation. The act of simply understanding is a powerful elixir in alleviating anxieties, whether such fears stem from an imaginary bogeyman or from terrorism.

Right now, because our country is so polarized and we need to come together as a nation, we have to stop demanding that others think he way we do. It is just a point of view. It doesn't have legs. It's not going to hurt you. By encouraging open discussions, we can begin to understand where the person's heart is, which is what forms relationships, not where they religiously or politically stand. Understanding what another person's soul is like can go a long way in cementing the relationship, even in the face of political and philosophical differences. The reason I say that is because the commonalities that each of our souls have with one another are love, compassion, and empathy—the building blocks necessary to have our country come together as a nation.

When relationships are formed, they involve matters of the heart, not of the mind. We don't say to a prospective lover, "My brain is crazy about you—let's get married." Hardly. Need I say more?

Since it doesn't appear our president is going to lead and guide us in our thinking, so that we come together as a nation, we must do it. To enhance our thinking and work together so that our country becomes whole again, to minimize our differences and maximize our similarities, we need to promote these discussions ourselves. Even in the midst of a heated political discussion, this can be done. By appreciating what we all want to do—which is not only to debate the political issues, but also to get in touch with our caring and loving natures and share such feelings with one another—we can engage in verbal and nonverbal communication that says we're all in this together and want not only the best for one another, but for the country as well.

Open discussion works and goes a long way in correcting misunderstandings and stereotypical and even prejudicial thinking because shared thinking enhances intimacy, which is very much like what happens in talking therapy.

Communication Is Key

The job of psychotherapy is to make the covert, overt—in other words, make the unconscious manifest. Those who seek therapy are encouraged to verbalize their thoughts so they get them out into the open, and the thoughts don't continue to plague them by remaining underground. As long as they remain in the unconscious, they will continue to be bothersome, because what's under the surface continually strives for expression.

As far as terrorism is concerned, we are all in this together. The only way we're going to regain our perspective and we feel better about our uncertain future is to stop being so self-absorbed. This is accomplished by looking beyond ourselves and becoming more concerned about all people, whether they be loved ones, friends, neighbors, or perfect strangers. The motto we should follow is, "Love everyone as thyself."

In order to heal our country's wounds, we need to stop preaching the merits of individualism at the expense of what is best for our community and our nation. We must begin to think like John F. Kennedy, who said in his inaugural address on January 20, 1961, "And so, my fellow Americans: ask not what your country can do for you—ask what you can do for your country."

We also need to adopt Abraham Lincoln's belief that "Right makes might" and abandon the trigger-happy belief of the current administration, which is "Might makes right." For, if we continue along the current course, terrorism will eventually defeat us.

When we ask ourselves what being an American means to us, it is my hope that the answer is resounding and spoken in unison. Being an American means being part of a whole. Being an American means valuing the well-being of your fellow citizens, as well as that of yourself and your family. Being an American means coming together to find solutions that will brighten the future of our once-great country.

THE PROBLEM WITH EXTREMISM

I've made the argument that America needs unity to effectively deal with terrorism; I've implored each American to reach out to others, to share ideas and fears, and to think beyond his or her individual needs to the needs of an entire nation.

Of course, these ideals are easier described than implemented. As we struggle to stand united, what aspects of human nature threaten our success? One formidable obstacle is extremism.

What Is Extremism?

John W. Gardner, architect of Lyndon Johnson's "Great Society," said, "Political extremism involves two prime ingredients: an excessively simple diagnosis of the world's ills, and a conviction that there are identifiable villains back of it all."

This quote captures the essence of our current drift toward political extremism. It exposes the motivation and willingness to pursue narrow policy paths without regard to nuance, consequences, or representation.

If we define "extreme" as "farthest removed from the ordinary or average," it is safe to say that most people would be comfortable using the term "extremism" to describe terrorist movements, theocratic governments, cults, and radical fringe groups. Most Americans would be appalled at the idea of our government being equated to a terrorist movement or a rigid theocratic regime … yet, considering how moderation is being drowned out by those groups who embrace more strident and extreme positions, eventually our government could adopt those positions that are antithetical to the people's interests.

This may be particularly true when you consider how the various political talk-show hosts, both from the extreme right and left side of the political spectrum, describe those political positions different from their own. What they consistently do is attack their opponent's character and quickly jump to erroneous conclusions, simply by assassinating and labeling him or her as being a "flaming liberal," "conservative extremist," or any other pejorative term. These hosts imply that with these terms, they have captured the essence of that person's character. Labeling carries with it so much surplus meaning. The malevolence is not in what they say about their cause, but in what they say about their opposition.

One of the extremist's tools of the trade is character assassination. By questioning their opponent's motives, biases, prejudices, values, or a host of other qualities, they may besmirch their opponent's character to such an extent that the listener will turn a deaf ear to what he or she may say in rebuttal.

Once the extremist has the listener's support and buys into what the talk-show host says about his guest, then whatever is said in support of his position is accepted as gospel.

Unfortunately, the talk-show host frequently uses arrogance and intellectual intimidation to sell his line of reasoning to his viewing or listening audience, all at the expense of his guest—which may be entertaining to the viewer or listener, but doesn't further intellectual discourse or critical thinking. What is tragic about all of this is that the important political issues of the day are never seriously and fully discussed; only the talk-show host's political biases and agenda is supported and promoted. Where's the democracy in that? How are Americans to reach out to one another in a political climate that revolves around theatrical polarization?

"Extremism in the defense of liberty is no vice," was Barry Goldwater's catchphrase when he ran for president against Lyndon Baines Johnson, in 1964. I can remember Goldwater uttering those words when he gave his acceptance speech at the Republican convention in San Francisco.

That part of his statement is often quoted, but he went on to say, "And let me remind you also that moderation in the pursuit of justice is no virtue."

To preach extremism in any context or venue is something I cannot and will not embrace. It doesn't matter what political party professes such a belief; it is simply anathema to me and, as a result, is something I will argue against whenever such an idea is expressed.

So many political ills of the world have occurred because of extremism. It is a breeding ground for racism, bigotry, and prejudice. Dictatorships and fascism thrive on extremism.

Johnson and the Democrats painted Goldwater as a trigger-happy extremist who was willing to drop bombs whenever and wherever necessary to defend the United States' interests.

The Democrats capitalized on the country's Cold War fear of nuclear annihilation and our increasing involvement in Vietnam's civil war. They developed a television commercial showing a young girl standing in a field plucking petals from a daisy. A background voice recited an ominous countdown. Finally, the child evaporated in a mushroom cloud. The viewers were asked to vote Democratic because "the stakes are too high for you to stay home."

The irony of the Democrats' statement is that, like Goldwater's pronouncement, the Democrats' declaration was pretty extreme as well.

Later, Goldwater acknowledged that the campaign against him effectively exploited the public's fear of his militancy. "In fact," he said with sardonic wit, "if I hadn't known Goldwater, I'd have voted against the SOB myself."

Johnson defeated Goldwater in a landslide. Goldwater carried only five southern states and his home state, Arizona.

He was unapologetic about his extremism speech, feeling that protecting freedom was what this country was all about. "We'll go to any extent to protect it. I know people were thinking 'nuclear' when I said [extremism], but ... I think it had to be said, and I never lost any sleep over it."

Ironically, Johnson escalated the Vietnam War, and it dragged on until 1973. Goldwater felt that Johnson's Vietnam policy cost the country far more money and lives than if he, the supposed warmonger, had been elected.

At the time Barry Goldwater ran for president, I was a dyed-in-the-wool conservative Republican. I thought what he said made a lot of sense. I was thirty-two, fresh out of graduate school, and beginning my career as a psychologist. Why shouldn't Goldwater impress me? I was primed to accept whatever he said. That's what party members do, don't they? Besides, I was at a different place with my life then. Today, I measure my life differently and question what my country does more frequently. The young man I was in 1964 didn't have time to think as deeply about politics. Today, I can't afford not to.

As I said in my opening remarks in this chapter, today I wouldn't be able to support Goldwater because of my feelings on extremism. Whether his extremism statement was a political ploy, I don't know, but considering where my thoughts are today, that statement would cause me not to support him, because it is particularly important to take any politician's statements at face value. Otherwise, what can you believe?

Outgrowing Extremism

I began to question my political affiliation a number of years ago, when I started working on my memoirs. That was done near the end of a struggle to find out what was really important in my life.

Throughout my youth and well into my adult years, I saw my father as the cat's meow. He could do no wrong. He was what every son would want in a father. He was truly bigger than life. In that sense, as a little boy, every time I looked at my father, it was like I was looking at him through a magnifying glass. To me, he was a giant.

Like any little boy who loves his father deeply, I wanted to be just like him. By thinking and acting like him, I thought, I wouldn't have a thing to worry about. Because my dad appeared to do things so well and seemed to be so pleased with himself, all I hoped was that if I played at being Dad, the things I liked about my father would rub off on me.

Well, as you know, that's not how things work, but for a boy of four or five years old, I thought playing the part made it so.

The problem was that I had a hard time thinking and acting like my father. No matter how hard I tried, I always fell short of the mark. When that happened, I would dust myself off and try again. Maybe if I just tried harder, then things would work out. Well, the inevitable would happen again. So ... it became a vicious cycle. It went something like this: I would try harder. I would fall down. I would pick myself up and the cycle would repeat itself all over again. I was not a quitter. I was going to continue to do it until I made it work. This endless cycle continued throughout my developmental years.

It was only after I began working with a fellow psychologist, Richard R. Waite, that I began to put the pieces of the puzzle called life together. It was then that I stopped this repetitive, self-defeating behavior.

What Dr. Waite did for me was to help me appreciate myself for who I was.

I might look a little like my father, but that's where the similarities stop. I learned that, in many ways, I am the opposite of my dad.

I realized the answers to life's questions reside within me, rather than within what I might consider some higher authority, like my father. I began to depend on my own judgment in how I sailed my own ship of state.

Being a conservative Republican like my father didn't fit my persona, so I became a Democrat. It didn't take me long to become disenchanted with the Democratic Party also. Today, I'm an independent with Democratic leanings. It's been important to figure out what I believe in and stand up for it, but avoiding extremism on either end of the spectrum has also become part of my political philosophy. The extremism I witnessed in both parties clearly hindered political progress and heightened tension unnecessarily.

My transformation from Republican to Democrat to independent was a slow one. It was not until I began to examine and compare the differences in my core values as compared to the values that my father and brothers held that I was no longer able to accept the philosophy and basic tenets of the Republican Party.

When they were living, my father and two brothers were staunch, conservative Republicans. My brother Doug owned, operated, and edited a small weekly newspaper in Wisconsin. During the months prior to his death, he wrote editorials that were increasingly critical of the Republican Party.

Reading his editorials gave me an opportunity to appreciate how Doug felt about a number of issues that were dear to his heart. He was not one to hide his feelings. Doug was the kind of brother who told it like it was; he was a man of principle and conviction.

Doug's last editorial was published on November 28, 2002,[29] a few days after his death. He expressed his feelings about the corporate scandals that were making headline news in this way: "Corporate biggies prove you can't buy happiness." He pointed to corporate scandals and greed in order to criticize the idea that money equals happiness. Instead of highlighting successful executives as role models, Doug pointed to the common American.

"Some of the happiest, most satisfied people in this country are people with modest family incomes," he wrote. "They have love. They have achievement. They're happy with a modest car and home that is warm and an occasional vacation to South Dakota or Michigan. Money and the accumulation of it for more, more and more is a drug no less addictive than smoking and biting your fingernails."

Also that year, Doug wrote about the Martha Stewart insider-trading scandal, in which Martha Stewart was accused of selling ImClone stock based on a tip from the CEO. My brother criticized Stewart's response to the allegations—or lack thereof.

"The woman who seemingly is omnipresent—on cooking and craft segments during morning news shows, on her own TV show, in the magazine racks, on book covers and in K Mart—suddenly has nothing to say," he observed.[30]

Doug criticized that nonresponse, inviting her to stop hiding behind her lawyers. "She should fire them and simply face the music," he wrote. "Either she broke a securities law or she did not. She should tell the truth, take her licks and move on."

In both articles, my brother criticized corporate greed and encouraged personal accountability and ethics in business. Integrity

[29] Doug Lyke, "Corporate Biggies Prove You Can't Buy Happiness," *Ripon Commonwealth Press*, November 28, 2002. Used with permission of the Lyke family.

[30] Doug Lyke, "Martha Stewart Should Speak Up," *Ripon Commonwealth Press*, September 19, 2002. Used with permission of the Lyke family.

was important to him, and it should be important to everyone, regardless of their political leanings.

In his editorial "Women Know When It's Moral to Buck the Team," he had this to say about female whistle-blowers who have brought various corporate scandals to light, including Sherron Watkins of Enron.

My brother pondered,

> Maybe women really do have more backbone than men. It took courage to expose mismanagement, corruption and fumbling. Nary a man stepped forth. Perhaps in their cowardice they thought they would be labeled as "stool pigeons" or "not team players."

> The values and fortitude it takes to do the right thing doesn't come from any particular male or female gene. Being a whistle blower is an equal-opportunity responsibility.[31]

My brother even took on what he saw as America's arrogance on the world stage, criticizing President Bush for failing to send anyone to the World Summit on Sustainable Development in Johannesburg, South Africa, until the final day.

> "How can we expect the rest of the world to hear us if we are unwilling to share the world stage?" my brother asked. He noted a recent victory of Argentina over Team USA in the World Basketball Championship.

> "Guess we're not such hot shots after all," he concluded.[32]

My brother would have made a lousy politician. Doug knew what he believed and wasn't afraid to make his thoughts and feelings public, regardless how unpopular they might have been. My brother was a man of great integrity, an attribute that is sadly lacking in America's political arena today. At the same time, Doug was not an extremist. He didn't fall in line behind a president just because

[31] Doug Lyke, "Women Know When It's Moral to Buck the Team," *Ripon Commonwealth Press*, November 7, 2002. Used with permission of the Lyke family.

[32] Doug Lyke, "America Is Acting Mighty Arrogant," *Ripon Commonwealth Press*, September 12, 2002. Used with permission of the Lyke family.

that president was Republican; he decided these issues for himself, weighing them out carefully. He demonstrated that one can have strong political beliefs without giving in to extremism.

The reason Doug steadfastly remained a Republican was because he lived in small Wisconsin towns all of his life. Consistent with his small-town orientation, he believed in the ability of people to act rationally and make decisions in their best interest. He also believed that neighbors should take care of one another and not rely on state or federally mandated programs. Because of the way he and his wife conducted business and their relationships in that town, these things worked out. And though not a perfect system, people in need in a small town are more likely to get help when they need it. The scale of needs and resources are so much clearer than in large metropolitan areas. Doug also lived in a state that, in the main, generated thoughtful, just, and consensual policies.

Doug not only talked the talk, he walked the walk. He was very active in local politics and served on many local boards and committees throughout his life. He served on the local school board for several years.

Instead of taking an extreme point of view on local political issues and concerns, he was always willing to compromise and, by doing so, thought in terms of what was needed to get the job done.

A good example of how he put Republican thinking into practice would be his inclination to reject federal education guidelines because they interfered with local educators in best determining what and how to teach the community's children.

One of the things we can learn from my brother's life experiences is that to rigidly adhere to a party or a governmental policy and believe you have the formula for solving all problems that can be applied in each and every situation, regardless whether it's on the federal or state level, can make you an inflexible citizen who does not have the best interests of America at heart. As responsible citizens, we must be sufficiently flexible and adaptable by keeping an open mind in any political situation. When a decision is necessary, we can follow our heads, hearts, and integrity in order to make the best possible decision for our country.

One of the reasons for my brief stint as a Democrat was because in a large community—like Denver, Colorado, where I live—there are people who are vulnerable and who might well fall by the wayside if the federal government doesn't enforce better legislation, rather than leaving it to the states or local community to do so. Compared to the Republicans, I felt the Democrats were more inclined to be responsive and compassionate toward the needs of the less fortunate. Being a Republican in Wisconsin, and living in a town such as Ripon, worked for my brother.

Another reason for my abandoning the Republican Party was the party policies that my brother Doug and I felt were contributing to corporate corruption—his distaste for which was clear in his articles. There was also the unresponsiveness in caring for and responding to the needs of those less able, the unfairness of the president's tax cuts ... and certainly, the Republican administration's Iraq war policies.

I recognize I haven't said anything about my other beloved brother, Ned. Not doing so does not imply for a minute that he didn't have an influence in my life, for like my mom, dad and brother Doug, he too had as big an influence as they did, but in a different way.

Human Tendencies Toward Extremism

I don't believe that the difficult beginnings of my political journey make me an anomaly. We all need to emulate others in an effort to be all that we can be in this short life of ours. What we do is pick out the traits we admire in others and try to incorporate them into our own personalities. Our role model can be a teacher, a politician, a friend, a brother, a sister, a mother, a father, a loved one, or a host of other people in our lives that we admire and respect. It can even be a therapist.

Because we come into the world feeling incomplete, we all have this need to emulate others. That is why it's so important for our parents to help us understand what our strengths and abilities are, so that we can play to our strengths in an effort to live life to the fullest. When we as parents or mentors do that, we obviously have to use language to be understood. It is important to appreciate the power of words. Labels take on a life of their own. For example, in describing your particular political position, the problem with using party labels is that there is so much surplus meaning to the terms that they may not accurately reflect the views espoused by the holder.

In our zeal to emulate someone we care about, we must be careful not to go too far—into the realm of extremism. Sometimes, our need to identify with a certain political party or ideal can turn us into political caricatures who are too polarized to accomplish anything useful.

For a moment, reflect on your own political position and decide whether you're a Democrat or a Republican. I'll bet you conclude that in some instances you think like a Democrat, and at other times, you think like a Republican.

Many of my friends say they think like a Democrat on social issues but like a Republican on fiscal matters, speaking as if both categories are mutually exclusive. What is implied is that all Democrats are fiscally reckless. What is implied is that any government project backed by Democrats is financially unsound.

Faulty reasoning like that may compound itself by further thinking that because there are more socially conscious, sensitive, aesthetic people who are Democrats and more Republicans are seen as pragmatic, bottom-line-oriented businesspeople, it stands to reason that there is a greater likelihood that Democrats, rather than Republicans, will recklessly spend money on pork-barrel projects because they don't have any sense when it comes to being fiscally responsible.

What a ridiculous and extreme conclusion to reach!

Such faulty logic may not be done consciously, where you reason it out in such vivid detail, but rather unconsciously, or subliminally. When that type of reasoning occurs, it can be lethal. What it does is destroy sound critical thinking.

This is just one of a myriad of examples that could be hypothesized to show how stereotyping through labeling can begin to take on a life of its own and veer into extremism. What has happened as a result of years of thinking this way is that the two political parties of today represent the extremes, rather than the moderate positions they once promoted.

Divisive labels continue to damage American unity. To add insult to injury, politicians have now fine-tuned their party's terminology and introduced another dimension to the equation: moderate, liberal, and conservative.

By attaching a conservative or liberal label to your favored political party, you simply compound the problem by promoting extremism. It forces the listener to simply hear the most strident part of the message—the part of the label that states "conservative" or "liberal." The major part, "Democrat" or "Republican," is lost in the translation.

The Democrats recognize the abuse they've received by being defined as liberals. The very term "liberal" implies irresponsibility. They have now replaced the term with the word "progressive."

On the other hand, being conservative suggests making prudent and wise choices, whether it be formulating policy or using government funds in a nonwasteful manner. The conservative talk-show hosts have a field day describing any Democrat as liberal. They might describe him or her as being a bleeding-heart liberal, but never a progressive. That would be too positive.

If you talk to someone who's not like you (whatever that means), the more you talk about being a Democrat, or a Republican, the more it becomes like walking on quicksand. After you announce your political persuasion, it doesn't matter what you discuss. The label that is different than your friend's has already stigmatized you. The more you talk, the deeper you sink into the sand. Eventually, you'll be up to your neck, and your cry for help will fall on deaf ears.

Political labels minimize the similarities between groups and maximize their differences. That being the case, what we do is single out the aspect that we don't agree with and maximize its significance, as if that reason alone is sufficient to reject that party's political philosophy in total.

My father always accused the Democrats as leading us down the road to socialism. He simply would say, "We can't afford all the government programs the Democrats want to enact; it's fiscally irresponsible."

Why are humans so prone to extremism? What mechanisms drive that tendency, and how can we recognize and correct these issues? If we hope to replace extremism with a more measured approach, we must first understand this human inclination toward the former.

Tragically, when a political position is adopted, it's human nature to pick out reasons for continuing to think that way and ignoring reasons for thinking any other way. In order to understand such inconsistency, we have to look at the theory of cognitive dissonance, or the tendency to look for a rationale that supports your thinking and ignore those reasons to think otherwise.

If there is cognitive dissonance existing in your political beliefs and attitudes, or between your attitudes and behavior, you will either change your attitude by thinking, "Actually, now that I think about it, I didn't really believe that ..." or get new information to support your attitude: "But here's some other evidence that confirms what I originally thought ..." Or you will minimize the importance of the conflict: "It doesn't really matter, anyway ..."

Usually when it comes to political party affiliation, the battle lines were drawn years ago. Consequently, the moment anxiety is experienced because cognitive dissonance is present, the angst is dealt with by

1. Devaluing contrary thinking.
2. Using selective avoidance by directing one's attention away from information that challenges one's attitudes.
3. Using selective perception and focusing on those attitudes that others hold in common with your own, and in that way, reducing the anxiety of feeling you're the only one who thinks that way.

It is through one of these three means that anxiety is reduced.

Devaluing contrary thinking: This is frequently done by pejoratively labeling the point of view contrary to your political persuasion. "Oh, he's a flaming liberal." This removes credibility from the idea in question and prevents you from having to explore more fully the thought that might potentially differ from your thinking.

Using selective avoidance: I have friends who won't watch CNN, NBC, CBS, or ABC television channels, and will only watch Fox, because they feel all the channels except Fox are too liberal in their thinking. Many see the Fox network as being owned and operated by the Republican Party.

Using selective perception: "I like you because you think like me." It's just human nature to organize into like-minded groups.

Growing up, if we had a loving, caring relationship with our parents, we wanted to please them. Therefore, we tried hard to see things from their point of view. When we did, through our actions or words, our parents would show their approval by smiling or making an appreciative comment, suggesting they approved what we did or said.

One of the reasons conservative talk-show host Rush Limbaugh has such a large following is because he speaks with such certainty. His followers can feel calm and secure when he talks to them. In an uncertain world, that in itself is very appealing. He is a radio father figure. He always seems to be able to put a positive light on political happenings of the day, and in the fairy-tale world he talks of, at the end of the day, the conservatives are always triumphant.

The conservative Republicans, whether through their politicians or talk-show hosts, love to assign the liberal label to Democrats. By doing so, they can stigmatize all Democrats as evil spendthrifts.

Their eternal mantra is "Liberalism is bad. Conservatism is good."

Developing Moderation

The way to avoid such extremist thinking is to realize that we all operate in this world—whether it is in the world of politics, or any other world we call life—with a prejudicial and biased way of thinking. We come to the table with a preconceived or biased attitude or belief even before the thinking begins. These biases are based on both our beliefs and our experiences and may invariably influence our thinking and decisions. That's part of the human condition. It can't help but be so, because we have to operate with certain prejudices or biases in order to progress in our thinking. As soon as we begin our thinking with, "I believe this to be the case ..." our biases begin to operate. The only way to keep from getting premature closure on a subject is to keep an open mind. Closed-mindedness certainly doesn't enhance progressive thinking.

If you want to avoid political extremism, you have to admit your biases and remain aware of them, so that you can listen to other points of view and work toward a compromise.

Biases and labeling can affect how we feel about terrorism. For example, when the word "terrorist" is used, what may immediately come to mind is some mentally imbalanced man or woman who represents the fringe element of the Muslim religion and therefore need not be taken seriously. Nothing could be further from the truth. The label "terrorist" should begin the conversation, not end it. The only way our government is going to be able to wisely deal with the terrorists is if we more fully explore why they behave as they do. And what we can do to stop them from taking lives.

The fundamental difference between a conservative Republican, a moderate Republican, a moderate Democrat, and a liberal or progressive Democrat is the amount of governmental interference allowed at either the state or federal level. The degree of meddling at either of these two levels determines what political persuasion is represented.

When I reread what I just wrote, I noticed I used the word "meddling" when describing government "interference"—another intrusive word. Unwittingly, I used uncomplimentary wording, which set the stage for people to think negatively about what I was going to say on the subject. Let's try using two other words in place of the ones I used and see how you might react to that same paragraph.

"The fundamental difference between a conservative Republican, a moderate Republican, a moderate Democrat, and a liberal or progressive Democrat is the amount of governmental *involvement* allowed at either the state or federal level. The degree of *participation* at either of these two levels determines what political persuasion is represented."

Regardless of whether you're a Democrat or a Republican, isn't the second identical paragraph much more palatable than the first when substituting the two italicized words for meddling and interference? Recognizing our biases and correcting them as well as we can will help us speak in a less inflammatory and more engaging manner.

Remember John W. Gardner's observation that extremism involves the "conviction that there are identifiable villains" behind everything?

Our biases and labels further that idea. But if we examine politics more fairly, we have to admit that there is no blameless political party.

At the national level, both Republicans and Democrats of all stripes participate in pork-barrel spending, where they gain funding for projects—some of them worthwhile, but many irrelevant and unnecessary for people outside the district for which the pork was designated.

A good example of such spending was Congress approving $223 million to build the infamous Alaskan bridge to nowhere.

Fortunately, the Senate had enough sense to ultimately reject the proposal. However, the fact that Congress initially approved the spending makes those who voted for the bill all liberal Democrats, regardless whether or not they were Republicans or moderate Democrats.

At one point or another, Democrats and Republicans have swapped positions on a variety of issues. To the degree that happens, both parties are inconsistent with their images.

For example, Republicans often are accused of wanting to influence the religious views of others through legislation that limits gay rights. That doesn't really seem to be in favor of an individual's right to self-determination, which for years has been the Republican Party's mantra.

The "tax and spend" Democrats, at least in the Clinton administration, exhibited fiscal responsibility and cut government spending.

Besides bias and labeling, another source of political extremism between the two parties involves tension along class lines. Generally speaking, when compared to the Democrats, the Republicans tend to be people of means.

Some Republicans who are in that category may view themselves as people who made the grade. They tend to be the captains of industry. They are people who hold down white-collar jobs. In contrast, the Democrats are more inclined to hold down blue-collar or what is generally thought of as working-class positions. The Republicans tend to be the movers and shakers of industry. Their allegiances are more tied to that of big business, whereas the Democrat's allegiance would be to the working class. With labor and big business being what they are, polarization between these two groups can sometimes be a foregone conclusion.

Together We Stand, Divided We Fall

The way to minimize labeling and stereotyping is to suspend judgment when talking to others who don't hold the same political beliefs as you. For example, the best way to bridge the gap that exists between the two different parties is to make a conscious, thoughtful, purposeful effort to keep as open a mind as you can when you hear a point of view that is contrary to the way you think.

More specifically, let's say that for whatever reason, you're against same-sex marriages and feel that, before the law, they should not be treated in the same way that heterosexual marriages are handled. Let's say I share the opposite view.

The only way to breach the barrier to agreement and appreciation of the other point of view is by having an open mind. That's not easy, because if you hold a point of view different than the other person, you have an unconscious resistance to even hearing what's being said, let alone accepting it.

Even if I were to cite studies in our hypothetical argument that support the idea that same-sex couples are taxpaying, law-abiding community contributors who are well loved and well respected by their families, friends, neighbors, and employers ... even with that kind of support, unless you say to yourself, "I'm going to try my very best to appreciate this other point of view," a change in your thinking will not occur. Incidentally, I started to write "the opposition" rather than "this other," illustrating how labeling can interfere with keeping an open mind in any political discussion. This is because if I had viewed the person I was talking to as my opponent, I would view him or her as an adversary, which would only further impede the bridging of the philosophical gap. As has been implied in our discussion of political parties, labels tend to divide rather than unite this country. We should begin to look at Americans not as representing political parties, but rather, as the individuals they are, gauging what they can do to help fight this war on terrorism. Since the advent of terrorism, we need to be more concerned about the welfare of all our people and respond to all human need than ever before.

Terrorism is so foreign to each of our lives. It is so insidious, and it creates so much fear and anxiety in each of our psyches, that we need the emotional support of everyone in order to help sustain ourselves in the advent of another terrorist attack. All of us can find the time to volunteer in soup kitchens, give blood, give money, donate food, and donate clothing. It's our moral responsibility to administer love, care, and comfort to everyone, regardless of social class, race, color, or creed.

The struggle against extremism seems to describe a battle between the unrestrained passions of man and his ability to reason. This being the case, should we settle for a government where passion rules the day? Should we settle for simple diagnoses and simple solutions or confront our complex world armed with the wisdom of reason and deliberation?

Even the question of whether "extremism" qualifies as a definition of our government should sound the alarms of democracy. A country of such rich diversity of ideas, cultures, race, creeds, and philosophy should shudder to its core and demand a change of course if its governing body is even close to resembling an extremist government.

Author and philosopher Aldous Huxley credits a large portion of the world's misery to three pillars of extremism: idealism, dogmatism, and proselytizing zeal. He wrote, "At least two thirds of our miseries spring from human stupidity, human malice and those great motivators and justifiers of malice and stupidity, idealism, dogmatism, and proselytizing zeal on behalf of religious or political idols."

Another famous philosopher, Aristotle, said, "The virtue of justice consists in moderation, as regulated by wisdom."

And yet another less famous philosopher of dubious distinction, Karl Rove, said, "I don't know about you, but moderation and restraint is not what I felt when I watched the twin towers crumble to the ground, a side of the Pentagon destroyed, and almost 3,000 of our fellow citizens perish in flames and rubble."

Hmmm ... let's see ... whom to emulate?

PUBLIC OPINION AND THE PRESIDENCY

According to Lincoln, "Public sentiment is everything. With public sentiment, nothing can fail; without it nothing can succeed. Consequently he who moulds public sentiment, goes deeper than he who enacts statutes or pronounces decisions."

A president's response to public opinion is important; it takes integrity and leadership to remain flexible enough to respond to public need, while also remaining principled enough to resist the temptation to give into the people's every whim. Lagging public support drains a president's political capital and makes it more difficult for him to persuade others to follow his lead.

In a 2006 Associated Press poll of 1,003 adults, President Bush's approval rating had dropped to 36 percent—the lowest of his five years and three months in office. The remaining 69 percent of the Americans polled said this country is on the wrong track.

Along with a number of political analysts, I too believe President Bush and Vice President Cheney will go down in history as the worst president and vice president we've ever had in American history, so ... Mr. President, polls do matter.

As of December 26, 2006, the death toll of our troops in Iraq had risen to 2,978—five more than died in the 9/11 attack. To add insult to injury, as had been predicted in one of the cited polls, a number of people believed Iraq was experiencing a civil war.

Clearly, at the present time, our president couldn't say, as he has said time and time again, "absolutely, we're winning in Iraq." The midterm elections were a clean sweep for the Democrats, which was a clear message of the American public's response to our president's failed Iraq policy. Our country wanted the troops to return home.

Our president has made it abundantly clear that he doesn't pay public opinion much heed when it comes to his principles and positions.

On August 27, 2004, President Bush was interviewed by *USA Today*. In part, he said the public knows who he is, and added, "They know I'm not going to shift principles or shift positions based upon polls or focus groups."

In spite of the public's protestations, once the "decider"—as the president likes to call himself—decides, he's not going to budge. What's so sad is he appears to feel that his contrary and stubborn nature is an asset, rather than a liability. He seems to take great pleasure out of being contrary for contrary's sake.

The reason President Bush wanted others to believe he didn't read polls is because he wanted to demonstrate to the American public that he was in charge.

What he said and what he did appeared to be two different things. Although he wanted it to appear as though the American people's reaction to his policies didn't affect him—since, as Tony Snow, President Bush's press secretary, said, "You cannot conduct a war based on polls"—that inane statement betrays what really concerned the president.

Contrary to what the president said, just the opposite is true. President Bush appeared too self-absorbed and concerned about his personal image to be able to look beyond himself and directly address the issues that are so troublesome to the American public.

Again, President Bush is an example of what we don't want in a future leader; again, we need look only to great leaders of the past to get a clearer idea of the characteristics desirable in future candidates.

Lincoln and the Public

It's obvious from what has been written about Lincoln that throughout his life, he tried hard to be responsive to human need. He was indeed an other-centered and caring man.

Even though by the end of the Civil War, the deaths and casualties surpassed any other conflict in American history, President Lincoln was the most beloved president this country has ever had. He was loved because he had the ability to keep the Union together and abolish slavery, two very ambitious and difficult goals to achieve. Even under great odds to the contrary, he did all of this while still looking beyond himself, which was evident by his responding and caring for the Confederate and Union forces equally.

Since Lincoln treated both friend and foe alike, he never held a grudge or harbored ill will toward those who opposed him. Even when people called him names such as a "big ape" or a "buffoon" or any other derogatory comment, he would not let that affect his ability to get the job done. In his way, he managed to be both impervious to useless public commentary while remaining tuned in to what the public needed, thus achieving a delicate balance. He had a plan and a strategy in how he was going to govern and what he wanted to accomplish while being president; therefore, he wasn't going to let name-calling or any other character assassination comments keep him from accomplishing his goals, whatever they might be.

At the same time, the reason Lincoln had confidence in his ability to make good and wise decisions is because he always made such decisions by listening to his public, taking their wants and desires into account whenever possible, and using both his heart and his mind first before coming to a decision. He always recognized that two factors had to enter into his decision-making process: the need to use his intellect, which was well honed and sharpened by the time he became president, and the need to use his heart, gauging how he felt about what he was going to do. How would his decision affect the populace? Would the decision further the goals and desires of all Americans?

By the time of Lincoln's assassination, he was considered by many to be "the most popular man in the republic."

Yes, by the time Lincoln was assassinated, he indeed had won the hearts and minds of many more than the simple majority of the people. He had convinced many, friend and foe alike, that the Civil War was indeed worth fighting for, to preserve the Union and free the slaves from bondage.

Whenever a presidential decision involves the loss of life and limb, the American public's approval of that decision is of vital concern. After all, some of those Americans will have to fight that war.

From Bad to Worse

Since President Bush realized, at some level, the American public was not satisfied with the way the Iraq war was progressing, his concern was further exacerbated by his lack of an exit strategy, which simply made him feel even less adequate and less in control.

The polls suggested that the president didn't know when the U.S. troops were going to be able to leave Iraq. The president continued to state his tired mantra, "As Iraqi troops stand up, U.S. troops will stand down." Since the Pentagon suddenly decided to no longer make public how many Iraqi troops had been trained, this suggested they had no idea of when American troops would withdraw from Iraq.

Yes, the American people were deeply concerned about the loss of life, limb, and treasure that occurred in Iraq in the time our soldiers have been over there.

If President Bush had had a greater sense of empathy and compassion for what the troops were going through, he wouldn't have been so cavalier in deciding that we needed to wage war with Iraq.

In 1944, when Roosevelt wanted to keep fighting until the German army was destroyed, over 70 percent of Democrats and Republicans supported that decision, whereas, in 2007, bipartisan support could not be obtained for the Iraq war.

Since public image was so vitally important to the president, and because he is concerned that his voters realize he personally does not have everything under control, it is surmised that deep, deep down in his heart of hearts, our president wondered if he was indeed in charge and was capable of making decisions as commander in chief.

He acted like the little boy or girl who goes into a dark and forbidding cave with a little flashlight and repeats over and over again, "I'm not scared, I'm not scared, I'm not scared ..."

Before President Bush speaks before the public, instead of saying, "I'm not scared," he might say to himself, "I am the president, I am the president ..."

Interestingly, the public is painfully aware of President Bush's discomfort when he is expected to speak in any public gatherings. It is for that reason that he has held the fewest number of press conferences than of any president beginning with Eisenhower. Please keep in mind that President Bush is a public servant, just like any other person who works for the government. Therefore, his job is to answer your questions—no doubt about it.

But President Bush considers himself, not the American public, to be the decider. The fact that the president wanted to make it abundantly clear that he was indeed in charge and made the decisions suggests that he believed others might be in doubt about who sails the ship of state.

In the many books and articles published about the president's decision-making processes with regard to matters of state, there emerged a common thread among the authors, observers, and analysts. In their effort to understand, most recognized that President Bush's resistance to considering the complexity of an issue, his tendency to disregard dissenting opinions, and his consolidation of the process in the hands of a select, secretive, trusted few is his modus operandi.

Despite the image President Bush wanted to project, he was not the sole decider. In an op-ed in the *Los Angeles Times* on May 7, 2003, print and broadcast journalist James Moore, co author of the book *Bush's Brain*, had this to say about Rove:

> As the president's chief political advisor, Rove is involved in every decision coming out of the Oval Office. In fact, he flat out makes some of them. He is co-president of the United States, just as he was co-candidate for that office and co-governor of Texas. His relationship with the president is the most profound and complex of all the White House advisors. And his role creates questions

not addressed by our Constitution. Rove is probably the most powerful unelected person in American history.[33]

A Vote Revisited

In the 2004 presidential campaign, candidate John Kerry was castigated as a flip-flopper, largely for his habit of altering his position on issues as the circumstances dictated and warranted. This quality was successfully portrayed by the opposition as a weakness and widely viewed by the populace as a detriment to the candidate for the office of president.

But how many voters who weighed this label heavily in casting their ballots would now, in the light of current events, regret their decision? Was there a collective failure of the electorate to consider that the complexity and dynamics of global politics, representative governance, and domestic issue demands possibly overtaxed the decider in chief to the extent that our president was paralyzed and was either unable or unwilling to make nuanced decisions and flexible implementations?

The way future voters can avoid basing their voting decisions on tricky slogans is to recognize that "One sparrow doesn't make a summer." Translation: you must base your voting decisions on a multitude of factors before deciding on one candidate over another.

No War Without Consensus

It is vitally important to have or acquire public agreement if a president declares war with another country. This was particularly true when President Bush preemptively declared war with Iraq.

The story of mankind is interlaced with the history and the concept of war. Warfare has served to satisfy our most primal instincts of self-preservation and self-interest. Some observations of that history are that wars very seldom go according to plan, that there will be more wars after the last one, that there will be unintended consequences, and—most importantly—that people, combatant and civilian alike, will suffer and die. With those thoughts in mind, I feel that the decision to go to war should be the most exhaustively considered,

[33] James C. Moore, "Counting Votes While the Bombs Drop," *Los Angeles Times*, May 7, 2003. Used with permission of Allen Roland at salon.com

strenuously debated, and deeply reasoned position any government will pursue. Sadly, I believe that our government's decision to adopt a policy of preemptive war did not hold to that template.

President Bush has given a myriad of reasons why he preemptively declared war on Iraq. As of yet, the majority of the public is unwilling to buy any of the rationale he's put forth for going to war.

To select strong and competent leaders in the future, voters need to examine President Bush's behaviors in order to better understand what motivates his actions and causes him to make the statements he does.

Weak Justifications

Ego defense mechanisms work in service of the ego. By that I mean, it helps keep our self-esteem intact. The mechanisms like denial, repression, and intellectualization, to mention but a few of many, help keep us from feeling bad about ourselves. Instead of saying, "Boy, did I screw up! I'm sure a dummy," a statement that would assault our sense of self-esteem, we might say, "Gee, I had to do that, because if I hadn't, such-and-such would have happened." If what you did was not socially acceptable and therefore shouldn't have been done, and you didn't consciously know what the reason was for your action, you were using one or more of the defense mechanisms available to you.

Even though our president offered many reasons for going to war, such as the now-questionable existence of weapons of mass destruction, the explanations he gave may not be the true reasons, but, at best, rationalizations for doing what he did. I say "at best" because if his reasons were indeed rationalizations, he had no conscious control in deciding what to say when explaining why war was necessary. It was plausible, but not the real reason for the war.

If that were the case, he would not consciously know what the real reason might be. He simply failed to think through the problem sufficiently enough to know. But it seems reasonable to at least suspect that Bush was intentionally being duplicitous.

As a president, Lincoln was very honest with others. In that sense, what you saw was what you got. That was one of the reasons he was so loved as president of the United States. People could trust him. What people heard was what people got.

Adam Khan, the author of *Self-Help Stuff That Works*, said the following about Honest Abe:

> Lincoln was one of the few great men who really was great. Before he became president, Lincoln spent twenty years as an unsuccessful Illinois lawyer—at least he was unsuccessful in financial terms. But when you measure the good he did, he was very rich indeed. Legends are often untrue, but Lincoln was the real thing. George Washington never chopped down a cherry tree, but Abraham Lincoln was honest.

Khan went on to describe several incidents in which Lincoln represented his fellow poor citizens, charging very little or even working for free. In one instance, he even paid the client's hotel bill and funded her return trip home.

"He was a fool, perhaps, by certain standards," Khan observed. "He didn't have much, and it was his own fault. But he was a good human being by anyone's standards."

Honesty makes you feel good about yourself and creates trust in others. It improves your relationship with yourself and with others. It's not much in fashion these days to talk about the benefits of honesty and decency, but the benefits are there and they are valuable and worth the trouble. If American voters are wise, they will seek an honest, humble leader who remains open and accountable to the American people."[34]

Love as a Means to Equality

What makes a Lilliputian (U.S. citizen) tick? No, I'm not talking about its literal heart, but rather, its metaphorical one. Metaphorically speaking, our fictional Lilliputian should indeed have a heart, for it's love that makes the world go around. Love is the principal force behind human life. In medieval theology, it was held that love set the universe in motion. Love is the essence of life; without it, we die.

---

[34] Adam Khan, *Self-Help Stuff That Works*, http://www.amazon.com/Self-Help-Stuff-That-Works-Adam/dp/0962465674. Used with permission of the author.

When we compare our lives to that of other countries throughout this world, we do indeed need to appreciate how very fortunate we are as a nation.

Speaking for myself, I feel very blessed. I realize that if I hadn't grown up here, in these United States, and had the parents that I was fortunate to have, my life would have been much different. My parents and this country have given me so much. If any of you can empathize with me about how blessed we are, then you need to think about what you are going to do to show your appreciation for having the opportunity to be living in this great country.

I have to ask myself that question every day. Whatever I do to show my appreciation will never come close to matching the chance happening of having been born here rather than in any other country in the world. It is the Constitution, the Declaration of Independence, and the Bill of Rights that have allowed me to be all that I can be. To be truly self-actualized, every U.S. citizen needs to be given the opportunity to thrive in a similar way.

How can we channel our love for America in a positive way? Well, we could start by loving all fellow Americans, not just the ones who look and dress the way we do.

Some ethnic groups, like African Americans, while technically having been given the same opportunity that I've been given, are not on a level playing field with me. Why? It's simply that racial prejudice and bias has not ended here in America. Why is there so much intolerance shown? Why should there be so much hatred and scorn shown the African American community by others? When are we going to grow up as a nation and begin to appreciate, respect, and love the differences between each other?

We'd better start appreciating whatever cultural differences exist between the two races, because what differences might exist aren't worth mentioning. It is those cultural differences that are not only the most interesting to observe, but can teach us the most because they expand our appreciation for the breadth of humanity, a quality that is so important for any political candidate to possess. We should cherish those aspects of a people that are different, because that makes them unique. Wouldn't it be boring if we were all the same? Absolutely.

Throughout years of slavery, some of America's brothers and sisters were treated as property right after they got off the ships and started working as slaves for their masters. What chance did they have to enjoy the potential benefits and opportunities this great country supposedly had for all Americans?

Just imagine the impact that the label "slave" had on each African American's self-concept. What a dehumanizing experience. Obviously, the reality that the label signified and implied was far worse and shameful than the label itself.

If we really want to love our country and give something back in thanks for the amazing opportunities this American life has offered us, we need to make our country better through tolerance and love. Our nation needs to finish what Lincoln began, which is to abolish racial discrimination in this country. It is not only the morally correct thing to do, but also will help bring this country together as a nation.

Just as Lincoln had a great love for all people that drove them to champion freedom for all, it's my contention that, today, love still drives us. It's our ability to love one another that makes life worth living. Without love, where would our lives be? Or would we have a life at all? Obviously, the answer to that question is no. Love does indeed make the world go 'round ... yet, considering the way we treat one another and other countries, I can't help wonder what priority we and other nations place on just simply trying to get along better with one another.

Relationship Therapy

These ideals and philosophies don't just apply to our nation, but to our entire world. Getting along requires compromises. We, as a nation, can't always expect things to go our way.

Using a marriage as an analogy, pretend our nation is married to another country—say, China. Most marriages have at least some little hitches in them; none go completely as planned. If that is the case, what determines whether professional counseling is in order is the degree or severity of the discord between the two parties.

When a couple experiences stress in their relationship because of a clash of ideas, they go through predictable stages that can be placed on a continuum, which measures the degree of differences they are experiencing. The continuum goes from the least stressful, which is a disagreement, to the most stressful, which is open violence.

In order for peace to again be restored in the relationship, some type of resolution of differences needs to take place.

The level of differences can be displayed in this way:

Disagreement → argument → conflict → open conflict (physical violence)

The first step would be disagreement. If that doesn't get resolved, the disagreement could escalate into an argument, a verbal exchange that can be resolved by the parties involved. The next level of escalation could be conflict, a prolonged clash of opinion that may need a third party to resolve it. The final could be open conflict, where either one or both couples engage in open violence. In that case, the opportunity to resolve the differences and save the marriage would be pretty minimal. The vast majority of those cases end up in the divorce court.

Unfortunately, in the case of our marriage to China, we can't split by getting divorced; we are indeed married to each other "'til death do us part." Obviously, we can't allow our differences to escalate to open violence, for if that occurs, since we are both nuclear powers, it would be the end of life as we know it.

How can we as voters and Americans deal with these conflicts constructively and find effective solutions to global clashes, thus preventing war and encouraging peaceful the cohabitation of our planet?

Putting our marriage to China aside for a moment, let's say you are married, and you and your wife or husband come to me, in my role as a clinical psychologist, for marriage counseling; I would encourage each of you to explain how you looked at your marriage and what changes you'd like to see take place.

Let's say that I start the session by asking you who made the referral and what brings you to my office. You start to explain your problem to me. Invariably, when you start talking, at some point in time, your spouse will interrupt and say, "No, that isn't true." I will then have to ask that your spouse let you speak, as this is how you look at the relationship.

It always takes several reminders before either one gets the message. What brought you and your spouse into my office in the first place was that neither one of you were listening to what the other was saying, because you both were so preoccupied with trying to get your own point across. So the same scenario that took place at home was again played out in my office. How are we going to be able to make the necessary compromises if we don't know how your spouse feels about the situation?

In other words, we need to learn how to empathize, or put ourselves in the other fellow's shoes, and in that way, truly appreciate how that person feels and what that person needs. Usually when empathy occurs, compromises can be made, and the marriage can be saved.

If what brings couples to my office is that they have needs which have not been adequately met in the relationship, then generally, that problem can be resolved.

However, if a couple comes into marriage counseling, and their belief systems are different, their marriage generally is doomed. That is because beliefs are defined as values or standards that are not subject to compromise or modification. If you and your spouse don't share the same values and priorities, how can the marriage survive?

Now, in the case of our marriage with China, even though our belief systems are diametrically opposed—since they value their communist ideology and we value democracy—we have to learn to coexist, because what other alternative do we have? We certainly don't want our differences to escalate to open conflict, because the nuclear power that we both possess makes outright violence an unthinkable alternative.

Like in any marriage-counseling scenario, the couple will stay in counseling as long as there's hope for change. Whenever that is viewed by either the husband or wife as no longer a possibility, the counseling ends, because one or the other will not wish to continue with therapy.

Though today, China's government, or giant, is communist, that doesn't mean it will always remain so. Like people, governments also can change. That's what happened with Russia and some other once-communist nations.

Though we would like China's government to eventually change their political ideology to be more consistent with our own, that's not what we should diplomatically focus on. What we should be interested in promoting is how we can both live peacefully with one another.

In order to achieve that, we should continue to be a strong trading partner, accept their help in dealing with North Korea, help maintain peaceful coexistence with Japan and Taiwan, and back off lecturing them on human-rights issues, which will resolve themselves as China's young people will experience benefits of free enterprise and greater intellectual freedom.

Applying Lincoln's Wisdom

If we take Abraham Lincoln's adage seriously, perhaps something good might happen. He is quoted as saying, "'A drop of honey catches more flies than a gallon of gall.' So with men. If you would win a man to your cause, first convince him that you are his sincere friend. Therein is a drop of honey which catches his heart, which, say what he will, is the highroad to his reason."

As Lincoln suggests, the high road to his reason is to capture a man's heart. How do you touch a man's heart? You do that by showing him that you care and respect him by showing genuine interest in him, showing him that you want to learn more of what he thinks and believes, and that by acquiring such knowledge, you understand his way of thinking.

So ... believe it or not, when today's politicians are out on the campaign trail and are doing their thing as politicians, which is to garner votes, what they should be doing is expressing a political kind of love toward their constituents, if they want to hear where their voters are coming from—and in that way, capture their votes.

This sounds nice, but what does "a political kind of love" even mean? Well, Eric Fromm, a twentieth-century psychologist, felt there are four key ingredients to love: caring, respect, understanding, and knowledge. I agree with this assessment and consider each element to be a valuable, productive part of political love.

Whenever Lincoln put on his political top hat and played the part of a politician, he was a master in employing all those qualities that make up political love. In that respect, he was the quintessential politician.

In America's hypothetical marriage to China, political love needs to exist between us in order for an amicable and successful union to occur, in which we coexist in harmony.

Negotiating Successfully

Because President Bush appears to think in such an absolute way about issues, and because his tolerance for ambiguity appears to be very limited, his type of thinking is the antithesis of good negotiation.

I would imagine that whenever President Bush attempts to confer with China's president, he hardly utilizes caring, understanding, respect, or knowledge in order to enhance their relationship, so that both parties feel like winners at the negotiating table.

In order for successful negotiations to take place between two countries, both countries need to know where the other one is coming from, or why it believes as it does, and what some of its fears and anxieties might be. A true diplomat is one who's able to achieve at least part of his goals and objectives without the other person feeling like he has been had.

But are we being too simplistic in placing our faith in love? Well, if what Gandhi says is true, that "love is the strongest force the world possesses, and yet it is the humblest imaginable," we've got to examine this whole subject of love a little more.

Reason suggests to me that if our nation was a little more loving and caring toward other countries by showing them respect and humility, that would go a long way in enhancing the likelihood that we could get along better with one another. We need to do less talking and more listening, and offer a sense of admiration and appreciation for who our comrades are and what they represent.

When I was a practicing clinical psychologist, if you, as a client, came to me for psychotherapy, I would have to find something I liked about you in order to continue to work with you to resolve the conflict that brought you into my office.

How you presented yourself would determine how easy or difficult it might be for me to see something I liked. I might end the first hour by concluding that the only thing I liked about you was your eyes. I might say to myself that you have the most beautiful eyes I've ever seen. Obviously, my fondness for you has to be genuine and sincere if the rapport is to grow.

By humility, I mean feeling a sense of modesty and respectfulness in that we as a team are going to work together to figure out what the best way might be to help you feel happier and more content with your life.

Obviously, I would not act arrogant by thinking that I indeed knew how to fix your problem, and that the only way to do it would be for me to tell you what you must do to resolve your difficulties. When it comes to diplomacy, that Father-knows-best approach doesn't cut it with me.

Since one of the basic premises of my book is to describe our giant, our nation, as comprising all the voters in our country, and because each voter represents a mythical Lilliputian, we need to look at our individual selves to understand what we should expect from our president, who represents our giant.

Remember, our greatest insights are our own projections. By that I mean, whether we're talking about counseling, parenting, diplomacy, or listening to a politician, we form our opinions about what to think and say by seeing a little of ourselves in the people we're relating to. Therefore, in the case of the politician, it is by identifying with that person that we can not only understand, but also know how to react to what is said.

"When the power of love overcomes the love of power the world will know peace." That quote is from Jimi Hendrix, the musician, singer, and songwriter.

How can we apply these lessons on love, humility, and tolerance to reducing the threat of terrorism? Notice I said reducing the threat, not eliminating it, for terrorism will continue to be a threat beyond even the foreseeable future. That being so, the world's goal should be to reduce the threat, so that it becomes manageable, so that we are better able to defend our shores from terrorism in the future than we are able to do today.

Terrorism will not be reduced significantly unless we have the cooperation from the world's family of nations.

If we begin to treat the family of nations as we would treat any member of our flesh and blood, we would stop and view nations that don't agree with us with a greater degree of respect and appreciation. This will only work if, instead of a Father-knows-best treatment that reduces those nations to the status of our children, we begin to look at other countries as adults who have grown up and had families of their own. We need to respect their maturity and where they're coming from.

We need to do that because we can't fully appreciate the trials and tribulations of each of the other family members and what they are experiencing with their individual kin. If they act differently than we would, we need to try to understand what kinds of issues they are struggling with in their own country and, in doing so, we can empathize with them, and our discussions or negotiations could progress in the way we would all desire.

How can we get other countries to work with us if we don't show them that we care for their welfare as well as our own? The best vehicle that can be used to accomplish that goal is leading by example.

In order to reduce the threat of terrorism in this country and around the world, we need to treat France, or any other country that we're talking to, with respect and humility. We can do that by listening intently to what each country is saying to us. If we don't understand what they're saying, we need to ask them to clarify what is being said, all the time suspending judgment regarding their statements.

If negotiations are involved, we need to be willing to compromise, since it is vital that we get not only France, but any other nation, to realize how important it is for us to work together, if our war on terrorism will be successful.

I know we can't, and shouldn't, show other giants or nations unconditional love, for that would be foolhardy and give them license to behave any way they wish, if they know they have our trust and believe that they will always be protected by us. We must send them the message that we want to work with them for *peace and the good of human kind and for the survival of this planet.*

All races, colors, and creeds in the United States should be proud to say they're an American. Right now, for some ethnic groups, we as a nation still have a long way to go to justify some of our people making that statement. We must begin to be more caring and loving of our fellow Americans and our fellow nations than we have been in the past, if we as a nation expect to survive the rigors brought to bear by terrorism.

THE BEST THINGS IN LIFE
ARE FREE

This chapter is about what Americans value.

Even taking individual differences into account and accepting the possibility that extrinsically, money is valued and contributes to your sense of well-being and job satisfaction, acquiring money for money's sake may have limited value for you in the long run. It's what you do with your wealth and its intrinsic value that may determine what part the value of money plays in contributing to your happiness.

Let's say that you and your husband, wife, or lover come to my office for psychological counseling. You are a housewife or househusband. You have three preschool children. You describe yourself as the caregiver in the family. And that your partner is the breadwinner. You bring in the sheet music for the song "The Best Things in Life Are Free." You say you get ridiculed by your partner for liking the song, and you want me to read the lyrics so that I can better understand your situation.

When I further inquire about your circumstance, you say there isn't enough intimacy in the relationship. Your partner then chimes in, "I don't understand what the big deal's all about. I'm a good provider. I bring home a six-figure salary. President Bush's first-term tax cut made my take-home income that much more. As far as I'm concerned, life doesn't get any better than that!"

After I talk to you both for a bit longer, it becomes obvious that you don't relate to one another. You don't have a loving, caring relationship. You don't value the same things, nor do you share the same basic values.

It is no wonder the breadwinner laughed at the lyrics. The idea of anything free having value seems ludicrous. To the employed partner, the worth of anything is related to how much it costs. If it's free, then it is perceived as having limited value.

I'm as guilty as the next person in the way I assess the value of something. I use the cost of the item as a parameter. If it costs a bundle, it's worth a lot; if it costs little, its worth plummets accordingly. If I want to buy a gift for somebody, I focus on its price. If it's too low, I immediately reject it as inappropriate—yet, that might have been the perfect gift.

In 1968, President Richard Nixon said, "In the next twenty years, we shall become much richer, but will we really be any richer as people—happier?"

According to Matthew Herper, the answer is no.

Herper wrote an article for Forbes magazine titled "Money Won't Buy You Happiness." In it, he says:

> It's official: Money can't buy happiness.

> Sure, if a person is handed $10, the pleasure centers of his brain light up as if he were given food, sex or drugs. But that initial rush does not translate into long-term pleasure for most people. Surveys have found virtually the same level of happiness between the very rich individuals on the Forbes 400 and the Maasai herdsman of East Africa. Lottery winners return to their previous level of happiness after five years. Increases in income just don't seem to make people happier—and most negative life experiences likewise have only a small impact on long-term satisfaction.

America can be a materialistic place; sometimes, it seems as if the American dream has slowly morphed into the American pursuit of lots of expensive stuff. So perhaps you're surprised by the revelation that a poor herdsman is, on average, just as happy as Bill Gates.

As citizens, we need to recognize the money myth and adjust our priorities accordingly.

Herper continues, "Why doesn't wealth bring a constant sense of joy? 'Part of the reason is that people aren't very good at figuring out what to do with the money,' says George Loewenstein, an economist at Carnegie Mellon University. 'People generally overestimate the amount of long-term pleasure they'll get from a given object.'"

Having lots of money can even make you less happy, if it pulls you from the neighborhood, job, friend group, or hobby that you love. Even if life as a recent lottery winner is just as fantastic as you expected, human nature dictates the novelty will inevitably wear off.

As Herper cleverly observes, "You can get used to anything, be it hanging by your toenails or making millions of dollars a day."[35]

Psychologists have a name for the eventual wearing off of pleasurable experience: it's called habituation. When the novelty of the positive experience disappears, the corresponding joy and gratification dissipates as well.

Those who are poor and in need of money to take care of their everyday needs value the acquisition of money much differently than those who are financially well-heeled.

Clinical psychologist Clayton E. Tucker-Ladd, PhD, had this to say in his online book, *Psychological Self-Help*:

> Money—while, in general, people living in a wealthy, free country are clearly happier than people in a poor country, making a lot of money is usually an ineffective way to achieve happiness. In fact, once we get into a materialistic mode of acquiring 'things,' the result is often less happiness, maybe even compulsiveness, competitiveness, boredom, or meaninglessness in the long haul.[36]

---

[35] Matthew Herper, "Money Won't Buy You Happiness," *Forbes*, September 21, 2004, http://www.forbes.com/2004/09/21/cx_mh_0921happiness_print.html Reprinted with permission of Forbes.com, © 2007.

[36] Clayton E. Tucker-Ladd, PhD, *Psychological Self-Help*, http://www.psychologicalselfhelp.org/Chapter6/chap6_27.html. Used with permission of the author.

Though the message in the song "The Best Things in Life Are Free" may sound dated, it is as true today as it was when the tune was written in 1927.

Some might say that such a sentiment is too dated and doesn't apply to the real world of today. Well, that's true—it doesn't. But maybe that's what's wrong with this country. Maybe, just maybe, we should look inward and appreciate what this nation offers us intrinsically. This country has great physical beauty, much of which is protected as national parks. We have a public-education system, a fair justice system, and our greatest asset: free speech.

All this talk of money and happiness is key to our expectations of the American government and the ideals we expect it to uphold.

Pursuing Happiness

Inside the Declaration of Independence is a small passage:

> "We hold these truths to be self-evident, that all men are created equal, that they are endowed by their Creator with certain unalienable Rights, that among these are Life, Liberty and the pursuit of Happiness."

If money does not equal happiness, what does the Declaration mean by the term "happiness"—that which our Founding Fathers claim we all have a right to pursue? *Webster's New Universal Unabridged Dictionary* defines happiness in this way:

> 1. the quality or state of being happy. 2. good fortune; pleasure; contentment; joy.
> -Syn. 1. 2. pleasure, joy, exhilaration, bliss, contentedness, delight, enjoyment.
> -Ant. 1. misery.

What I've tried to make abundantly clear is that you can't buy happiness. According to the dictionary's definition of what it means to be happy, happiness involves intrinsic rather than extrinsic factors. It involves a state of mind or an attitude.

Tucker-Ladd, in his book *Psychological Self-Help*, summarizes several ways to seek a happy life:

1. Don't make the mistake of believing that being a big success will automatically make you happy. Being a genuinely caring person with good friends is a much better way.
2. Learn to control your time and your behavior. Have a daily to-do list.
3. Act like a happy person—smile, greet people, be outgoing and optimistic, even if you are a little down. Acting sour and unhappy keeps you feeling that way.
4. Find respected tasks to do that use your talents and challenge you to do your best ... flow!
5. Every day do exercises you enjoy to the point of "working out."
6. Learn to thoroughly rest. Get plenty of sound sleep. An alert, relaxed body feels good.
7. Attend to friends, loved ones, and the people you are privileged to serve.
8. Also, empathize with and respond with help to strangers in need. Happy people are sensitive and giving.
9. Take time each day to remember people and institutions who have helped you. Count your blessings. Express your gratitude.
10. Join caring groups that support your being your best self and give you hope.[37]

You can increase your happiness quotient by either giving or being a recipient of someone else's love, caring, or devotion. Being empathetic to, and responding by helping, strangers in need also enhances your chances of experiencing joy in your life.

I've said that America needs to return to the ideals that once made it great. Nothing is more fundamentally American than our forefathers' emphasis on the pursuit of happiness. Today, Americans may still think they are pursuing happiness, but the truth is that they're more interested in accumulating material possessions. Happiness has nothing to do with "the more the better, and the happier you will be."

---

[37] Clayton E. Tucker-Ladd, PhD, *Psychological Self-Help*, http://www.psychologicalselfhelp.org/Chapter6/chap6_27.html. Used with permission of the author.

Today, many of us try to be happy at someone else's expense, which is simply a form of self-aggrandizement.

In his book *Lincoln on Leadership*, Donald Phillips says that

> Lincoln possessed a true gift when it came to communicating his feelings and emotions. That talent can be readily observed in one of his shortest and most moving speeches, his farewell remarks to the people of Springfield who'd gathered at the railway station to see him off to Washington.

> At eight o'clock on the morning of February 11, 1861, the president-elect arrived at the depot with his family to find that more than a thousand of his friends, neighbors, and colleagues had gathered to say good-bye. Moved by their presence, and feeling somewhat obligated to say a few words, Lincoln made the following impromptu speech:

> "My friends, no one, not in my situation, can appreciate my feeling of sadness at this parting. To this place, and the kindness of these people, I owe everything. Here I have lived a quarter of a century, and have passed from a young to an old man. Here my children have been born, and one is buried."[38]

Because we're the richest country in the world and have more creature comforts than any other nation on the face of the earth which was certainly not true in the 1800s—you'd think we'd have more time to look beyond ourselves and be more loving and concerned about all people's welfare, not only in this country, but throughout the world. But that is not to be.

Even by Lincoln's own admission, he undertook the presidency "with a task before me greater than that which rested upon Washington." In the most trying time in American history, Mr. Lincoln was able to look beyond himself and give an impromptu speech filled with love, care, and feeling, to a "thousand of his friends, neighbors, and colleagues."

---

[38] Donald Phillips II, *Lincoln on Leadership*, 149–50. With permission of Warner Books. © 2004 by Donald Phillips II.

Materialism isn't the only roadblock on the American path to happiness.

A National Plague

Egocentrism and narcissism are national plagues in our country. Just as with many plagues, the end result is death—not of the afflicted individuals, but of our nation.

The symptoms of these self-centered maladies may include taking advantage of others for one's own personal gain, driving while talking on a cell phone, cutting in line, and talking prejudicially about people who are not like oneself.

The costs of catching this malady are devastating. It is the preoccupation of self at the exclusion of most others; a self-love that has no limits; a feeling of entitlement; a lack of humility; an inability to empathize; and a tinge—or, in many cases, more than a tinge—of arrogance.

This virus is passed down from generation to generation.

Unfortunately, this disease is very hard to treat, because the ailment develops at such an early time in your life. If left untreated until ten and a half years of age, it becomes a chronic condition and is almost impossible to treat successfully. This is because the personality is pretty well formed at that age and is very resistant to change.

There may be a ray of hope that the country is moving in another direction. Recently, some of the young people of our country have begun to reach out to communities in need and offer them a helping hand. College students who might have spent spring break partying instead went to New Orleans and the Gulf Coast to help rebuild that battered region.

A Note to Parents

When your children leave the nest, what you as a parent want for them, more than anything else in the world, is for them to be happy. Your happiness is a result of your children being happy. Since you now know that money doesn't bring a perpetual sense of happiness or well-being, even if you extrinsically enjoy making it, you need to remind your children to look elsewhere to determine what it is that creates a sustaining feeling of inner peace and contentment from within.

The antithesis of selfishness and egocentrism is becoming other-centered, or caring for people other than yourself.

A true and sustaining appreciation of life, which involves a "feeling of inner peace and contentment from within," can only occur through reflection and introspection. When you can make such feelings your own by thinking about how they came about and why you feel like you do, then, by reaching out to help others in need, you heighten your sense of well-being. Because it makes you feel so good, it eventually becomes an automatic response to the human condition.

I contend that a prolonged sense of happiness comes from intrinsic factors—those factors that reside in your very being. It is at the core of your existence. In that sense, it is that which separates you from all other animal species. It helps define your soul and who you are as a person. When expressed, it not only nourishes your spirit, but gives you great joy and a sense of well-being. That something is unconditional love—what life is all about.

According to Victor Hugo, "the supreme happiness in life is to know that we are loved."

Hugo was a novelist, poet, and dramatist of the nineteenth century. He is considered by many to be the most important French Romantic writer of that period. As was true in the 1800s and continues to be true in the twenty-first century, giving and receiving love is the pathway to happiness.

Love in its purest form involves caring, emotional intimacy, and physical intimacy.

Abraham Lincoln has been presented as the ideal American president. How well did he show that he cared about the American people?

Lincoln not only talked the talk, but he also walked the walk. In his book *Lincoln on Leadership*, Donald Phillips noted, "Lincoln often attended private funerals, whether it was the infant son of his secretary of war (Edwin M. Stanton) or for eighteen women killed in an explosion at the federal arsenal. During his presidency, Lincoln visited the wounded in hospitals and private residences and attended funerals any time such an occasion presented itself."[39]

The caring part of the equation involves being compassionate and concerned about the other person's welfare. Lincoln was a master at showing empathy and concern toward those in need—not only toward his friends and loved ones, but toward perfect strangers as well.

Emotional Intimacy

In emotional intimacy, your loving self is verbally expressed without fear of censorship or chastisement. You are able to be yourself in the relationship. In other words, you're respected for who you are, just by the mere fact of being you.

If desired, you're able to share secrets and feelings that you wouldn't necessarily share with a perfect stranger. I say "necessarily" because, on occasion, Lincoln publicly expressed his feelings freely, regardless of where he was at the time. For example, when Lincoln learned of the death of his sister, he openly wept, regardless of who was there to witness his grief.

Lincoln did not confine his grief to only those who were loved ones, friends, and associates. He expressed his deep love and caring for all whose lives touched his. His anguish and grief was particularly evident when learning of the men on the battlefield who lost their lives because of the war's terrible toll. American voters would be wise to select a president who could maintain a beneficial level of emotional intimacy with the American public. Such a candidate wouldn't be afraid to speak freely or express his or her emotions. Such a candidate would want a relationship with the American public—one full of caring and empathy. The empathy aspect is especially important when you realize that the American presidency includes the ability to send thousands of American troops to their deaths.

Lincoln's empathetic understanding of the horrors of the Civil War helped him make decisions with an understanding and appreciation what his actions had on friend and foe alike. Clearly, he didn't take lightly his job as the Union's commander in chief. Because of his great empathetic ability, he knew only too well the inestimable price

---

[39] Donald Phillips II, *Lincoln on Leadership*, 20. With permission of Warner Books. © 2004 by Donald Phillips II.

paid in terms of human suffering and sorrow that comes with any war—a war that he so very much wanted to avoid having, even prior to becoming the president of the United States.

A discerning voter will likely to be able to spot and appreciate a presidential candidate's sense of empathy. Intimacy, however, is another story, thanks to the boundaries existing in modern culture.

On average, in the 1800s, Abraham Lincoln, as well as society as a whole, enjoyed a greater sense of intimacy than what is experienced in our culture today.

Using today's standards as an indication of same-sex impropriety, some behavior that was considered commonplace in the 1800s would be viewed with dismay in our twenty-first century.

When traveling, it was not unusual for men to share their beds. It was considered a luxury to have private quarters. Besides, in many cases, there simply was no room in the inn, so men were required to sleep together if they wanted anywhere to sleep at all.

The nineteenth-century male was much more open in expressing his feelings of intimacy toward both sexes than is true today. The expression of such feelings such as affection, love, and passion was commonplace in that era. Tragically, compared to today's standards of propriety, that kind of behavior appears to belong to a bygone period in American history.

An example of the kinds of open expression of feelings would be what transpired by two members of President Lincoln's cabinet: Secretary of War Edwin McMasters Stanton and Secretary of Treasury Salmon P. Chase. Chase had sent Stanton a letter that was filled with emotion. Stanton's reply was that it "filled my heart with joy; to be loved by you, and be told you value my love is a gratification beyond my power to express." He went on to say that "To love and to be loved, is a necessary condition of my happiness ..."

Prior to becoming president, Lincoln was a lawyer and traveled the circuit throughout the state of Illinois. At that time, many of his friendships were made during his shared experiences with his fellow lawyers. They would journey together for eight weeks each spring and fall. At the end of the day, they would gather at a local tavern, and Lincoln would regale everyone with his stories. Inevitably, a crowd would gather, and because he was able to tell the stories with such humor and glee, he developed a statewide reputation of being a storyteller par excellence.

His storytelling reputation garnered a number of friends and devoted followers, all of which helped him immeasurably when he began his political life in earnest.

Lincoln, by his very nature, was a very loving person who expressed his compassion, joy of life, and even his sorrow freely. His honesty in expressing caring, along with emotional and physical intimacy, stands as an example to us all of how we should be unafraid to express our deepest feelings.

Love, Sweet Love

You now have an intellectual understanding of what I mean when I talk about love. You now know it may involve caring, emotional intimacy, and physical intimacy. You also realize you may be loving if you express only one of the components that make up the love equation.

Love is a marvelous elixir in each of our lives. In my mind, loving and being loved is the essence of life. It is what makes life all worth living. It is the fuel used from which all that's good and right in the world evolves.

And the way we all can experience happiness, love, and compassion needs to be shown to not only our family and friends, but to total strangers as well, regardless of race or ethnicity.

You also realize there is no more powerful antidote toward making this divided nation whole again than following Lincoln's belief, as pronounced in the Declaration of Independence, "that all men are created equal ..."

It appears that frequently, Mr. Lincoln had the Declaration of Independence in the back of his mind whenever he made a presidential decision. On the one hand, the Declaration stressed the importance of respecting the individual's undeniable and independent right to pursue life, liberty, and happiness. Yet, on the other hand, throughout President Lincoln's life, his overriding desire was to preserve the Union and abolish slavery. At times, this required giving up his own independent and selfish interests for the good of the community—and, ultimately, the nation. In order to do that, he encouraged factious groups to come together, settle their differences, and treat each other with love and compassion.

Realizing this is the greatest country on earth and that we are indeed privileged and fortunate to be Americans, we too can express our gratitude by what we do for others, just like Lincoln. We as a country need to put aside our differences and work for the common good. This is no time to be selfish and uncaring toward the needs of others. We must reach out and give a helping hand in any way we can to assist not only those less fortunate than ourselves, but also anyone who needs assistance, regardless of their personal situation. If we can help, we should do it unconditionally.

There are many resources that list volunteer groups. These run the gamut from serving in soup kitchens to caring for the disabled. Almost anyone could find some group to volunteer with.

By helping others, you are considering the needs of your country as well as your own personal self-interests as well. It should be rewarding enough, realizing that perhaps you have provided a sense of safety, security, love, and support to another person in these very difficult and trying times.

INTEGRITY

In my book's preface, I spoke of my age and the feeling that as I reach the twilight of my life, as my senses have begun to fail me, and my mental agility is not what it used to be, the only thing I have left is my integrity. If I've tended to business by honoring who I was, the only thing I will have intact as I face death is my integrity. My integrity represents the template of my life. It is the standard from which all other comparisons are made. When people say, "He lived a good life," they're talking about integrity.

When people realize they're going to die soon because of severe illness or for other reasons, they frequently show they have submitted to that understanding by saying they're at peace with themselves, or are ready to go, all of which implies they've tried to be true to themselves and their ideals.

We all like to be well thought of by others. That's true with everybody. It doesn't matter what your personality is like. You can be an extreme introvert or extrovert; it makes no difference. You still want to be liked. That's part of the human condition.

What Went Wrong?

If that's so, why have so many politicians violated that maxim? Before their term is up, why do so many civil servants, from the president on down, frequently do some shameful things that have disgraced and dishonored the esteemed office they occupied? What is it that causes them to deviate from the straight and narrow to such an extent that they engage in disgraceful and scurrilous acts that cause them to no longer be able to hold their head up high and proclaim, "I'm proud to be an American"?

It's because when they were in office, their rhetoric didn't match their deeds. Whether you're a parent or a politician, you never can get away with saying, "Don't do as I do; do as I say." That's because parents or politicians must always remember that their children or the American citizenry are watching them. In the case of the politician, the people they serve are looking for them to lead by example. For the president, the responsibility becomes even that much more demanding, for not only is the American public looking toward him for moral guidance and direction, but the world at large is also judging his actions. After all, he's the leader of the free world. That's an awesome responsibility.

In his book *Lincoln on Leadership*, Donald Phillips writes,

> In a way, Abraham Lincoln represented the summation of those leadership qualities that had helped to form a nation. The last great leader before industrial change, Lincoln stood for all that was right, honest, and self-evident. As a boy, his heroes were the Founding Fathers, and he studied the history of that young nation that was so devoted to human rights. He grew up in poverty and had a binding link to the common people. He was innovative at a time when the age of discoveries and inventions was just beginning. He was patient, persistent, consistent, and persuasive rather than dictatorial. But, without a doubt, the foundation of Abraham Lincoln's leadership style was an unshakable commitment to the rights of the individual.[40]

Such a description of Lincoln's character should help you understand why few of today's leaders even remotely approximate the high ideals which Lincoln embraced. One of the reasons is because today's politicians are primarily interested in money, power, or fame, rather than responding to the needs and concerns of the common people.

---

[40] Ibid., 2–3.

Compared to those Americans who live and die with integrity, unfortunately, very few of them are politicians. Hopefully, voters can learn to apply their own ideals about integrity to governmental elections, restoring integrity in a place that has been lacking for far too long.

In general, Americans already value integrity. It defines the essence of our being and what we as a nation value. There's no greater compliment than someone saying that you lived your life with integrity, because it is the most treasured quality for anyone to possess. Unfortunately, now that many of the politicians aboard today's ship of state seem to have lost their moral compasses, imperiling their passengers, the crew and the captain (Congress and the president) have taken the people's vessel into hazardous, uncharted waters.

Today's politicians too often seem to lack integrity or make it take a backseat to greed and intolerance. Does the quote "I am not a crook" ring a bell?

The crumbling of America's integrity isn't limited to just the political arena. I think if we were honest with ourselves, we would all agree that for most of us, we, as individual Lilliputians, have allowed our lives to go astray to such an extent that our sense of integrity or personal honesty and conviction has not been maintained. Consequently, at the end of the day, we can't say, "I'm proud of who I am and what I did today, for today I lived my life with integrity."

Adhering to Ideals

The reason many of us can't say that is because, during the course of our day, we allow ourselves to be tempted in a way that violates our sense of self and what's important to us. If you put a high priority on being honest and being true to yourself and your ideals, then you can see how, in any given day, it's very difficult to uphold those ideals, rather than that which is expedient or self-serving in some other way.

A good example of how we all jeopardize our sense of integrity on a daily basis would be when we violate the traffic laws, whether it be putting the pedal to the metal and driving too fast, driving through a yellow or red light, or violating a myriad of other laws of the road.

Of course, the above example is overly simplistic. I don't think any of us say at the end of the day, "Yikes, I'm a bad person because I went five miles over the speed limit today!"

No, I'm talking about a more serious kind of violation, where we knew what we were going to do was wrong, but we did it anyway.

Let's take a look at how politics as a whole lacks integrity. Notice I say "as a whole," because not every civil servant lacks integrity.

One particular way in which many politicians lack integrity involves their dishonesty. Plenty of duplicitous politicians won't hesitate to say one thing even when they believe the complete opposite. Those people are two-faced and blatantly dishonest.

A good example of those kinds of shenanigans, here in 2008, is where the politician suddenly switches from supporting a woman's right to choose whether or not to have an abortion to deciding suddenly to support the exact opposite, voting in favor of banning abortions entirely unless the life of the mother is in jeopardy. That's a perfect example of political expediency, or the wish to pander to that party's extremist base in order to win that party's nomination for presidency.

What stimulates politicians—and people in general—to be less than honest? For politicians, it's frequently the desire for money or power. Our society doesn't really value honesty and straightforwardness as much as it once did. The politicians, from the president on down, are the templates that are used to measure what society values. Unfortunately, many politicians who represent us on Capitol Hill are not by and large honest folk. Because many of them seem to be motivated by accumulating wealth, political muscle, or a combination of the two, it seems like hardly a day goes by that the media doesn't end up reporting a political indiscretion or scandal of one kind or another.

The papers are filled with stories about politicians who have engaged in unethical or quasi-ethical activities in Congress. Foreign junkets, poor voting attendance, collecting an unreasonably high fee for speaking to special-interest groups, looking for tax loopholes to help them avoid paying their taxes ... the list goes on and on.

The way the voter can prevent politicians not worthy of serving from gaining office is to watch and listen to each of them with a critical eye and ear. That is to say, listen to what they say and observe how they say it. If they don't have a vision for the country or haven't done their homework in terms of what they want to do for America, then they're suspect. Until you're sure that they're in politics for the right reason, they should not get your vote.

We all look to our elected officials to steer our ship of state in such a way as to avoid the rocks and shoals of corruption and greed. If the president and Congress are not providing the guidance necessary to avoid the dangers that would cause our vessel to spring a leak because of dishonesty and scandal, how are we, the electorate, going to keep our own heads above water? How will we avoid drowning in the sea of moral degradation and ruin? If our elected leaders try to get away with it, whatever "it" may be, why shouldn't we do the same, since they set the standards for what we as a nation hold dear to our hearts?

It is easy to see how politicians can jeopardize their own sense of integrity by saying what the other fellow wants to hear, rather than following their hearts and doing what they believe is right. When we do that in order to cause situations to turn out as we want them to, we sacrifice many of our cherished personal values along the way. You might as well do a paint-by-numbers version of your life, filling in your thoughts and actions however you are told. This approach deprives you of owning what you do. It's like when you were young and your parents told you what to do in order to have you act like a responsible citizen, and you did it—not to please yourself, but to please your parents. Later, when you blend your parent's values with your own, you then do what you think is best, according to your value system, rather than what others tell you to do. You then own the experience and, as a result, feel proud of yourself.

Clearly, because this is a complex society we live in, and depending on our life situations and belief systems, we are pulled in various directions when it comes to preserving our integrity. That yin-and-yang kind of experience puts a great strain on our sense of integrity. How we respond when we are tempted depends on whether we have the courage of our convictions and whether we follow our moral compass. If you avoid doing the expedient thing or responding to your avaricious and selfish nature, but rather do the right thing, even at personal expense and loss, you will find yourself among a small minority of Americans.

Win at all Cost

The ill conceived Iraq war is an example of a war that many politicians from the president on down feel we need to "win at all cost." They say that we must do that in order to protect our honor and prestige as a nation. But at what cost in American lives lost and maimed or the treasure spent to come out of the conflict saying, "We won, so now we can go home." If it was an "ill conceived" war to begin with, then our country's integrity has already been jeopardized.

Usually the issue of winning or losing is one that more aptly applies in sports. Frequently, if, in a sports contest the participant can conceal the truth in his or her action, he or she will do just that. An example that immediately comes to mind is when a football player catches a ball and knows it hit the ground before having control of it; he is trained to keep his mouth shut and hope the replay will not reveal his dishonesty.

On July 5, 2008, I had the rare experience of watching two Americans, the William sisters, Venus and Serena, play for the women's Wimbledon championship on TV. What made it so extraordinary was that they were two competitors who played their hearts out without sacrificing their sense of integrity.

The way they played the game made me feel proud to be an American. That's why I said viewing the match was such a "rare experience" because for the past number of years, I've had very little to be pleased about when it comes to the way America acts when being on the center stage in the International Arena.

Vince Lombardi, considered to be one, if not the greatest football coach of all times once said, "Winning isn't everything, it's the only thing." This is a mantra of dubious distinction. What is implied is that if you lose a contest, then, by definition, you're a loser.

Contrary to what coach Lombardi said, you can still feel like a winner even if you lose a competition. It all depends on how you feel about yourself before competing. If you feel like a winner going in, you'll feel like a winner going out, regardless of the outcome.

Using the coaching metaphor, in the case of George W. Bush, his coach is his Vice President, Dick Cheney. Even though President Bush is the central player in the drama that has unfolded in our government ever since he became president of the United States, judging by the results of his presidency, he has been miscast as the 43rd president of the United States, not only here in this country, but internationally as well. The reason for that is because he clearly doesn't fit the part. He is a method actor who never learned his lines, nor delivered them with any passion or conviction. That's because his drama coach, Vice President Cheney, has written the script that he's expected to play. To the degree that President Bush claims as his own in word and deeds what his coach has given him, he has sacrificed his sense of integrity, the most important quality that presidents must have if they are going to be trusted not only by their fellow Americans, but by the international community as well.

Increasing Rebellion

Integrity isn't the only item in short supply. Right or wrong, we have also quit having respect for authority.

In the 1970s, draft-age young adults began to rebel against the establishment. Such slogans as, "Draft beer, not boys," "Hell, no, we won't go," and "Make love, not war" were a few of the slogans that were chanted at anti-war demonstrations. When Lyndon Johnson was president, a chant that was frequently heard was "Hey, hey, LBJ, how many kids did you kill today?" The Vietnam War was what drove President Johnson out of office. He wanted desperately to end it, but didn't know how. It was for that reason he refused to run for a second term.

As a result of that war, the Vietnam generation taught the next generation to question authority in general and the reasons for going to war in particular. Young people began to realize how tenuous life was, particularly when they were expected to fight a war in a distant land—especially, if in their minds, the reasons for going to war were not clearly articulated and the morality of what they were expected to do was open to question.

Based on what I said earlier, it would appear that some of the Vietnam War protesters were following their sense of integrity when they protested the war.

They began to question authority in a way that had never happened before. As the first children to come of age with the threat of nuclear annihilation, their future didn't seem as predictable as was true in their parents' generation. They were less inclined to simply accept what their parents said was so. Many exhibited a healthy skepticism of what they could expect from society, and what society in turn could expect from them. They no longer believed that success was inevitable if they did what their parents told them to do, which was study hard, follow the Calvinistic ethic, and work hard toward success.

I was a member of the preceding generation and was taught that if I kept my nose to the grindstone and did what my parents told me to do, I was bound to succeed. It worked for me.

Today, the future is much less predictable than it was when I was a young adult. We have to be much more flexible and adjust our thinking to meet the ever-changing demands of society. This has caused us to be less introspective and reflective than was true in earlier generations. In order to deal with the real world today, we need to constantly strategize to meet the ever-changing demands placed on us in our workplaces. Those changes may involve more schooling, technical training, abrupt career shifts … or even, heaven forbid, layoffs.

Because of the ever-changing world we live in, our society can't afford the luxury of being introspective and searching our souls to make sure we preserve our sense of integrity. That doesn't make it right, but it's just the reality for anyone who must work to make a living. As a result, we have become more pragmatic and realistic. This is important to understand, because in order to stay gainfully employed, we now do things to please the boss.

If we are going to hold our politicians to a high standard of integrity, we must hold ourselves equally accountable. Compromise that doesn't cause any harm is understandable, but no one can allow a great wrong to occur and use the yuppie defense of "I was only trying to pay the mortgage."

There's a huge difference between putting lipstick on a pig to beautify a product for a prospective buyer and using substandard materials that could potentially harm or kill people just to increase profit.

The Importance of Integrity

Psychology defines "integrity" as a sense of wholeness, where one is undivided. This definition suggests it is a part of our personality that can't be compromised or tampered with without vast damage to our sense of self. To change it, even ever so slightly, would seriously violate what you cherish as a human being. Since it cannot be divided or transposed in any way, it stands in and onto itself.

Frequently, when we admire famous personages like Lincoln or Washington, or ordinary people like ourselves, we admire them for their senses of integrity. So if you have a sense of integrity, you have all that's valued and good in the world.

Because fame, power, money, and control do funny things to us all, whether we're talking about politicians or ordinary folk like you and me, it's very difficult to maintain and sustain our senses of integrity over a lifetime. This is particularly true for senators, congresspeople, and presidents, for in almost all cases, their sense of integrity is jeopardized and abused by the time they leave office. The assault on their integrity is so great, and their integrity is compromised to such an extent, that they can't stand tall and say to themselves and the world that they served their country honorably when they were in office.

We all know why that was so: they didn't follow their moral compasses when they were serving. They said what they thought their constituents, the voting public, wanted to hear in order to remain in office, rather than voicing what they truly believed as they helped sail our ship of state through the political waters.

Salmon Chase was an American politician and jurist in the Civil War era. He served as an Ohio senator, the Ohio governor, the U.S. Treasury Secretary under Lincoln, and the chief justice of the United States. When it came to slavery, he used his power and influence with integrity. Chase focused his energy on the destruction of what he felt was a conspiracy of slave owners to seize control of the federal government and block the freeing of the slaves. Chase pursued this just course, even under the deluge of contempt and derision that rained down on him.

Chase fulfills all of my criteria for integrity. He showed the courage of his convictions by speaking out in favor of abolishing slavery in a more forceful manner than even did Lincoln (who, at the time, held a more moderate viewpoint on the slavery issue). He also was willing to act and speak out on behalf of what he knew in his heart was right, even in the face of much opposition, scorn, and ridicule. At the time, he was unequalled in being a leader who strove to abolish slavery and who supported the equality of various ethnicities before the law.

John Adams, the second U.S. president, once said, "Power always thinks it has a great soul and vast views beyond the comprehension of the weak; and that it is doing God's service when it is violating all his laws."

Like an earthquake, what the president does or doesn't do reverberates throughout this country and affects each of our lives to one degree or another. Or, if the quake is large enough, these actions may affect the world as well. Therefore, if the president really wants to represent all America's interests, he needs to be as transparent and as honest as he can be. By doing that, he will not only unite this country again, but also help us once more look at our country with pride and faith that our president is doing the people's business by uniting, not dividing, this country.

False Appearances

Books have been written about President Nixon's flawed character—that he thinks one way and, when in public, says something to the contrary. Nixon's secret White House tapes certainly bear this out. All too often, appearances are everything to our politicians. This was certainly the case with Nixon. While in office, he had been often compared to a used-car salesman. He wasn't concerned about what was under the hood; that wasn't what counted. Just getting the car sold was all that mattered.

Well, that also was true as far as Nixon's welfare program was concerned. He wasn't genuinely interested in getting a law enacted that would truly help and assist the needy, but rather, he was interested in the political splash he could create by enacting such a program. It was all show.

Especially disturbing to me is Nixon's obvious duplicity in what he thought and what he said. If there is anyone whom we expect to be honest both inside and out, it is the president of the United States. He is supposed to represent truth and hope for a better tomorrow—not only for the people here in these United States, but also for the world at large.

An Open Book

When it came to honesty, Lincoln and Nixon were complete opposites. In Lincoln's case, he was quite up-front with his thoughts and actions. Unlike Nixon, who thought one way and acted in another—all for political gain and to advance his hidden agenda—Lincoln was honest with his public—and, whenever the occasion so warranted, shared his thoughts openly and forthrightly with the American public. His thoughts matched his actions.

For example, when Lincoln was pondering the whole Emancipation Proclamation question, he was more than willing to tell his cabinet what he planned to do, even though the majority of nine to one opposed enacting his Emancipation Proclamation at the time he chose to do it.

Whereas Lincoln's transparency was the rule, rather than the exception, Nixon mentally calculated what the vote would have been if he had let his cabinet vote on his welfare-reform decision. Because he had decided beforehand what he was going to do with the measure, he neither told his cabinet what he was thinking nor took to heart what they said in opposition to it. That behavior was not only patronizing, but also dishonest. It was disingenuous because he only paid lip service to what was discussed and recommended. He never intended to take seriously what his cabinet said. That was a deceptive and devious way of running the government.

As it turned out, even though Nixon's announced welfare program was not conceived from his heart, and he couldn't care less whether it was enacted into law, it was widely embraced by the American people.

It's too bad Nixon couldn't have embraced his welfare reform, as the majority of Americans had done. If that had been the case, it wouldn't have ended up being a political stunt, and he wouldn't have damaged his sense of integrity in the process, since the legislation would have represented his genuine and honest thinking.

When we understand integrity in politicians and ourselves, we can understand how to be good Americans.

All our actions, opinions, and aspirations stem from our sense of identity. The important thing is for us, the voting public, is to have healthy senses of selves. Then we'll be able to more accurately vote for the kinds of candidates that can bring this country together—and as a result, speak in one voice as to what is needed to bring America back to its former greatness.

The Moment of Truth

At the end of our lives, how will we feel when we gauge our own lifelong integrity? The field of psychology examines that common introspective process.

Psychologist Erik Erikson received his professional training under the tutelage of Sigmund Freud's daughter, Anna Freud. After he graduated from the Vienna Psychoanalytic Institute in 1933, he came to the United States. It was here that he developed his own psychoanalytic theory, quite different and distinct from Freud's psychoanalytic stages of development. Erikson focused on the development of one's self-identity.

Erikson's last and final stage of his eight stages of development is called "integrity vs. despair."

Before I continue, I want to make it crystal clear that when I talk about Erikson's psychosocial stages of development, it is with the understanding that these are stages that everyone goes through. No one is exempt from passing through each of the eight stages of development and resolving the conflicts pertinent to each stage. I say this because if you have not successfully passed through the last and final stage of development, integrity vs. despair, it will be apparent to you or anyone else that you haven't resolved the conflict and will suffer the emotional and psychological consequences of not having reached resolution.

The final stage occurs in late adulthood, at about sixty to sixty-five years of age. It is during that time when we review our life experiences and decide whether or not we made good or not-so-good decisions as we progressed through our earlier life cycles. When we do that, we will access our life's challenges—our defeats as well as our victories. Our reckoning comes when we add up all our pluses and minuses.

A successful resolution of this stage is where you end up saying, "If I had my life to live over, I'd live my life the same now as I did then." That would suggest that you indeed did live your life with integrity, following what was in your heart as well as what was in your mind.

The central task of that last stage of development, late adulthood, is to maintain our sense of who we are and what we stand for, which is our ego integrity, so that even in the face of physical and mental decline, and realizing that we too will die, we feel satisfied with how our lives turned out. We have no regrets, since we lived life to the fullest; at the same time, we still looked beyond ourselves, as exemplified by our nurturing, caring, and loving of others as well.

In order to feel we've lived a complete life, we must remain not only responsive to our own needs, but, when able, remain quick to respond to other people's concerns as well.

Past Missteps

Even back in more idyllic times, our integrity as a nation was a bit tattered.

During the Second World War, it was not difficult for us and our allies to know why we were fighting Germany, Italy, and Japan. We were fighting them to protect our sense of integrity, or what we believed in as a nation. It could pretty much be summed up in the Declaration of Independence: "Life, Liberty, and the pursuit of happiness" for all Americans.

Unfortunately, even then, the "all" part of that text wasn't always applied. Many Americans were excluded from realizing the same degree of life, liberty, and happiness that others were experiencing.

On December 7, 1941, Japan attacked Pearl Harbor. In a very real sense, with Japan's attack, our territorial integrity was assaulted, and we had to respond. So Congress declared war on Japan on December 8, 1941. Nazi Germany declared war on the United States that same day, December 8.

Since the Second World War and until 9/11, the reasons for our military involvement with other nations were less obvious, because we were never directly attacked until 9/11. Nevertheless, in every case, the threat to our nation's integrity has been cited as the reason for going to war. In the future, why we go to war must be clarified.

Hand in hand with the idea of integrity is the idea of accountability.

In August 2004, the U.S. Department of State's Bureau of International Information Program's Web site posted its principles of democracy, part of which involves government accountability:

> Government accountability means that public officials— elected and unelected—have an obligation to explain their decisions and actions to the citizens. Government accountability is achieved through the use of a variety of mechanisms—political, legal, and administrative— designed to prevent corruption and ensure that public officials remain answerable and accessible to the people they serve. In the absence of such mechanisms, corruption may thrive.

These days, our government rarely seems accountable to anyone. Despite the low public approval rating, the Bush administration continues with its unpopular military plans. When we think of a lack of accountability on a governmental or individual level, we think of corruption.

When we don't hold our governmental officials accountable, we nurture corruption. Too many times, various governmental servants aren't punished for their illegal and underhanded activities. If we don't do something about that, then we are all at fault.

The public has an obligation to monitor government action by reading newspapers and news magazines, watching the political shows on TV, and writing to officials to make their opinions known.

It is everyone's responsibility to determine what parameters they use to differentiate acceptable from nonacceptable behaviors that are integral to each person's sense of self, as well as society's expectations. Of course, no one is perfect, and everyone slips up occasionally. For our purposes, we are going to confine our thinking to those times when we engage in acts that are antithetical to our sense of integrity, or behavior that is at someone else's expense, and call such actions self-aggrandizement.

In order for our nation to remain a democracy, our government and capitalistic system needs to act more responsibly than it has in the recent past. With each day that has gone by since Nixon's presidency, we have continued to lose sight of the principles that protect our country's integrity; we have lost a little bit more of the essence of what has made this country special. This loss is occurring at an alarming rate. Almost daily, our media gives us examples of government and civilian corruption in which the parties involved show a complete disregard for the well-being of others. This kind of self-absorption has become so prevalent in American life that it could almost be considered a major industry.

We must return to the basics that made our nation the greatest country in the world. By doing that, we will again begin to realize that our Constitution, Bill of Rights, and Declaration of Independence were written for all Americans, regardless of their race, color, or creed.

In order to preserve our integrity at the national level, we must respond to the needs of all Americans, not just the special-interest and lobbyist groups who fill the favored political party coffers with big bucks. As American citizens, we must not only embody integrity, but be careful to vote it into the White House as well.

WHAT IF ABE LINCOLN WERE ELECTED PRESIDENT IN THE YEAR 2000?

Why should the question posed by the title of this chapter even be raised, here, in the beginning of the twenty-first century? Because our system of government is broken, and we need to do something to fix it. The split between the two parties is a very serious matter—so critical that in future elections, the voter should seriously consider voting for any candidate who pledges to make this divided nation whole again.

Just how important are future elections? Well, let's look at the state of the Union.

The two-party system is not functioning as it should. The Republicans and the Democrats are contentious. They are not unified in how they should combat terrorism. They get nothing accomplished when Congress is in session.

Our federal deficit is five trillion dollars. Due to interest compounding, the total amount of the national debt increases by about ten thousand dollars per second.

Our military budget is the highest ever. Our military expenses alone for the year 2007 are estimated at $563 billion. The budget for the Iraq and Afghanistan Wars are conservatively estimated at $100 billion.

The preemptive Iraq war is still raging, with no end in sight. The war casualties on both sides, amounting to thousands of dead and injured, continue to mount.

Osama Bin Laden is still at large. The legalities of government wire taping have yet to be resolved, and we condoned torture to extract information from suspected terrorists.

Many countries of the world shun us, and the goodwill we've been able to engender over the years is at its lowest ebb.

As a potential threat economically and militarily, China has yet to be reckoned with.

North Korea's nuclear arsenal continues to menace the world. Iran's nuclear ambitions are obvious.

Aside from the war, the handling of Katrina and the other southern storms was a disaster.

Satisfactory immigration laws have yet to be enacted.

By the year 2052, it is anticipated that we will no longer have enough funds to finance the Social Security program.

There is now the largest gap ever between the rich and the poor in this country.

Medical costs for the average U.S. citizen are out of control.

And last, but not least, in June 2007, the NBC *Wall Street Journal* poll reported that only 23 percent of the American public approved of the way Congress operates. President Bush received a 29-percent approval rating. Assuming the polling represents an accurate sample of how our citizens feel toward both their Congress and president, that means that less than a quarter of the public approves of their Congress and slightly more than a quarter of the same population approves of how our president is handling our country's business.

The list above illustrates the mess that American voters and politicians have gotten themselves into. The question now is, what sort of politician will be able to get us back out again?

Enter Abraham Lincoln, Stage Right

We have discussed the ways in which Abraham Lincoln was a great president. It is my thinking that not only this country, but also the whole world, would have been much poorer without Lincoln's leadership during the critical Civil War years. At that time, what

America represented for the entire world to witness was Lincoln's humility, empathy, intelligence, and love for all of us, regardless of our ethnic, racial, or social economic levels. He was indeed a giant among men.

Please remember, there have been many presidents since Lincoln who have done marvelous things for this country. I only mention Lincoln as extensively as I have because many historians consider him to be the greatest president of all times, so why shouldn't I use him as the gold standard by which all other presidents are compared?

Lincoln was not a highly experienced politician in 1860, when he was elected. His eminence didn't come from his political skills; they came from his nature and his moral fiber. That is why I've discussed him in such depth—and why I am examining the impact such a man would have on our country today.

Most people would agree that Lincoln was an incredible leader who had a major impact on American history. But what if Lincoln were running for president today? Would he still be elected? Would his values, like honesty and integrity, be enough to heal our ailing country?

It is very possible that Lincoln would not have a chance to be elected, what with the need to be financially backed by big money, the media's penchant for thirty-second sound bites, and Lincoln's physical characteristics. He had a high, squeaky voice, and he suffered from Marfan syndrome, the symptoms of which include unusual height, disproportionate arms and legs, long fingers and toes, and many other characteristics. The mentioned symptoms gave him an apelike appearance. With today's TV scrutiny, it doesn't take much of an imagination to realize what his opponents would do with that kind of an image!

Unfortunately, even his beard wouldn't save him this time around.

The idea of Abraham Lincoln being passed over for the American presidency based on his appearance is a sobering one indeed. Has our system become so cosmetic and superficial that one of America's greatest presidents wouldn't have a chance? What can we learn, as voters, from such a disconcerting truth?

The voter needs to constantly keep in the forefront of his or her mind the importance of listening to the message and trying not to let the candidates' superficial factors such as looks and voices interfere with the message. Is it a pitch, or is the message expressed in such a way that generates a feeling that the candidate is sincere and genuine in what he or she is trying to say to the voter?

A Trusted Candidate

If Lincoln's previous history followed him into the twenty-first century, and we knew now what we knew then about Lincoln—and if God would allow us to borrow him, so that in the twenty-first century, he could once again grace us with his presence—I believe Americans would want him as our president. The reason I say that is because today there is a wide center in this country that is tired of the battle that the extremes are having—a battle that is tearing this country apart. Lincoln's major goal as president was to unite the country, as witnessed by taking into his cabinet three of his political opponents. He empathized with the populace, who yearned for the day when the country would be united again.

With the political climate and the deep division that exists today, you might question Lincoln's willingness to become president again. There's little doubt in my mind that he would accept the challenge. He would accept it because he would recognize it was his duty to God and country to again serve his beloved nation. With his sense of integrity, he couldn't help but accept God's invitation. This dedication and sense of duty is exactly what American voters need to find in a candidate today.

Today, playing politics takes priority over solving problems and dealing with the world of ideas. Now, it's how you play the game that will determine if you'll be elected to high office. In the nineteenth century, politics was not of great concern to Lincoln. In fact, even before he became president, he was interested in ideas, rather than in projecting the correct political image (whatever that might be). He might have struggled to pass the gatekeepers of either party, who would be shocked at his honesty and frightened by his straightforward style of speaking, but he would find himself embraced by an American public hungry for his brand of statesmanship.

It was because he was such a compassionate and empathetic man, that in many of his decisions, he used not only his head, but also his heart, to determine what was best for the country.

That is precisely what's wrong with our twenty-first-century politics: too many politicians of the day don't use enough of their hearts in making decisions. They deal with only their favored constituencies, thereby ignoring the needs of America as a whole.

Certainly, in the case of Congress, it's important to be responsive to the needs of the state that you represent and the political party that helped put you in office, but there is also a need to do what's good for the country at large, and in that way be responsive to all Americans, for that is the only way we're going to come together as a country.

Lincoln was a thinking and empathetic president—his two greatest strengths—and he wasn't concerned with outward appearances, which is certainly not true in today's political world; his persona, or public image, was the least of his concerns. His concern was how to reach his viewing and listening audience, the American public. That was not a difficult thing for Abe to do, because he had made communication, whether it be written or verbal, his top priority throughout his life.

So ... how he appeared before the public was the least of his concerns, and it showed. By that I mean, whenever he spoke to the community, his hair looked disheveled, and his clothes didn't fit; even if his suit was new, more than likely than not, when he put it on, it would look wrinkled, and he would look as if he had already outgrown it, since it would appear to be one or two sizes too small for his long, gangly frame.

Shallow, or Just Misunderstood?

Today's voters may be seen as apathetic and concerned only with superficial aspects of candidates, but what I believe is that they are just numbed by the banality and lack of sincerity the candidates exhibit, and people wouldn't even think about Lincoln's physical appearance because they would be mesmerized by his passion and message of hope for the future.

I feel that way because the voter would be voting for Lincoln for the right reasons—those being not only what was in his mind, but also what was in his heart. He was able to win so many people over because he struck a chord with them. He spoke from his soul about what needed to be done to make the Union whole again.

When on the campaign stump, if today's politicians would speak not only what's on their minds, but equally importantly, what's in their hearts, voters would be more inclined to listen to what was said and would be less inclined to assume what they heard was simply more of the same campaign mishmash.

Because so little gets done by either the legislative or executive branches of government, it's difficult not to be critical of either the president or Congress. What is disconcerting is that President Bush seems to act as a catalyst in adding to the cacophony and mean-spirited attitude that exists on Capitol Hill. Instead of being a unifier, he's a divider. The last thing a president should do is worsen the political climate of his or her administration.

A good president would adopt the policy of Harry S. Truman, who had a sign on his desk that said, "The Buck Stops Here." Like Truman, Lincoln also took full responsibility for his presidency, regardless of whether he was at fault or not. If his cabinet did something not to the public's liking, Lincoln would quickly assume full responsibility for the action by saying or implying it was his fault.

If Lincoln were elected in 2000, how would the Iraq situation have been handled?

Hegemony for control's sake, or to protect our vital energy interests where there is not an immediate threat to our lives and property, are not sufficient reasons to wage war. This is not a new concept, but modern times have certainly added credence to it. Lincoln showed this kind of thinking prior to the onset of the Civil War. He anticipated that a conflict between the North and the South was probably going to occur even as he gave his farewell address to a thousand people in Springfield, Illinois—he said, with a heavy heart, that his job as president of the United States was even greater than Washington's. The job he was speaking of was the preservation of the Union. Five weeks after Lincoln's inauguration, the South fired on Fort Sumter, and the Civil War began.

"Right Makes Might"

At Lincoln's inauguration on March 4, 1861, he said he hoped to resolve the national crisis (Civil War) without warfare. On April 12, the Confederate Army fired the first shots on Fort Sumter, which marked the beginning of the Civil War. For political reasons, Lincoln felt it was important not to fire the first shot. So, it's obvious that he wanted to avoid a war with the South if it could possibly be prevented. Because he was such a loving president, conducting war was hardly part of his personality. One can only imagine the deep sorrow that he felt when he heard reports of the death and casualties occurring on both sides of the battlefield. Yet, that didn't deter him from doing what he considered right. Instead of taking the position that might makes right, using his own words, he said, "Right makes might."

In part of Lincoln's first inaugural address, he stated,

> I am loath to close. We are enemies, but friends. We must not be enemies. Though passion may have strained, it must not break our bonds of affection. The mystic chords of memory, stretching from every battle-field, and patriot grave, to every living heart and hearthstone, all over this broad land, will yet swell the chorus of the Union, when again touched, as surely they will be, by the better angels of our nature.

Rather than looking at the Confederate troops as his enemy, he looked at them as friends. That powerful poetry spoke to Lincoln's heart and sensitivity to his fellow man. But more to the point, this quote clearly shows his reluctance to go to battle with the South. It also demonstrates his wish to preserve the bonds of affection, even if war between the North and the South should occur.

After 9/11, the then-divided states briefly became united again. Like our country's unity, the world's support was short-lived. The Iraq war represents the turning point where many of the things that were good about America began to disappear and be replaced by even greater division where optimism and hope were replaced by fear and shame.

If Lincoln were president during this period in history, he would not preemptively attack Iraq. If he even were strongly urged to consider doing so, he would have encouraged his cabinet to thoroughly discuss the pros and cons of such action, as well as get input from key congressional leaders from both parties, so that a sound conclusion could be reached.

Please keep in mind that when he was president in 1861, his cabinet comprised people who didn't necessarily agree with his views, because some of the cabinet members were presidential candidates whom he had defeated. Following his earlier model, here, he would also make sure that both parties were well represented in his twenty-first-century cabinet. He would realize that by having as diverse a point of view as possible and listening to opinions from both sides of the aisle, he would be able to formulate policy that would be most representative of the nation as a whole.

The reason I feel he would summarily reject the idea of attacking Iraq, and would not even consider it unless there were reasons unbeknownst to anyone else, is because of how he looked at himself, as well as how he viewed his role to be as president of this country.

First of all, Lincoln saw himself as someone who unites the country. He would recognize that going to war in Iraq, particularly preemptively, would be a very divisive thing to do. Remember, Lincoln waited until the South fired the first shot, making war his only option.

He had been a student of American history prior to becoming president. He deeply admired what our Founding Fathers accomplished in writing the Constitution, Declaration of Independence, and Bill of Rights. He would no doubt continue his interest in American history if he became president in the year 2000. Consequently, as he did when he was president in the 1860s, he would realize how important it was to have a sense of history in making daily decisions. Without knowing why and how past presidents made policy, the errors of the past are bound to be repeated.

For example, during the Cuban missile crisis, Robert Kennedy advised his brother, then President John Kennedy, against bombing or invading Cuba, since to preemptively attack Cuba was "not something the U.S. would do." Well, that was true until President Bush entered the scene and preemptively attacked Iraq. In this case, Lincoln, out of hand, would have agreed with Robert Kennedy because, as you'll recall, he chose to wait until the Confederates fired the first shot before he allowed the Union troops to commence firing.

Lincoln would look at the 9/11 attack as being quite a different and unique problem from what this country had experienced before. As a result, he would seek counsel from a wide range of people—politicians and nonpoliticians alike. As was true when he was president in the first go-round, he would appear to take forever and a day to make a decision, but when the decision was made, it would be sound and well reasoned. His gift with words, which was reflected in any of his public pronouncements, added additional weight to his speeches. As a result, people knew he was a man to be trusted—a man they could depend upon to do the right thing.

President Lincoln said that on January 1, 1863, he planned to sign the Emancipation Proclamation. Many questioned his resolve to do that, but Frederick Douglass, the leading black abolitionist of the day, had no doubt that Lincoln would go through with his pledge, for he had intimate knowledge of his good friend's character. And he was right. With great boldness and clarity of heart, Lincoln signed the document.

You might say, "Well, that's true with President Bush as well. He doesn't give up ground once he decides a course of action he believes our country should follow." Well, the kind of thinking Lincoln engaged in was quite different from that of President Bush. Lincoln had a mind that was remarkably free from illusions or the kinds of deceptive perceptions that distort reality to such a degree that they cause erroneous conclusions to be reached. He did not rely on magical thinking to connect the dots. Because he wasn't defensive about who he was or what he was about, he had no reason to fabricate reasons in order to arrive at a conclusion that he wanted to come to in the first place, even before his intellectual inquiry took place. In making decisions, he never was personally invested in the outcome of his inquiry, as President Bush appears to be.

If Lincoln were president when 9/11 occurred, when and how he planned to share with the American public his thoughts about how he was going to wage war on terrorism would be critical. He certainly would not describe the war as the "decisive ideological struggle of the twenty-first century" or as a "war between two civilizations." He would realize that language would only inflame the terrorists and frighten the public.

Since Lincoln was such a student of history and always tried to use what history taught him in solving current problems, he would use less provocative language when discussing the differences between the two camps (ours and the terrorists'). Since, when he was president, he always had in the forefront of his mind how he could best bring the North and the South together again and in that way eliminate the bloodshed and destruction that was occurring on both sides of the battlefield, and because he believed in reconciliation whenever possible, he would always put the olive branch front and center whenever he discussed issues related to terrorism.

Lincoln had a great sense of seizing the right moment at the right time. For example, he freely admitted that he signed the Emancipation Proclamation into law at just the correct time. He later said, "It is my conviction that, had the proclamation been issued even six months earlier than it was, public sentiment would not have sustained it."

A Much-Needed Plan

I wonder what will happen if not just a few thousand lives are lost by a terrorist attack, but millions. How are we as a nation going to react to that kind of catastrophe? At the moment, we don't have a clue what is necessary for us to endure that kind of trauma. That's because there's a lack of presidential leadership. Terrorists have fragmented this nation. We are all seeking some kind of hope that our predictable world will remain predictable. We need to engage in more selfless activities by looking beyond ourselves and comforting others less able to care for themselves. Successfully combating terrorism requires a community effort where we as a nation stand shoulder to shoulder and collectively help and nurture each other in a way that will be comforting and strengthening. There is indeed strength in numbers.

The Gestalt principle that the whole is greater than the sum of its parts is certainly true in the case of dealing with terrorism. Terrorism is an opportunity—yes, an opportunity—to begin to look to and help others in a way we as a nation have not done since the end of the Second World War. In order to do that, we need to not only follow our faith's teachings, but also use Lincoln as an example of a leader to emulate. Now, I know what you're saying: "How can we do that? He's no longer living among us." Yes, that's true, but his spirit lives on, and the traits historians admire in him can be found in future presidential candidates, if American voters are willing to look hard enough at the candidates and at ourselves. We individually and collectively, as a nation, must incorporate some of the principles and beliefs that Lincoln had during one of the darkest moments in our nation's history.

Unfortunately, our current era is not much brighter, with terrorism threatening our way of life and with corruption rampant in our government. At times, it's difficult to feel optimistic.

"The only thing we have to fear is fear itself," said Franklin Delano Roosevelt in his first inaugural address. That phrase was used in response to the Great Depression. FDR had campaigned against Herbert Hoover in the 1932 presidential election by saying as little as possible about what he might do if elected. Roosevelt's first inaugural address outlined in broad terms how he hoped to govern, and he reminded Americans that the nation's "common difficulties" concerned "only material things."

Our common difficulties now are different, but just as severe as during the Great Depression. It's serious because, at the moment, we have no unified plan to deal with terrorism. What we need is a president who will help explain how he plans to deal with terrorism. A good mantra to follow would be Roosevelt's "the only thing we have to fear is fear itself." We can apply that same quote to our twenty-first-century war on terrorism, for that is exactly how we need to be thinking today.

WHAT DO WE
AS A NATION VALUE?

It's important to know what we value as a nation, because those priorities drive us and determine why we vote for certain candidates. After all, in order to get elected, all politicians try to appeal to what they think are your values and desires.

Since they don't have a crystal ball, and because they can't appeal to each individual's needs and desires, they provide you with what they think you should value, then drive those concepts home in hopes that you will buy into their program.

For example, prior to the presidential election primaries and caucuses, peripheral issues might be presented to the voting public. Such inside-the-beltway concerns as stem-cell research, abortion, or prayers in the schools will be discussed. Frankly, those kinds of issues should not even be up for debate when a candidate is yet to be chosen to run in the general election.

Rather than discussing those kinds of issues, candidates should spend time discussing issues that are more immediate and important to all Americans, such as those issues affecting one's security and quality of life: health care, the Social Security problem, terrorism, war policies, immigration, and so on.

Shouldn't the choices made at the caucus level be based on national concerns and interests, rather than provincial issues? These are the primaries that will determine our presidential candidates.

Before I answer the question posed by the title of this chapter, we need to look at some of the factors that made this country what it is today, because, after all, that's where our values come from. What forces propelled this nation into its status as the greatest country in the world? When you stop to think of how young a country we are, it's pretty remarkable what our nation has been able to accomplish. Not only are we a young nation, but we are not even as big geographically as some other nations. We're only half the size of Russia and smaller than Canada.

The point of comparing the United States' geographical size with that of other countries is to illustrate that size alone does not a country make. Indeed, a number of factors are involved, such as the availability of natural resources, the population (the United States is a nation of immigrants from the four corners of the world), the type of government (which in our case is a republic, being a capitalistic system), and last, but certainly not least, having the finest governing documents in the world: the Declaration of Independence, the Constitution, and the Bill of Rights.

I am quite sure that if these exceptional documents were not available, we would never have attained the degree of success that we were able to attain, nor would we have the stature among other countries that we command. Our prestigious history and relatively rapid progress as a nation have taught us that these documents represent a lot of wisdom and protection.

At the close of 2006, both the president and Congress's approval ratings were in the low thirtieth or high twentieth percentile, with the president's rating one or two percentage points higher than that of Congress. Congress was described as a do-nothing Congress. That may be an unfair portrayal, because they were doing something. They, along with their leader, George W. Bush, were, without thinking, diminishing what this country stands for, especially our sacred right to personal liberties. For example, in a frenzy of reaction to terrorism, they approved warrantless wiretaps and searches into our once-private records. . If something is not done soon, we will not recognize what our Founding Fathers and the patriots of this country had worked so hard to establish, defend, and protect. Over the years, many gave their lives for a cause they deemed worthy of their sacrifice, so that we could continue to enjoy the freedoms they so gallantly fought to protect.

Our government forgot that with freedom comes accountability. The best way the president and Congress can act responsibly is to serve as good role models for the American public to emulate. As depicted in the media, what with all the scandals, corruption, and petty bickering that goes on in the halls of Congress, there's not much worthy of duplication.

Identification is not just an abstract term in psychology that has little or no meaning in the real world. The concept is central to why we behave as we do. That is the principle that explains why little girls act like their mothers, and little boys want to be like their fathers. That is also how we, as adults, act like those who we wish to model our lives after. Throughout the book, I've used Abraham Lincoln as the gold presidential standard because he is the quintessential role model for all of us, me included, to emulate. Our future politicians must serve as role models as well; it's time that modern government began providing some patriotic inspiration to the American people.

Learning of Lincoln's life, his trials and tribulations, and the true giant of a man that he was, has restored my faith and belief in America, because I know excellence can be attained if we have the right man or woman at the top. It's all about leadership and possessing the values and beliefs that our Founding Fathers embraced—the same kind of values Lincoln possessed, which were the kind that any American would be proud to own, regardless of whether they were Republicans, Democrats, or independents. The reason? It was because of his desire for all Americans to attain a degree of happiness during the time we have on earth, so that before they die, they can say, "I am proud to be an American and feel so blessed to be part of this nation and what it stood for."

This desire for America becomes self-evident when one reads about Lincoln's life. He never seemed to concern himself with petty issues. He was too big for that. Nor was he concerned with his public image. He was just himself. He didn't have to play a role and be somebody different than himself, because he had a good sense of self. He knew who he was and treasured what he did with his life. Here was a man who had less than one year of public education, struggled and rose from the depth of poverty and despair, and became president of the greatest country in the world. Talk about a self-made man!

It would have been easy for Lincoln to lose his perspective if he weren't such a principled man. Take the slavery-versus-Union issue. He was unwilling to make unwarranted compromises in order to avoid civil war. He could have jeopardized his sense of integrity by agreeing to do what might be considered the political thing to do, which was avoid the Civil War in the first place—or, if war ensued, make certain slavery concessions to the Southern states in order to avoid further bloodshed. We know if he had avoided fighting the Civil War altogether, that would have been done at a fantastic cost to his sense of integrity, because he would have had to acquiesce to the South's demands. As we all know, that was not done, because Lincoln was unwilling to compromise his cherished views on eliminating slavery or preserving the Union. No wonder he remains the best presidential role model in American history.

When you consider the pro-slavery contingent was just as adamant in feeling they were right as the abolitionists, it was amazing Lincoln maintained his principles. He did this by refusing to succumb to either one of those factions. Rather, he took what he heard and adjusted his thinking to reflect the reality of the moment as he saw it to be. For example, during the first several months of the Civil War, Lincoln chose to not make eliminating slavery an issue, since he said the purpose of the war was "to preserve the Union," not to eliminate slavery. It was several years into the Civil War before Lincoln signed the Emancipation Proclamation.

Lincoln was a deep thinker. He frustrated a lot of his cabinet, because he took so long to make up his mind on things. That's because he wished to hear all sides of the issue before arriving at a decision. I'm surprised Lincoln was not labeled as the Great Cogitator, since he thought so deeply and carefully about issues. As he pondered what was best for the nation, he remained centered through his capacity to think critically, his integrity, and his empathetic ability. Lincoln's ideals about serving the nation both as a whole (resisting war) and as a group of individuals (freeing slaves) are still relevant today. In order to appreciate why we became the greatest, most powerful nation in the world, it's important that we understand the difference between individualism and democracy.

The Modern Dangers of Individualism

According to the *Webster's New Universal Unabridged Dictionary*, individualism means

> 1. A social theory advocating the liberty, rights, or independent action of the individual. 2. The principle or habit of or belief in independent thought or action. 3. The pursuit of individual rather than common or collective interests; egoism ... 6. Philos ... b. the doctrine or belief that all actions are determined by, or at least take place for, the benefit of the individual, not of society as a whole.

That same dictionary defines democracy in this way:

> 1. government by the people; a form of government in which the supreme power is vested in the people and exercised directly by them or by their elected agents under a free electoral system. 2. A state having such a form of government: *The United States and Canada are democracies.* 3. A state of society characterized by formal equalities of rights and privileges ...

Since our Founding Fathers settled this country, individualism has reigned as king, and those who support individual initiative and inventiveness have been richly rewarded. Our country was founded on the belief that the rights of the individual and independent action need to be respected, as opposed to common or collective interests. According to the concept of individualism, all actions have been determined by—or at least take place for—the individual, not society as a whole. That's what the capitalistic system is all about. To an extent, isn't that philosophy antithetical with democratic principles, which is that supreme power is vested in the people and exercised directly by them, or by their elected agents under a free electoral system? The Constitution starts out, "We the people of the United States, in order to form a more perfect union, establish justice, insure domestic tranquility, provide for the common defense, promote the general welfare, and secure the blessings of liberty to ourselves and our posterity, do ordain and establish this Constitution for the United States of America."

Presently, "we the people" has been replaced with "we the corporations." In fact, from almost the beginning of America's history, individualism has been a double-edged sword that protects the rights of individuals while also creating an environment in which ruthless corporate capitalism can thrive by claiming those same rights. Ironically, this has allowed corporations to all but take over, infringing upon the rights of actual individuals while pushing their own corporate agendas.

Robert Reich, former Secretary of Labor, once said, "There's no longer any countervailing power in Washington. Business is in complete control of the machinery of government." That is to say, the lobbyists have become so strong in this country in being able to influence legislation that businesses, rather than "we the people," now exercise a predominant influence on policy.

When this country was founded and under the domination of England, the original thirteen colonies were chartered by the king of England to extract timber, animal pelts, and other resources to benefit England, not the colonies. That being the case, the charters were not written to create democracy or promote the welfare of the colonies, but to make a profit for England. As a result, the abuse of power was rampant. Unfortunately, this kind of abuse of power continues in government today, where the rights of the common man are ignored in favor of corporate interests.

One of the precipitating causes of the Revolutionary War was the king's raising of the tea tax. This resulted in the colonies needing to raise their prices to pay the taxes. All of this resulted in them not being able to compete with the British East India Tea Company.

I'm sure many of us remember reading in school about the slogan "no taxation without representation" and remember how that issue precipitated the Boston Tea Party revolt against higher taxes.

Even in the colonial days, corporations played a large role in politics. The taxing of our tea by England was in itself a mistake and should never have been done, but the king, because of pressure from his own tea company, raised the taxes in the American colonies even further. This was even doubly wrong, because in both instances, the

English government and the British East India Tea Company were working in their own self-interests without bothering with the needs of the king's subjects, who happened to have settled in America. No wonder "we the people" decided to revolt.

Governmental corruption is not a twenty-first-century phenomenon. Throughout the history of our country, there have always been a few officials who sought to take advantage of their position for personal profit. Corruption was even present immediately after the colonists sailed over to this country. Not all corporations who were given the charters from the king of England obeyed what was stated, which required that the corporations be "obligated to obey all laws, serve the common good, and cause no harm." Initially, the colonies made sure that the same kinds of abuses that they suffered under England were not repeated again. However, that was short-lived. The culprit in this saga was land.

Land was the source of wealth. This realization contributed to schemes, bribery, and speculation by some colonists in an attempt to profit by illegally influencing the local and royal politicians. There were other types of corruption, but land was the major one.

During the Civil War, it was difficult to police corporate activity. The reason for that was obvious: the progress of the war captured everyone's attention, allowing the unscrupulous ample opportunity to line their pockets.

In fact, President Lincoln was very concerned about fraud and dishonesty. In 1864, he said,

> I see in the near future a crisis approaching that un-
> nerves me and causes me to tremble for the safety of my
> country. As the result of the war, corporations have been
> enthroned ... An era of corruption in high places will
> follow, and the money power of the country will endeavor
> to prolong its reign by working upon the prejudices of
> the people ... until wealth is aggregated in a few hands
> ... and the Republic is destroyed.

Following the Civil War, a battle of a different nature emerged as states competed against each other with weakened chartering requirements designed to attract corporations and their money. This bidding war reached such a magnitude that President Rutherford Hayes issued the following striking statement in 1876: "This is a government of the people, by the people, and for the people no longer. It is a government of corporations, by corporations, and for corporations."

Presently, the people's attention is diverted by terrorism and world instability; once again, those who wish to profit illegally and immorally are at work.

In 1953, Charles Erwin Wilson, GM president, was President Eisenhower's Secretary of Defense. This was during General Motors's heyday, when it was considered the largest corporation registered in the United States in terms of its revenues as a percent of GDP (gross domestic product). Wilson was asked during the hearings before the Senate Armed Services Committee if, as secretary of defense, he could make a decision adverse to the interests of General Motors. He answered yes, but added that he could not conceive of such a situation "because for years I thought what was good for the country was good for General Motors and vice versa."

I can recall how the statement was misquoted. The day after Wilson spoke, there were headlines in many of the newspapers across the country that quoted him as saying, "What's good for General Motors is good for the country."

Frankly, I don't think that "What's good for General Motors is good for the country" is necessarily true for the country as a whole. It wouldn't matter whether he said it in the early fifties or today. It all depends on what he means when he says, "good for the country." What segment of society is he talking about? Obviously, what's good for General Motors is good for the stockholders, but what about the nonstockholders, the poor, the disadvantaged, people like that? How does GM help them?

Now that corporate involvement in the government has only intensified, I believe we as a country have come to a national crossroad. We can either adhere to the principles enunciated by individualism— principles on which this country was founded and that have served part of our citizenry very well since our nation was born—or we can change our focus by addressing social concerns, and in that way, be more inclusive by passing legislation that affects a greater portion of the population.

When our Founding Fathers wrote the Constitution, I'm sure they didn't make provisions for the great disparity existing between the CEO's salaries and what the wage earners of today receive.

On April 12, 2005, the *One World* online publication published an article written by Abid Aslam titled "U.S.: Pay Gap Widens Between CEOs and Workers." In it, he said that in the year 2004, the "CEO raises once again dwarfed those of the average worker ..." He further said, "the nation's chief executives walked away with more than $20 million, excluding windfalls from option exercises."

Aslam went on to say that whereas the CEO's pay rose 12 percent in 2004, the rank-and-file worker's pay rose 3.6 percent, "further widening the world's gaps between executive and labor pay." Aslam reports that this was not far off from *Business Week* magazine's fifty-fifth annual executive pay scorecard numbers of 11.3 percent for CEOs, a number described as "not far off the rise in shareholder gains'" last year.[41]

In 2006, it was reported that the CEO salaries increased 12 percent from what it was in 1980. The CEOs' salaries are 130 times greater than workers' salaries.

Just to add salt to the wound, take a look at this fact: on April 30, 2006, on *Meet the Press*, it was reported that Exxon Mobil Corp. gave their retiring CEO, Lee Raymond, a nearly half-billion-dollar (400 million) parachute. It seems to me that anybody who can command that kind of money wouldn't even need a chute! He should be able to not only walk and run, but also fly. Perhaps he can teach Superman a few tricks!

If we consider Raymond's 2005 paycheck of $51.1 million and include it with his $400 million severance pay, that's equivalent to receiving $141,000 a day, or nearly $6,000 an hour, which even includes Saturdays and Sundays, when he wouldn't be working at all. It seems the least they could do is not pay him for weekends.

On April 14, 2006, in discussing high gas prices, ABC News reported that last November, when Raymond was still CEO of Exxon, he told Congress it was a matter of supply and demand,

---

[41] Abid Aslam, "U.S.: Pay Gap Widens Between CEOs and Workers," April 12, 2005, Http://us.oneworld.net/article/view/109279. Reprinted with permission of OneWorld US. OneWorld.net is an online hub for people who care about the world beyond their own borders.

further adding, "We're all in this together ..." If that's true, why doesn't he share some of his parachute with us, since he doesn't need it? He could buy us all parachutes, because we're the ones who can't fly. The truth is that corporate individualism does not create a situation where everyone is "in this together." It deepens the divide between classes.

Oh, incidentally, in addition to his severance package of $400 million, ABC news reports that Raymond will receive stock options, a $1 million consulting deal, two years of home security, personal security, a car and driver, and use of a corporate jet for professional purposes. I wonder what else they can do for the poor man; we certainly don't want to leave him destitute now, do we? In order to justify this obscene retirement package, ABC News reported that a company spokesman said that it reflected "a very long and distinguished career."

Now, I ask you: is what you just read something we as Americans can be proud of? Was this what the forefathers intended when they promoted individual rights? Is this corporate involvement in government best for our nation as a whole, particularly when you consider how that CEO salary could help so many people who are unable to realistically fend for themselves and take care of their basic needs?

No wonder there's such a division in this country between the haves and the have-nots. How are we going to come together as a nation when those kinds of disparities exist? At what point does monetary compensation go from being fair to not only excessive, but obscene?

I don't wish to squelch the American dream that we all have a right to be as monetarily successful as we so choose to be. The freedom to do that is not what I question. What I do have concerns about is when we delude ourselves into thinking that only money in itself is a measure of success, devoid of any of the reasons why that kind of prosperity was able to be obtained in the first place.

When that kind of shift is made, and success is measured by the number of lives that have been helped rather than merely how much money was made, then our definition will broadened to where it becomes more meaningful to our nation as a whole, because we are all able to see a relationship between acts of kindness and money. When that happens, we are all able to share in the joy that is represented in the giving, and that act in itself will go a long way in closing the great division that exists in this country.

Raymond is just one of a plethora of examples I could cite where some people are being rewarded too much in proportion to what they contribute to society. That holds true with not only the corporate world, but also the entertainment industry as well. Whether we're talking about sports or Hollywood, the monetary reward is set by supply and demand, which is what the public is willing (or not so willing) to pay to be entertained.

The only way to stop this money insanity is for the American public to stop paying those outrageous prices to be entertained; however, we know that will never happen.

So, what's the big deal? Why does it matter how much we're willing to pay the entertainer, or CEO, to reinforce their already inflated egos, which tell them that they're something very special? Because it sends the wrong message to our young people that what we value in America is the almighty dollar.

Dollars and Sense

We must remember that money is not the root of all evil; the *love* of money is the root of all evil. We need to look beyond what money can personally do for us and think in terms of how we can use our financial resources to help others ease the pain and hardship they have to endure. When we can do that, then we are truly rich, both as individuals and as a nation.

What are the high-profile corporate executives, the Hollywood stars, and the sports figures who make millions of dollars a year doing to help those who are financially strapped live a happier and more satisfactory life?

I believe that greed is not a natural attribute, but a behavior learned by observation of those around us. One of the ways greed can be curtailed is by having people of influence write newspaper and magazine editorials when excesses are noted, and they should paint a vivid pejorative picture of how being paid an excessive amount of money for any reason does not convey status or elevate a person in the eyes of the community but makes them objects of scorn.

Please, don't misunderstand me. I realize that many millionaires contribute their fair share to worthy causes, but there are likewise too many millionaires who see their worth as being how much money they can make and do nothing more with it other than indulge themselves. Now, that's not right. If, on the other hand, they go one step further and are willing to use a lion's share of what they make to help people in need … now, that's right. However, many of them don't do that.

I wonder how people who obsess over making money look at themselves and the world. You'd think there would be a point where they would no longer feel so driven to make more and more money, just for the sake of making it.

With the advent of terrorism hitting our shores and the grave possibility of a devastating strike, it seems it's time to change our value system from one of material goods to valuing human life and relationships in a way they haven't been valued since Abe Lincoln's time.

We don't want to be caught flat-footed by beginning to change our value system only after another attack takes place.

A Community Perspective

What's going to happen, besides utter chaos, if terrorists are able to get their hands on a weapon of mass destruction and successfully detonate it, killing millions of people? What will our nation do? What will you do? What will I do? There's are no easy answers to these questions. However, when governing our future activities, I do know that we need to think in terms of the common, rather than the individual, good. We can no longer limit our sphere of influence and interest to a few friends and our immediate family; we need to now think in terms of our community's well-being and concerns, starting with every member in our neighborhood. If you survive a terrorist attack, but the rest of your belongings are destroyed, you'll quickly change what you value in your life. It will no longer be your worldly goods. It will be how pleased you are that you survived the holocaust and that (hopefully) your loved ones did too. At such a time, you certainly would appreciate receiving more than just a little bit of TLC. Catastrophes have a way of reducing people to one common denominator. That's when you begin to appreciate the power of ongoing relationships, love, and care.

You don't need much more to experience joy in life and feel that your life is worth living than if you have three square meals a day and love in your heart. If you have love, you'll give it to others. After all, what else will you do with it?

Twentieth-century psychiatrist Harry Stack Sullivan said that we do not live in a vacuum. We need others to make our lives complete, because we cannot create our own self-definition. Who we are has to come from others observing us. Even the social recluse needs the love and care of others to feel worthwhile. That will certainly be true for anyone who might have survived a terrorist holocaust.

Up to now, in an effort to decide what's best for America, the captains of industry and the corporate world have been looking for new challenges outside the United States. And up to now, they have done very well for the individuals who were able to participate in the capitalistic system. But a number of Americans haven't been given that opportunity, simply because they didn't have the financial means. In fact, a number of Americans live substandard lives, based on anybody's benchmarks. I'm talking about the people who do not have the wherewithal for a minimally comfortable life.

Much still needs to be done to provide all segments of society with the same rights and privileges, including respect, that the majority enjoys.

The president, through speeches to the American public, could do much to focus on the need to level the playing field for all Americans by abandoning politics for a moment and speaking honestly about what we can all do to ensure the American dream for all. Every one of us can make a greater effort to be more accepting of different cultures and understand that we are all valuable ingredients in our national melting pot.

Why aren't some given what the rest of our country has? All should be shown respect and appreciation for who they are, rather than being labeled in a false, hurtful, and blatantly stereotypical manner. Much of society is too self-absorbed, self-centered, narcissistic, and fascinated with power to take time to look beyond themselves and get to know those who appear different from themselves. Their inability to do that keeps them from appreciating others for who they really are, rather than what they assume those people are like. So, it's due to ignorance—which is based on stereotyping, prejudice, and discrimination—that causes them to remain closed-minded in assuming they know all they need to know about a person. Because this type of thinking is based on ignorance, any American who thinks that way should be ashamed.

If we don't start being other-centered and give up being self-centered, we're not going to successfully deal with terrorism in the years to come. There is a great disparity between the haves and the have-nots. This country is so polarized politically, economically, and morally. How are we as a nation and a community going to successfully combat terrorism? The answer is we're not, if we don't come together as a country. In order to do that, we must remove the division that is hurting what this country stands for as articulated in the Constitution. When the Constitution starts out "We the people," that's what it means; *we* the people means just that. It doesn't read, "me the person," or "you the person." What it means is what it says.

Why can't we, as a nation, pick up the battle where others have left off—people like Lincoln, Martin Luther King Jr., and all the others who in the past have fought stereotyping, bigotry, and discrimination, replacing such destructive forces with love, understanding, and knowledge? Together, we can win this battle of prejudice and discrimination. However, we can no longer be passive. We need to actively challenge people who act in a biased and prejudicial way toward another human being.

We could start the healing process by smiling at and saying hello to perfect strangers. To quote the late comedian and pianist, Victor Borge, "A smile is the shortest distance between two people," so why not use it? Of course, that assumes you value others just by the mere fact that they're human beings. Or, to take it one step further, you value all life in general, as long as that life is not inherently harmful to you or other living things.

Because of what we have learned from our parents, school, media, and politicians, we are conditioned to be leery of those who are different from us. Some people turn that tendency into an entire sensationalist career in front of a microphone.

Political talk-show hosts engage in a lot of name-calling when they talk about people who they believe think differently than them. They may even pride themselves in taking the extreme view when discussing their particular political position. When comparing and contrasting their observation with that of their perceived opposite party's posture, they always describe their opponent's view in the most vile and reprehensible way.

Not all people who are of a party affiliation different than that of the host's are nearly as extreme as what he describes, yet, even a moderate Democrat or independent is described in the same way that a liberal Democrat may be characterized, which is with disdain and contempt.

I realize these hosts are on the air to entertain people, but considering the solemnity of the times, perhaps this rankling should stop. They should begin to think of the long-term damage they cause the country as a result of the diatribes and name-calling they constantly engage in when discussing viewpoints different than their own.

The best way to affect a change would be for print journalists to step up to the plate and write editorials—not just once, but many times—damning the extreme practices of these talk-show hosts and taking a stand for a more balanced display of views on radio and TV. Both the formal print outlets and individual bloggers should remind people how socially destructive many of these commentators are.

In Support of Taxes

Regardless of which political camp any of the talk-show hosts inhabit, they all have an opinion about taxes and what they think constitutes a citizen's fair share of support for our government.

Common sense suggests that if individuals or corporations accumulate wealth because of the support our government has given them, making it possible for them to acquire such riches, it seems only right for them to pay their fair share of taxes—keeping in mind, of course, that without such a government, the whole question of who should pay taxes and why would become a moot question, because, in most cases, their wealth would never have happened.

If there ever were a time when the concentrated wealth of the land should bear its fair share of our enormous federal expenses, it is now, what with the mammoth debt our government has accumulated—a debt which will have to be passed on to future generations, even if the wealthy do decide to pay their share.

Considering what our country has given each of us, and since our country was founded on the "we the people" principle, we must not only look after each other, but we must also pay our fair share of the tax burden as a way of giving back to this country. In that way, we can show our appreciation for what our glorious country has given us.

The Return of Affordable Health Care

Until fairly recently, when we thought about America, we thought it was a place of opportunity and safety. Compared to the citizens of other countries, we received the best care and quality of treatment, and it was affordable and available to most Americans. Well, not anymore!

Health care is becoming unaffordable for many Americans. For those medical problems that absolutely need attention, such as heart bypass operations or knee replacements, overseas travel is sometimes required just to find an affordable facility. For that reason, more Americans are traveling overseas to receive the necessary treatment, because the cost is one-third the cost here, in the United States.

Now, what do you think of that? What has happened to this country that its citizens have to go overseas so they can afford medical treatment?

There are many articles written about the U.S. medical insurance industry and how bloated and inefficient it is. Tales abound of the seemingly endless reams of paperwork that need to be completed for the most minor procedure, of doctors and medical practices that are awarded bonuses if they can avoid offering some preventative services … and, of course, the outrageous cost of prescription medication. Much of the high cost of our health insurance is due to the high cost of malpractice insurance doctors must carry.

Voters must demand that Congress stop pandering to the medical and pharmaceutical lobbies and enact legislation that helps the average citizen. I believe it's possible to put a cap on malpractice lawsuits, restrict the profit margin for prescription drugs, require insurance companies to simplify their paperwork, and even create a workable plan for universal medical insurance to cover anyone in need.

Defining Success

I would imagine many of you, like myself, have wrestled with the question of what we mean when we talk about success. Defining success for yourself has its benefits, political and otherwise; it helps you know what initiatives to support, what goals to work toward in your own quest for integrity, and what traits or accomplishments you admire in others.

But success has a very elusive definition. Success can mean so many different things to so many different people that it would seem futile to try to come up with a universal definition, but I feel compelled to try. I want to take a stab at what it means, because I've spent a very long time trying to define it for myself. And it was only after I wrote the closing chapters of this book that I was able to come up with a definition that works for me. I hope it suits you as well.

Please keep in mind that since I am a clinical psychologist, I come to the table with a built-in bias. Keeping that in mind, I think you might be able to resonate with what I'm going to share with you. First of all, I believe that human happiness, fulfillment, and the appreciation of the human condition is at the core of my thinking about any subject that involves life, whether it be religion, spirituality, politics, government, and so on. In fact, I would go so far as to say I'm concerned about maintaining the well-being of all life, including plants and animals as well.

By learning to appreciate myself for who I am, I feel like a complete human being who has tried to use his unique talents and abilities as fully as I could. What I didn't want to end up being, as psychiatrist Harry Stack Sullivan once said, is "an inferior caricature of what I could have become," because at my age, it's too late to change things. I don't deny that the journey involved a lot of hard work and many hours of introspecting, musing, and simply trying to decide how I could use what I was experiencing at the moment to enhance who I was—and after learning that, how I best could respond to human need.

The mantra of "duty to God and country," which is encapsulated in our sense of integrity, is invaluable in helping us understand how critical, in today's world, that concept is in each of our lives. I believe, like love, it represents the essence of our being. Certainly, those of you who choose not to claim any deity are still able to focus on your personal ideals and ethics and in that way maintain and nurture your sense of integrity.

My definition of success is as follows: It involves knowing who you are and what you're about. You need to know, as best you can, what your God-given strengths and abilities are, then play to those strengths. You must not try to be someone you aren't. You must have an empathetic understanding of the world, and generously use your compassion to help others whenever possible. So, with love in your heart and a keen understanding of yourself and others, and listening to your inner voice, your moral compass, all of which is part of your integrity, you will be able to steer your own personal ship of state through the seas of life without ever fearing whatever you might encounter. With peace in your heart, you'll be able to accept that which you can't change and be at ease with who you are.

The important thing is to remember that success involves not only being all that you can be and utilizing all of God's gifts and talents, but also, consistent with what I said earlier, fulfilling your obligation to be responsive to your country and the needs of others as well.

"There but for the grace of God go I ..."

There is a lot of power in the dollar. There is even more power in two dollars. As your wealth increases, so does your power. We, as a society, look at people who are wealthy with a certain amount of awe and respect. This is because not just anybody can make a lot of money. There's a number of factors that must come together to make that possible.

First of all, it helps if you are fortunate enough to inherit wealth— or, if you don't inherit it, you acquire it along your travels in life.

If you are driven to make a lot of money and don't have a wealthy donor to give it to you, never fear, the United States is near. Your chances of making a bundle are greatly enhanced if you were born into this country or have become a citizen of it, because you then have an opportunity to take advantage of all this government offers you. After all, our government was founded on the capitalistic system—where an idea or invention that others are willing to buy puts you on the track to make a lot of dough. In fact, depending upon how well received your idea is, it might even put you on the fast track, where you quickly pass go and collect much more than a mere two hundred dollars.

However, just being a U.S. citizen doesn't necessarily guarantee you wealth. In this day and age, you must also find investors for your project so that you can get the start-up capital to launch your endeavor—and even that doesn't ensure success. Timing is everything. What's critical is whether the idea you're marketing is timed so that the prevailing culture will accept it. It can't be ahead of or behind the times. So, there's a lot of luck involved in successfully marketing an idea that will eventually be a success.

Although it's possible to make it big in the stock market with limited cash, it's not very probable. It can be done, but it's very difficult. It takes money to make money; it's as simple as that.

The reason I said what I did was to illustrate how our capitalistic system works and why it has contributed to the wealth of so many venture capitalists and entrepreneurs here, in the United States. The capitalistic system symbolizes what can be done with good old American ingenuity and inventiveness.

Personally, I think that's all well and good, and should be applauded, but from my standpoint, that's not the end of the story about what success is. The missing link is what you're going to do with your money after you make it. That's the sixty-four-dollar question, so to speak. Are you going to indulge yourself or give it to some worthy cause or project? Are you going to use the money to help others in need or spend more of the same to make whatever you want larger, be it a home, car, or more cars, or a fleet of cars, more clothes, more shoes, more of everything? The idea that bigger is better is simply not so. Yet, today, this is the prevailing societal attitude.

The 9/11 attacks have changed everything. Our predictable world has become less than predictable. It's amazing that nineteen individuals could raise so much fear and anxiety in our country. You wouldn't imagine that would be possible to do that, but they did it.

If we benefited at all from that day in any way, even remotely, it was from the opportunity to reassess the values we hold and adjust to the questionable ones and reaffirm the good ones.

Hopefully we're smarter than we were before that fateful day. Now we have to adjust our thinking to the changing times. The reason we all experienced so much angst is because the terrorists rely on fear to accomplish their objectives—which is to kill as many innocent Americans as they can. It doesn't matter the sex or the age; they just want to destroy what we cherish in this country, which is each other. I say "cherish" with some reservation, because as of today, I don't believe we necessarily love one another as much as we love some of our inanimate objects, like money, cars, homes, and so on. But if we don't change our priorities, we as a nation will not survive terrorism.

In the early 1930s, my mother's father said, "The two worst evils of mankind are greed and intolerance." Well, since the advent of terrorism, we'll have a chance to see if he's right, now won't we?

So let's get with the program, America! Let's begin to reassess what we value in this country, which is each other, rather than material possessions and corporate prestige. By following our integrities and being loving and giving to all Americans, let's disregard our differences and see everybody only as our fellow citizens.

HOW TO CURE OUR GIANT'S IMPOTENCE

The way we cure our giant's lack of strength and power is not to give him one of those little blue pills, but to vote responsibly.

In order to do that, you need to do a number of things before voting. The first question is the most obvious, but still needs to be discussed, and that is whether you're going to vote a straight Democratic or Republican ticket. If you say that is what you're going to do because that's what you've always done, I would wonder whether you should vote at all. That's too simple an explanation for why you cast your vote as you do, year after year after year. Yes, many people do that, but that doesn't make it right. That method suggests that you accept, lock, stock, and barrel, everything either one of the two parties stands for, regardless. When you do that, you're not being fair to yourself or the American people. You didn't engage in critical thinking, because you didn't see any difference between and among the various candidates so that you were able to make discriminating choices. Are all the candidates that similar in thought that no discrimination was necessary, other than voting for those of one political party or another? Of course not. That's like saying you'll date anyone as long as that person is a man or a woman. Now, I'm sure you can be a little bit more discriminating than that, don't you think?

Religion as a Bias

We all have personal influences that sway our vote in one direction or another. Some of those influences might be religion, income, philosophy, personality, geographical location, and so on.

As a voter, it's important to be aware of your influences and biases, so that you can rein them in when necessary for the good of the country. Some factors in our lives affect our political stance more than others; religion is one of the biggest determining factors. Let's explore the relationship between religion and politics.

- Whether it should or not, religion plays a major role in the outcome of our elections and legislative process. It's pretty difficult for the Democrats to win if the majority of the electorate perceives them as not having God on their side. If a Republican can quote Scripture to help defend his political stance, who can argue with that? Since God can do no wrong, and if the Bible is used as the final authority, why do we need the Constitution, anyway? All we need to do is turn to God's teachings and everything will be all right ... right? It's not surprising that the Republican Party approaches issues from a religious angle. According to the Harris Poll conducted on February 26, 2003, when the religious and other beliefs of Americans were assessed, "a very large majority of the American public, and almost all (but not all) Christians believe in God, the survival of the soul after death, miracles, heaven, the resurrection of Jesus Christ, and the Virgin birth ..." The poll also reported that "majorities of about two-thirds of all adults believe in hell and the devil, but hardly anybody expects that they will go to hell themselves."
- The survey goes on to say that 90 percent of adults believe in God. Now that's some potential political power that the Republicans would like to take advantage of. But should religion even have an influence over politics?

I'm not saying there is no place for religious thought in politics. But, as with everything else in life, it's a matter of balance. One's church affiliation should not be the single most determining force to power our ship of state. At the moment, America's ship of state seems to have hit a rather lengthy becalmed stretch, since, for the past several years, Congress and the president have passed little in the way of legislation that will respond to many of the people's needs and wishes. Maybe God is doing his fair share in trying to make things happen, but he alone can't do it. That's because God didn't choose our president and our congresspeople; the people did. The question, then, is how can our civil servants use their religion in a way that will benefit the whole country? They should use God in a way that will help them make sure their ship of state's moral compass is pointing in the best direction and is responsive to the needs and wishes of all its people.

If I were a betting man, I wouldn't necessarily put any money on any particular party, regardless of its religious affiliations, because voting choices are still predominantly based on secular considerations. However, the political landscape is changing fast. If the Republicans have their way, it won't be long before they will have the political edge. It depends on whether the voting public puts a high priority on religious thought.

Since the Democrats and the Republicans are getting more and more polarized in their view of how our country should be governed, it has become a battle between the little people and the wealthy folks and special-interest groups.

It's interesting to note that the Democrats are becoming so concerned about the perceived belief that the Republicans have God on their side that they too are also using God. However, in their case, they take a more utilitarian approach in explaining how their God reinforces their belief, since responding to human need is paramount to their political belief.

The concern I have with emphasizing the importance of God in a campaign is that the factor might sway those uninformed voters who simply vote the straight party ticket. When pressed to explain themselves, they may latch onto one or two peripheral issues which in themselves are not sufficiently weighty to use alone to choose a president or member of Congress—issues such as stem-cell research, prayer in the schools, and evolution versus intelligent design. But to the conservative voter, one or more of those kinds of issues may be of great importance—issues such as the Iraq war, how we we're going to fight this war on terrorism, how best to respond to the needs of all Americans, including the poor, underprivileged, minority ethnic groups, the elderly, and the handicapped people who aren't even on the voting radar screen, because they are for individual rights as opposed to the rights and privileges for all Americans, as stated in the Constitution.

The Alternative of Humanism

Voters don't have to be religious to want the best for our country and its citizens. Humanism, a more secular discipline, is characterized by a strong interest in or concern for human welfare, values, and dignity. The humanist desire to promote the welfare of others is not rooted in religious faith, but in ethics. According to *Webster's New Universal Unabridged Dictionary*, the definition of humanism is

> 1. Any system or mode of thought or action in which interests, values, and dignity predominate. 2. Devotion to or study of the humanities. 3. (*Sometimes cap.*) the studies, principles, or culture of the humanist. 4. *Philos.* A variety of ethical theory and practice that emphasizes reason, scientific inquiry, and human fulfillment in the natural world and often rejects the importance of belief in God

Please note that from a philosophical standpoint, humanism "often rejects the importance of belief in God" just according to its definition. The reason that's important to appreciate is because if you believe God alone determines our thoughts and actions, then, by following his teachings and using the Bible as your nautical compass and navigational map, you might erroneously conclude that's all that's necessary to properly select political candidates.

What that does is entirely exclude the secular world from your thinking. Is that what our Founding Fathers had in mind when they wrote the Constitution? Of course not.

The Founding Fathers wished to avoid such problems. Making political choices solely in terms of religious thought short-circuits communication and further intellectual inquiry. This encourages closed-minded thinking, where your world is either all black or white, suggesting there is no room to examine and appreciate the areas of life that don't neatly fit into clearly defined categories. Since there are more of those areas than the ones you can speak about with certainty, how are you going to make good political decisions if you don't look at the fuzzy and murky parts of political thought? That kind of thinking fuels the flames that promote political extremism. We've got enough kindling already; we don't need any more.

To combat such extremism, keep in the forefront of your mind why you're voting for a particular candidate and make sure you're doing it for the right reason. Is it done because the candidate favors your religious persuasion, and therefore he or she makes you feel comfort that you have someone who embraces the same or similar religious thought that you do? Well, if that's the case, obviously, that's not a reason to support a candidate.

All religions encompass mythical or supernatural thinking that does not relate to the real world in the sense that what is discussed can be explained by natural laws. It is a belief in and reverence for a supernatural power or powers regarded as a creator or deity that governs the universe. What is also noteworthy is that many religious definitions include "matter of ethics or conscience" as part of the definition.

If religion is a formal, rigid belief system, then spirituality is its carefree cousin. Spirituality is more concerned with the spirit, the soul—those things that are not material in nature, but exist in our hearts and minds.

Whether we're talking about religion or spirituality, both hold in common a belief that cannot be scientifically proven, but has at the center of its system a belief in a "supernatural power or powers regarded as creator and governor of the universe."

A Common Concern

America's forefathers weren't the only wise men concerned with the relationship between morality and faith. Consistent with what has already been said, Mahatma Gandhi said that morality is important in any faith; otherwise it's not a religion. He said, "Man, for instance, cannot be untruthful, cruel, or incontinent and claim to have God on his side."

Gandhi was more than just a Hindu. When asked if he was a Hindu, he said, "Yes, I am. I am also a Christian, a Muslim, a Buddhist, and a Jew."

Obviously, he showed much tolerance and appreciation for religions other than his own. The necessary and possibly sufficient condition any religion must encompass is that it relates to right and wrong as derived from your personal conscience, rather than from what the law says should be done. In that sense, you can't be untruthful, cruel, sexually abusive, or unfaithful, or display any other uncontrolled behavior, and claim to have God on your side.

> Lincoln described himself as an "instrument" of a greater power – which he occasionally identified as the U.S. citizenry and at other times as God. He recognized the enormity of his challenge as Commander in Chief of his beloved country and said that he was entrusted with "so vast, and so sacred a trust" that he felt he had "no moral right to shrink." In that sense, he also allowed his conscience help him make executive decisions, for he once said, "When I do good, I feel good; when I do bad, I feel bad. That's my religion."

What is troublesome to me is when a religion shows intolerance for views that are different from their own. Former President Jimmy Carter, who was "born into a Southern family, nurtured as a Southern Baptist, and have been involved in weekly Bible lessons all my life," certainly has a strong religious background and belief system.

In his book *Our Endangered Values*, he speaks of the importance of tolerance and the acceptance of religions different than your own. In his book, he says,

> Since my mother and my wife were Methodists, I always assumed that equally devout Christians could have different worship and organizational customs and still practice our faith in harmony. It is disturbing to hear prominent Baptists make statements such as "You say you're supposed to be nice to the Episcopalians and the Presbyterians and the Methodists and this, that, and the other thing. Nonsense, I don't have to be nice to the spirit of the Antichrist" as Pat Robertson said on *The 700 Club*.[42]

---

[42] Jimmy Carter, *Our Endangered Values: America's Moral Crisis*, 19–20.
Reprinted with the permission of Simon and Schuster Adult Publishing Group. © 2005 by Jimmy Carter.

Carter is right to criticize such divisive talk, which is as inflammatory as referring to the Middle East as evildoers. What good could come of such combative discourse?

Regarding the rise of religious fundamentalism, President Carter said,

> In my 2002 Nobel speech in Oslo, I said, "The present era is a challenging and disturbing time for those whose lives are shaped by religious faith based on kindness towards each other." When asked by *Christianity Today* to explain this statement, I responded:
>
> "There is a remarkable trend toward fundamentalism in all religions—including the different denominations of Christianity as well as Hinduism, Judaism, and Islam. Increasingly, true believers are inclined to begin a process of deciding: 'Since I am aligned with God, I am superior and my beliefs should prevail, and anyone who disagrees with me is inherently wrong,' and the next step is 'inherently inferior.' The ultimate step is 'subhuman,' and then their lives are not significant.
>
> "That tendency has created, throughout the world, intense religious conflicts. Those Christians who resist the inclination toward fundamentalism and who truly follow the nature, actions, and words of Jesus Christ should encompass people who are different from us with our care, generosity, forgiveness, compassion and unselfish love.
>
> "It is not easy to do this. It is a natural human inclination to encapsulate ourselves in a superior fashion with people who are just like us—and to assume that we are fulfilling the mandate of our lives if we just confine our love to our own family or to people who are similar and compatible. Breaking through this barrier and reaching out to others is what personifies a Christian and what emulates the perfect example that Christ set for us."[43]

---

[43] Jimmy Carter, *Our Endangered Values: America's Moral Crisis*, 30–31.
Reprinted with the permission of Simon and Schuster Adult Publishing Group. © 2005 by Jimmy Carter.

In his continued critique of the more intense forms of fundamentalism, Carter pointed out some of the unfavorable common attributes: movements are led by authoritarian, arrogant males who dominate parishioners and devalue women; fundamentalists tend to retain beliefs that benefit themselves; fundamentalists are quick to condemn their opponents; fundamentalists are militant and temperamental; and fundamentalists stick to narrow definitions in order to differentiate themselves.

"To summarize," Carter observed, "there are three words that characterize this brand of fundamentalism: rigidity, domination, and exclusion."[44]

The late Senator Barry Goldwater, Mr. Conservative himself, had some harsh words to say about the extreme right of his party when, in September 16, 1981, he said the following on the Senate floor:

> There is no position on which people are so immovable as their religious beliefs. There is no more powerful ally one can claim in a debate than Jesus Christ, or God, or Allah, or whatever one calls this supreme being. But like any powerful weapon, the use of God's name in one's behalf should be used sparingly. The religious factions that are growing throughout our land are not using their religious clout with wisdom. They are trying to force government leaders into following their position 100 percent. If you disagree with these religious groups on a particular moral issue, they complain, they threaten you with a loss of money or votes or both. I'm frankly sick and tired of the political preachers across this country telling me as a citizen that if I want to be a moral person, I must believe in "A," "B," "C," and "D." Just who do they think they are? And from where do they presume to claim the right to dictate their moral beliefs to me? And I am even more angry as a legislator who must endure the threats of every religious group who thinks it has some God-granted right to control my vote on every roll call in the Senate. I am warning them today: I will fight them every step of the way if they try to dictate their moral convictions to all Americans in the name of "conservatism."

---

[44] Ibid., 34–35.

When Barry Goldwater died, the cause of church-state separation and individual freedom lost a great champion. His observations about extremism articulate its dangers.

Zero Tolerance of Intolerance

Extremism, whether it be in politics or in any other walk of life, is wrong and should not be tolerated. I know you can't stop it from occurring, but it's important to know when it is present. Radio talk-show hosts; whether they're of the liberal or conservative persuasion, routinely use extremism to get people to listen to them. Hyperbole in the service of extremism is the lifeblood for those kinds of hosts. It certainly gets the nonthinking electorate's attention. Labeling the opposition party by calling them flaming liberals, do-gooders, and cut-and-runners, as well as many more names that are much more lethal in their intent, are used to coalesce their political constituency. How does name-calling promote sound political dialogue? It doesn't.

People who call in to dispute what's said are immediately painted by the same brush as whomever was just mentioned, because the caller immediately is described in the same way.

Since it is generally accepted that politics and religion should not be discussed in polite society, we have to ask ourselves why. The answer is that those subjects are so emotionally charged that if they were discussed, some relationships might be fractured.

One of the positive results of my psychotherapy was my ability to take myself seriously, feeling that my thoughts, feelings, and attitudes, including my religious belief (or in my case, my spirituality), were as valid and worthy of note as anyone else's.

That being the case, I began to struggle with how so many religious beliefs, such as Christianity, Judaism, Islam, and Buddhism, to mention but a few, could exist side by side if each claimed exclusivity—claimed that their faith is the one and only belief to follow? For the life of me, I could not see how any one of the aforementioned religions, or any of those I failed to mention, had the corner on the market concerning the meaning of life as it applies to an afterlife or a belief of what occurs after death.

I resolved my dilemma by accepting at face value that there must be some truth in all faith systems. I cherry-picked from the vast array of religious thought those aspects of the dialogue that were simpatico to my way of thinking. By doing that, I was able to forge a belief system that seemed to fit who I am and what I believed to be important in my life.

Religious exploration must be undertaken carefully. Most religions are authoritarian in nature, and therefore may provide their believers with spiritual and moral role models who can bring highly positive influences both to their adherents and society in general. What many religions fail to acknowledge is that these role models may also provide negative influences. Those who seek spiritual guidance and inspiration are very vulnerable to those at the top, who are willing to be unscrupulous and unethical to gain or maintain money, power, and control, which may be motives for politicians as well. That's precisely why the politician who uses religion for political gain must do so with sensitivity and moral honesty—which many fail to do after they get into the political arena, where the winner takes all.

It is important for the potential voter to see the role religion plays in his or her life before entering the voting booth. A vote made according to religious bias is illegitimate, because that's not what the political issue is that the candidate is running on. That is why our Founding Fathers wanted to separate church and state issues. Issues principally related to the church are never legitimate to discuss in the political arena and should not be intermingled with those that are strictly political in nature.

Now that we've examined a potential bias in voters, let's examine the traits that voters should be looking for, both in themselves and in their elected leaders.

Integrity

In this book, I devoted a whole chapter to integrity. I frequently mentioned it in other contexts, because, like love, it is one of the most cherished and admired attributes that any man or woman can possess.

In order to develop a good sense of integrity, you need to know what you believe in—and, once you know that, stick to the principles that make up your unique personality. That is why Lincoln was considered a man of great integrity: He never wavered from what he thought was right, like his wish to abolish slavery. He was steadfast in his determination to accomplish that goal. However, he was unwilling to say one thing and do another. For example, he forthrightly said that if he had to choose between saving the Union and freeing the slaves, he would save the Union. In that sense, he had prioritized his life, deciding in what order he was going to accomplish his goals and then going about life thinking about how he was going to meet those challenges.

Today's politician is only willing to embark on programs that will either further his or her chances for reelection or enhance his or her legacy. They are statesmen no longer.

We can never take our self-worth for granted. It needs to be continually replenished by doing things that don't damage how we see ourselves. Once developed, our integrity remains as a constant, but what we do or say will either elevate or lower the sense of esteem we have of ourselves. Throughout Lincoln's political life, he appeared to know what he stood for and believed in—conclusions he reached through thoughtful reflection. He never appeared to waver from those principles.

While president, he once said, "I desire so to conduct the affairs of this administration that if at the end, when I come to lay down the reins of power, I have lost every other friend on earth, I shall at least have one friend left, and that friend shall be down inside of me."

That quote is a marvelous example of Lincoln's steadfastness in wanting to be true to himself, which is the essence of integrity. So, a voter should be seeking a candidate who keeps that desire in the forefront of his or her mind. By that I mean, any candidate should consciously ask themselves, "Is this what I would do even if I hadn't been elected to this office? Am I doing this to promote myself at another's expense, or am I doing this because it's the right thing to do?"

Particularly in the role of president of the United States, it is so easy to become enamored with your own self-importance that you begin to develop a kind of love relationship with yourself, which nurtures narcissism and arrogance, instead of developing a caring relationship with the country you wish to serve. Remember, the mere act of running for, let alone being, president of the United States is a pretty heady experience that can cause any person seeking that high office to lose his or her perspective.

Affect

It's important for public servants to be in touch with their feelings. By attaching some type of an emotion to their thoughts, they learn how important such thinking has been not only to them personally, but to their nation as a whole.

For example, it's conceivable that George W. Bush might have reconsidered going into Iraq if he hadn't gotten so engrossed in the pageantry of it all, but instead, appreciated the pain and suffering the survivors would experience if one of their loved ones died or became seriously injured as a result of fighting a war that has now, in 2006, proven to be a very serious mistake that should never have taken place.

Lincoln freely showed his emotions whenever he experienced them. He was very much in touch with his feelings. For example, at the onset of the Civil War, Colonel Elmer Ellsworth reportedly was the North's first casualty of the war. What precipitated his death was when the colonel pulled down a Confederate flag from the front of an Alexandria, Virginia, hotel in May 1861. The hotel owner, a Confederate sympathizer, shot and killed Ellsworth. At the time this happened, Lincoln was looking out of his White House window and witnessed the whole drama unfold. Lincoln cried upon hearing of Ellsworth's death.

If you can attach feelings to what you're thinking and doing, you'll take responsibility for your actions in a deeper way. That is particularly important when heavy and serious decisions need to be made, where lives are at risk. Remember, in the case of the Civil War, the pros and cons of seceding from the Union were debated for years before the war commenced. In the case of President Lincoln, the fact that he openly wept over Ellsworth's death indicates he thought very long and hard about involving the nation in a Civil War before it commenced.

Openly and appropriately displaying feelings, as Lincoln did so willingly, shows how human public officials can be. A proper display of emotion helps the public better identify with the officeholder, and in that way, appreciate the thought that must have gone into any serious decision—the message being that the decision wasn't made lightly.

I'm not suggesting that voters choose the person who shows the most emotion. I just want you to recognize that emotions do play a part in not only politics, but in your own life as well. What it does tell you is how much passion you have for the issue you're contemplating. If you get emotional, inwardly or outwardly; you then know that what you're hearing from a politician is important to you.

Compared to other politicians in government, President Bush's behavior hasn't appeared to change between his contemplation of going to war with Iraq and his waging war with that country. There's a serious and obvious disconnect. I'm not suggesting he remain solemn and serious in all public gatherings; however, I do think he should show a softer side of his personality when he discusses issues related to the Iraq war. Instead, he appears publicly defiant, saying that he's going to "stay the course" and constantly reminding everyone that "we can't leave Iraq until the job is done."

He also needs to stop waving at his political base whenever he's approaching or leaving the presidential aircraft, be it a plane or helicopter. Even though he cannot run again, he acts as if he is running. Is it more important to be well thought of than to act more somber when sobriety seems warranted? By behaving in a more solemn manner, he could convey the impression that he takes this Iraq war seriously, because he understands the consequences of his policy both home and abroad.

Therefore, in assessing the candidate's strengths, it is important to determine what his real self versus his public image is. Does a candidate use his or her heart when making decisions affecting our country's welfare?

Empathy and Compassion

Everybody, politicians and nonpoliticians alike, should have an ability to see a little piece of themselves in every person they talk to, as Senator Barack Obama once said. That's a little more personal way of defining empathy than to use the standard Encarta Dictionary definition, which is "the ability to identify with and understand another person's feelings or difficulties."

What I like about that definition is that in order to empathize with someone, you need to have had experiences similar to what that person has gone through, so you can better put yourself in that person's shoes. Or, if you haven't had that kind of an experience, your life's journey has been such that you can at least tangentially understand what he or she has experienced.

Much has been written about Lincoln's ability for empathy. He was a master at getting into another person's world and understanding what that person is feeling and thinking. He could do this because he allowed himself to be close to the emotional side of his personality. He was never afraid to associate his feelings with any good or bad experiences he had had in life, and he had plenty of both. The only way you're going to have that kind of proclivity available to you is to begin to think of how you feel about your past experiences, good or bad. If you haven't had an experience that mirrors what you're witnessing at the moment, you may not be able to fully empathize with it; however, actors and actresses can learn to play a part different from their personality, and in that way empathize with how they think the character they're portraying might act.

A byproduct of empathy is compassion. If you have empathy, you have compassion—another quality Lincoln had that is so valuable. When you have compassion, you have sympathy for the suffering of others, often including a desire to help.

When you can identify with what's happening to someone because you have had similar experiences, then that's empathy. If you felt an emotion along with empathy, then you also experienced compassion.

If our next leader sees himself or herself in each of us and feels the emotions that accompany such empathetic recognition, he or she is more likely to weigh decisions carefully and act in the best interests of the people, with a minimum of the bloodshed and suffering that has so divided our world.

Being concerned about individual rights, as well as having money, power, and influence, are all qualities opposite to a focus on adequately responding to the needs of the less fortunate and being empathetic and compassionate toward others. You can't be both at once. Frankly, that's why Democrats have the monopoly on caring for the less able and being an empathetic and compassionate party, compared to the Republicans, who appear primarily to be a party that favors individual rights, money, power, control, and influence.

I think it is an accepted fact that there are more Democrats than Republicans in the Hollywood crowd, at least on the creative side of the business. Actors and actresses need to assume various roles when they play their parts. In order to play the role properly, they have to be able to study the character they're portraying—and, through empathy, become that person. Perhaps it is because of their capacity to empathize and therefore be compassionate for people less fortunate than themselves that these people gravitate toward a political party that welcomes such feelings and makes such people and their party the object of derision by conservative talk-show hosts who favor the unsentimental reasoning of the Republican Party.

As a voter, you need to be discriminating ; don't just vote a straight party ticket. You should be aware of specific political ploys the politician uses to get you to vote one way or another. Your interest in supporting a candidate because he or she goes to church every Sunday, is against stem-cell research, and is an antiabortionist is not a sufficient reason to vote Republican. Conversely, if you're a Democrat, supporting a Democratic candidate as a protest vote against what the Republican politician stands for is not as good a reason for voting Democratic, as it would be if you supported your candidate because he or she reflected your Democratic principles. In other words, hopefully you have studied the issues sufficiently so that you can support a candidate in a positive and affirming way. It's better to be that way rather than oppositional. If you still can't decide, then leave that part of the ballot blank.

The best parameters to use when judging your candidate's merits are

1. Does the candidate have a heart (feelings)?
2. Does the candidate seem to have empathy?
3. Does the candidate have compassion?
4. Does the candidate appear to have integrity?
5. Does the candidate have at least bright normal intelligence, enjoy reading for reading's sake, and boast good analytical and synthesizing ability?

6. And last, but certainly not least, does your candidate have wisdom?

7. Then, when you put all those ingredients together, how does the candidate employ his or her feelings, compassion, empathy, integrity, and wisdom, in solving political problems?

If you're still at a loss as to who to support, think about the ideal political candidate—I don't know about you, but Abraham Lincoln immediately comes to my mind—then vote for a candidate who would most closely mirror that image. You then can't go wrong—assuming, of course, that you want to choose a candidate who will serve *all* the people.

WHERE DO WE GO FROM HERE?

"Seven blunders of the world that lead to violence:
wealth without work, pleasure without conscience,
knowledge without character, commerce without morality,
science without humanity, worship without sacrifice, politics
without principle."

—*Mahatma Gandhi (1869–1948)*

The person who is placed in a leadership position like the presidency assumes an awesome responsibility. His or her decisions can have far-reaching consequences—not only for his or her generation, but for many future generations as well.

In the case of our past presidents, if the decisions that were made turned out to be ill-advised, the future of our beloved country would have changed so very dramatically that what we are able to enjoy today, at best, would have become but a distant dream. That's why it's important for all Americans to participate in the elective process in order to give a man or a woman as overwhelming of a mandate as possible. This could indicate the majority of our nation's citizens respect and admire the chosen president, because he or she represents a good share of the collective values, interests, and aspirations we have for this great country.

I am not suggesting that he or she always do what the majority wants him or her to do. The president is in a much better position to assess what kind of decision needs to be made, because he or she is privy to much more information than the citizenry. But if a decision is made contrary to the will of the majority, and the decision chosen will have far-reaching ramifications, that decision better be the right one. If it's not, the consequences for our nation could be disastrous. It may take years to recover from the blunder, if recovering is even possible. In this book, I have reviewed problems like our massive national debt and criticized ill-conceived decisions like the war in Iraq. Our need for a great leader is dire; even with the best of leaders, the balancing of the budget certainly won't occur in my or my grandchildren's lifetime. The sooner American citizens use their voting responsibilities wisely and elect a new captain for our ship of state, the sooner we as a country will be able to turn it around.

A Key Role

In studying the history of this nation from its inception until the present, I was struck by the major role that presidential leadership played in determining the fate of our beloved country. More specifically, our quality of life and the path this country would have headed down might have been completely different if presidents like George Washington, John Adams, Andrew Jackson, and Abraham Lincoln hadn't been at the helm of our ship of state at their specific time in our nation's history.

These are but a few examples of the number of American presidents who showed audacity and boldness in the time of crisis—and by doing so, resisted the temptation to take the expedient path to help maintain their popularity or win themselves a reelection.

By not allowing their personal narcissism to determine their actions, they were able to make the hard decisions by doing what was right and best for the country. This was done by remaining steadfast, even in the face of character assassination and possible loss of reelection, as well as in some cases, the risk of impeachment and possible assassination.

These men have proven throughout history that a good leader can make all the difference. Unfortunately, so can a bad one. It is of utmost importance that American voters choose our future leaders carefully. These leaders must embody the traits discussed in this book, such as integrity, highly developed critical-thinking skills, and humility.

America must also set to work resolving its past mistakes.

Since renowned author Robert Merry, in his book *Sands of Empire*, speaks of the impossibility of establishing a democracy in Muslim nations such as Iraq, we must acknowledge the tremendous price we've paid for our mistake, both in treasure spent and lives maimed or lost, by peremptorily attacking Iraq. Before we are able to extricate ourselves from that untenable situation, it is estimated that in Iraq alone, we will have spent over $510 billion according to the Congressional Research Service.

Though I have spent much time in this book discussing the ill-advised Iraq war, it has been done because history will show that the war represents the defining moment when we as a nation began to slide down the slippery slope to becoming a second-rate power. The longer we stay in Iraq, the more slippery and steeper the slope becomes. The momentum increases each minute the bulk of our troops remain in Iraq.

President Bush has consistently and massively utilized the ego defense mechanism of denial to help him tolerate the onslaught of criticisms that he continually receives for the way he has handled his presidency. He has tried to carry out his responsibility as commander in chief of not only this country, but of the free world as well, with steadfast determination to do it his way, regardless of any substantial evidence to the contrary. He is not alone in the criticism that has been bestowed upon him, for like our president, Congress too has received overwhelming complaints and criticisms in the way they've conducted themselves in both word and deed. The Iraq war is simply the tip of the iceberg, and the unseen portion of the iceberg reveals how far off the mark America is regarding what it should be concerned about and is not getting done.

There is a myriad of unmet "we the people" issues yet to be adequately addressed by either our president or Congress. That is why President Bush and Congress's approval ratings are the lowest they've been since George W. was elected president of the United States.

Through President Bush and his administration's actions and inactions, and because of the damage the executive branch, along with the legislative and judicial branches of government, have done as well, it is critical that all of these governmental bodies immediately begin to listen to the "we the people" kinds of concerns and issues.

Time is not on our side.

If our appointed and elected officials don't begin to listen to America, our nation will not survive. We must come together as a country and not allow special-interest groups such as lobbies, large financial supporters of candidates, or religious groups dictate policy. Unfortunately, these deleterious and poisonous influences have been permitted to be part of the political backdrop for many, many years, and though such issues have been discussed extensively over time, the president and Congress have not shown a proclivity to rectify the situation. They all seem content in eating out of the same trough as the people who make the financial contribution eat out of, all of which results in helping sustain the status quo.

Lately, we have all heard a number of politicians say that our system of government is broken. So … what are they doing to fix the system? For some reason or other, our government seems paralyzed, unable to offer concrete recommendations on what needs to be done to make it run smoothly, or even run at all. It's one thing to say the system is broken; it's quite another to offer a solution on how to fix it.

No concrete recommendations are made to make our government deal with the people's business, because our current politicians are still acting like politicians rather than statesmen. They are only interested in doing what's necessary to get elected or reelected, rather than tackling some of the hard issues of the day, like immigration, global warming, Social Security reform, and so on. The list can go on and on, but I hope you get the idea.

The fact that all politicians start the campaign process all over again as soon as they get reelected doesn't make it right. The research I've done over the last four or five years has convinced me that we must return to the citizen's government like they had during the formation of the Continental Congress – where citizens would serve for a specified period of time and then return to their earlier and primary occupation. Term limits prevent an oligarchic form of government from occurring where the government is run by a few people and as a result, the Constitution as we know it becomes null and void.

The usual argument against this form of election process is that the government has become so vast and complicated that it takes several years to acclimate oneself to the routine required to run that elected office. If that's the case, they could make a provision for the retiree to be required to stay on board for the period of time necessary for the newcomer to acclimate his or herself. The time required for the person leaving office to remain could be determined by the two persons involved and of course, the length of time would be decided by the nature of the office being vacated. Initially, the amount of time necessary for the retiree to be available could be determined by trial and error. Eventually, a definitive amount of time for working together would be established.

One of the reasons term limits have value is it would require two people to work together, which in itself can nurture that sense of cooperation and working for something greater than themselves, namely the welfare and wellbeing of all Americans, not just those who the politician retiring was beholden to.

Instead of dealing with national concerns, our president and politicians spend the majority of their time discussing peripheral issues, such as stem-cell research, physician-assisted suicide, prayer in the classroom, evolution versus intelligent design, and abortion rights. It's very possible if we respected a diversity of opinion and the needs of all Americans, the issues I just enumerated would no longer require governmental interference.

We need to focus on issues related to our national security and survival now. If we don't, the concerns I just listed will not be on the politicians' radar screens at all, for the nation we once loved and cherished will no longer exist.

There needs to be a willingness on the part of the politicians to think in terms of what's best for the country, not for themselves. They must be courageous and forthright in dealing with the problem, even if it means not being elected or reelected.

Because of the advent of terrorism in this country and because the playing field for the African Americans as well as other minority groups is not level, we need to begin to empathize with those people who may be less fortunate than us, and in that way begin to think what's best for the community rather than just for ourselves. We'll need that neighborhood mind-set if we're to successfully fight terrorism, for the old adage "Alone, we cannot help but fail, but together, we cannot help but succeed" has never been more real than it is today, when scores of people can be eliminated by one weapon of mass destruction.

Since politicians are not stepping up to the plate to make right what is wrong in this country, our president must begin to vocalize what needs to be done and make laws that will effect those needed changes. Our future and way of life are dependent upon it.

We must indeed prove what Benjamin Franklin stated about America's great "experiment" in self-government, that it continues to be a success, for it to be a failure is unthinkable.

Again, time is not on our side.

What appears on our country's great seal, on official documents such as passports and is seen on the seal of the president, the vice president, Congress, House of Representatives, Senate and Supreme Court is the motto: "E.Pluribus Unum," which is Latin for "Out of Many, One."

If it appears in so many places of note, it seems like it's pretty important and should be a mantra that we honor and obey by not only our president and our governmental officials, but also all of us who are citizens of these United, now Divided States. This is particularly true when you consider what the motto means. When this country was founded in the 18th century, that saying, "Out of Many, One," suggests that out of many colonies or states emerge a single nation. Today, it means out of many peoples, races, and ancestries, has emerged a single people and nation.

Not to be overly critical, but where 's the community spirit and the belief that we as a country can work together by using the melting pot of people that represent America's spirit and integrity in a way that can benefit all of America, not just the privileged few.

During our more recent years, the motto "Out of Many, One," should be revised to say, "Out of Many, Many." Obviously, the oneness and sense of community and mission that Americans should share not only among themselves, but also the world, is sadly lacking.

We can start to rectify the situation by following what Theodore Roosevelt said in 1912,that, "The people themselves must be the ultimate makers of their own Constitution."

The president, Congress, Senate, Supreme Court and all the other indices that make-up our government at the national and local levels should start using our country's Constitution as their blueprint in making legislative decisions.

For we, as American citizens, we must draw upon our individual integrities, which represent each of our personal Constitutions, when deciding who best to run our country at the national, state, or local levels of government.

After the Constitutional Convention adjourned, a citizen asked what kind of government had been structured by the Founding Fathers, Benjamin Franklin is said to have answered…A REPUBLIC IF YOU CAN KEEP IT."

The Republic which our Founding Fathers envisioned, in reality, worked because our country was a place of liberty and opportunity for countless millions of people from all over the world. The reason the concepts worked as outlined in the Constitution was because they were based on enduring principles which recognized human foibles such as people showing a proclivity to respond to their own self interest rather than for the common or greater good.

This resulted in developing a system of checks and balances which is reflected in the Constitution. What that did was to protect the minority from the majority and the majority from the minority's actions or inactions. Our Constitution is not a perfect system, however, it's the best our Founding Fathers could create. The system is imperfect because neither the majority or minority desires are fully legislated. What it does is protect the interest of the few from the many and the many from the few. In order to attain that balance, where some legislation gets passed that benefit all Americans, compromises must be made on both sides of the aisle.

It was after the establishment of the Continental Congress and setting up of the Articles of Confederation that our Founding Fathers recognized that the thirteen colonies in general and colonists in particular were not interested in the common interest or the common good, or something that was bigger than themselves, which they called "public virtue," but rather, they were interested in promoting their own selfish interests, even at the expense of other's needs and desires – concluding that we as human beings are basically a very selfish, self-indulgent, and pleasure seeking lot. This kind of thinking would be very consonant with Sigmund Freud's hedonistic pleasure principle, which is that our natural inclination is to seek pleasure and avoid pain.

It was after the writing of the Articles of Confederation and the eleven years that transpired before the writing and signing of the Constitution that absolute pandemonium and chaos reined throughout the colonies. Rather than the colonists overlooking their own individual self-interests and desires, for the greater good, they were only interested in pursuing their own selfish needs and desires, even at the expense of others – which today is called self-aggrandizement.

A vivid illustration of how selfish and heartless the states were during the Revolutionary War were the squalid conditions the Continental Army had to endure during their efforts to fight the British. Rather than the colonies cooperating with one another for the greater good, which was to defeat British tyranny, they neglected the needs of the Revolutionary Army, which resulted in them being inadequately clothed and fed to the point where they nearly starved and froze to death. Instead of helping Washington's army defeat the British, they competed amongst each other, one colony against another, for trade superiority – resulting in corruption and exploiting the system at the Continental Army's expense.

As Daniel Webster said in 1837, "One country, one Constitution, one destiny." We now seem to have two "countries" named Republican and Democratic, and two distinct and polar opposite destinies; instead of passing legislation to respond to all America, these two "countries" are warring with each other to further their own political agenda, at the expense of what's best for the country. In the process, since both "countries" share a common Constitution, they essentially by-pass our nation's operating system because neither party is willing to make the necessary compromises in order to make the Constitution work.

Today, Congress and the president are not passing any legislation because neither political party wish to compromise with the other to get bills passed. Who suffers when that occurs? Not the politician, but rather, "We the people."

Even though in 1786, Washington wrote, "We have probably had too good an opinion of human nature in forming our confederation," today, in order to prove him wrong and fix our broken system, we need to begin to cooperate with one another – politician with politician, Republican with Democrat, citizen with fellow citizen, if we are going to save our Union from utter chaos and destruction.

The way our two party system operates today, when speaking of political parties, perhaps George Washington was right when he described them as "potent engines, by which cunning, ambitious, and unprincipled men will be enabled to subvert the power of the people and to usurp for themselves the rein of government."

The other example where some major changes need to be made is in energy independence. We need to reduce our dependence for oil from other countries and provide our nation with alternative energy supplies.

As long as we are dependent on other nations to help provide us with the energy necessary for us to maintain our standard of living, we will obviously have to continue to be duplicitous and sacrifice our nation's integrity in order to continue to tap into the overseas oil market. The duplicity rises when we are required to do business with countries we would have nothing to do with, if it weren't for the fact that we need their oil.

Since our major car companies are unwilling to make more fuel-efficient cars (like the hybrid models) in record numbers, our government must step in and legislate that it be done. Yes, you heard me right. We may have to sacrifice our individual rights for our nation's collective good.

Another thing we may do in order to ease the energy crunch is to require our major oil companies to build additional refineries using some of the massive profits they have accumulated over the years. Presently, what they say in order to maintain the status quo is that the reason the price of oil is so high is because of the classic supply-and-demand problem. There's a limited supply and a great demand, thus causing the price of gasoline to rise.

It's generally accepted that there are not enough refineries to process the oil into gasoline. We need more refineries. Since the oil companies are part of the problem, they should be part of the solution. Since they can afford to build more refineries and still maintain a profit, for the good of the country, they should step up to the plate and do just that.

Thirty-five or so years ago, the then-President Nixon urged our nation to become energy independent. What has happened since then? Nada. Our current president, President George W. Bush, has told us the same thing President Nixon espoused—namely, our nation needs to become energy independent. What significant steps have we, as a nation, taken since President Bush made that request? With the exception of offering rebates if you buy a hybrid car, nothing worthy of note has taken place.

We need an all-out national effort to search for an alternative energy source, much like what was done in the early phases of World War II. Through Albert Einstein's urging, President Franklin Delano Roosevelt got some of our country's leading scientists together to develop the atomic bomb. We should reenact the Manhattan Project—in this case, for peaceful, not destructive purposes. This collection of top scientists would look for and develop alternative energy sources.

Again, time is not on our side.

I say time is not on our side because if we don't soon figure out how to address these critical issues, we will never escape the political rut that is ruining our beloved country. Ultimately—sooner, rather than later—our country and way of life will be destroyed from within.

Past empires such as Rome may have been besieged by hordes that wished them harm, but it was the breakdown of the Roman government and the moral decay of its citizens that doomed Rome. If we fail to reclaim our government and allow our citizens' interests to be merely superficial entertainment, then we will suffer the same fate.

The value of money has replaced the value of love, charity, and caring for others as the parameter we and our fellow citizens choose to use as a standard of success and accomplishment. Since we won't survive the terrorism threat without all Americans working together as a community, it is time we looked beyond ourselves and stopped thinking about our egocentric and self-serving wants and desires. We must begin to think in terms of what we can do for others in a way we haven't conceived of for many years now.

By virtue of being human beings, looking beyond ourselves and helping others in need should be a natural progression of our life's development. If you think that's not your modus operandi, then think about how doing that may help you survive another terrorist's random act of violence. Because if, in the past, you've helped others in need, then they in turn will help you if the occasion calls for it.

Ambassadorship

We should realize that whether we are serving overseas, or are tourists, or are employed in a foreign land, we should consider ourselves United States ambassadors and act accordingly, since our behavior is put on display for the world's population to see and judge.

One thing we don't realize in this country is that we help grow terrorism by having armed troops kick in the doors of homes in small villages. We've all seen the TV images of women and children crying as soldiers search their home. The result is that young men and small boys in these families don't see the potential of democracy or that the troops are trying to help them. They see only their sister or mother crying, and they feel ashamed that they cannot protect them at that moment. As a result, they will later be willing to join any group that will help them reassert themselves and make them feel like men as they strike back at what has now become their enemy. Armed men going through their homes rob these young men of their pride, and that is an important factor in Mideast culture.

Empathy and compassion are so important in the world of politics today. One of America's problems is that, with the exception of the South during the Civil War, this country has never suffered the indignity of being occupied by a conquering force. Ask the French what it's like. One reason why they bluster and strut on the world stage today is because they are still trying to overcome the shame and humiliation not only of being occupied, but also in letting it happen so easily and helping their oppressors to send their Jewish countrymen to their deaths. Think about it—how would you feel if you had lived like that?

Political Realities

With a few notable exceptions, the thought woven throughout my book is that America's voting public provides the leads that our presidents are to follow. It is our job to tell our presidents what programs to focus on and develop within their administrations. As a rule, it's not the president who determines the direction in which our country moves, but rather, it's the people. It's the president's electorate, particularly his or her campaign contributors and supporters, that determine the presidential policy. Generally, America as a whole should be the decider (as Bush would refer to himself), not just one person.

The greatness and power of our country occurred because of both our democratic form of government and the capitalistic system. It was democracy that allowed our capitalistic system to flourish. On the one hand, the greatness of our nation exists thanks to our democratic system of government; on the other hand, our country owes its power to our capitalistic system.

Together, democracy and capitalism have been a dynamic duo, an unbeatable combination. So what's not to like? Nothing, as long as both systems work in concert with one another, much like a dance. However, when the capitalistic system misuses its power by throwing its weight around and stepping on its dancing partner's toes, a breakdown of our system of government results.

That is exactly what has happened today. Our democracy is broken. No one in our government wishes to recognize the problem—or, if they're willing to do that, knows how to fix it. This conundrum has caused the American public to lose faith in our president and Congress and in their ability to take appropriate action in dealing with any problem, let alone adequately respond to the needs and concerns of their citizenry.

In order to understand how we can mend our system of government, we must recognize that it is our country's willingness to support and nurture the individual spirit, not the collective will of the majority, that has greatly contributed to our nation's fortunes. However, such a system can allow people of great personal wealth to gain unfair advantage in controlling the government.

Modern politics is driven by money or economics, not by the people. To the extent that capitalism has allowed the dollar bill to influence our political system, the power has been taken from the citizenry and given to the corporations and the moneyed people, lobbyists, and special-interest groups. Therefore, through the power of the purse, these small groups influence what issues our politicians address and respond to. As a result, the will of the common people is left unattended. No wonder the vast majority of Americans are deeply disappointed in their government; their president and Congress never seem to hear or act on their needs and wishes. It's because money talks in a way that American citizens can't. Learning another language besides "money" would make no difference; the results would be the same. Because of the all-powerful and international voice of money, our government has continually turned a deaf ear to all those Americans who are crying to be heard. No wonder none of us can again say with pride, "I am fortunate to be an American, because my government is fair and just in the way it responds to the needs and desires of all people, rich and poor alike."

The higher a civil servant rises on the political ladder, from county commissioner to U.S. senator to president of the United States, the greater power they have over the American public. That being so, it is important that they utilize such authority with great empathetic understanding of the needs that all Americans have and respond to them in a way that is appropriate to the citizenry that they are privileged to serve. If they do that, they will act like statesmen and not politicians, for they will not be so concerned with how they will personally benefit from their actions or inactions. Rather, they will be doing what's best for the citizen and ultimately what's best for our nation. Of course, that's assuming the officeholder wishes to respond to all Americans and be evenhanded in the treatment of all those they serve. When that happens, we have democracy in action—the way our Founding Fathers intended for America to function.

Causes and Effects of Corruption

With corruption, there always is a lack of accountability.

What prompts corruption? Clearly, after many politicians get elected, they lose their sense of self and therefore their perspective. After all, that's a pretty heady experience to be elected president of the United States, or senator or congressperson, or Supreme Court judge. Even serving the president in an appointed capacity can boost one's ego to such a degree that pleasing the commander in chief takes precedence above anything else. After all, your boss is the president of the United States—it doesn't get any better than that!

The key to not going overboard with the implied and real power that comes with the office or appointment you are holding is maintaining your perspective. In order to do that, you must know who you are and what you're about. You must know what you believe in. You must not be willing to sacrifice your sense of integrity for some short-term goal and satisfaction. When you do use your inherent control and influence by virtue of the position you hold in government, it should always be used in a fair, just, and empathetic way in your effort to respond to your public, the American people.

In order to respond to the best in yourself, and in that way, resist the various temptations for personal gain that come with the office that you hold, you must have enough ego strength. This means having enough intellectual prowess and reasoning ability to avoid striving for a sense of superiority at someone else's expense. Because the personal gain is magnified and the temptations become greater the higher up the political ladder you find yourself, you have to be more vigilant and understanding of who you are and what you're about.

For a while, as you get used to your new job, you may need to get yourself in the right mind-set to perform the people's business properly. To do this, you might ask yourself, "Am I making this decision for personal gain or for the good of the country?"

The values in this country are cockeyed, and many elected officials, including the president of the United States, believe a person's worth is measured by the amount of money they make. Politicians who promote their personal agendas at the cost of the American public are misusing a power that has been vested in them by virtue of the office they hold.

Regardless of whether we're talking about a congressperson or a president, most politicians measure their success while they're on the world stage by how popular they end up being while they serve their people. Their worth is measured not only in how much money they've accumulated over their lifetime, but also how much prestige they've garnered while in office. When that is the major reason for serving in government, all of these wants and desires are usually sought at a terrible expense to the public they are expected to serve.

The expense comes in tax dollars spent on unworthy projects that cost too much and serve too few people, such as pork-barrel spending, salaries for politicians who have accomplished little or nothing while in office, financing for an unnecessary and bogus Iraq war, and so on.

Most wars are started for illegitimate reasons. If they typically began for reasons that were noble and right, there would have been a paucity of wars throughout our world's history.

President Bush has never appeared to know what he believed in while serving as president of the United States, nor did he seem to know what programs he wanted to strive for while serving as president. He has recklessly striven to widen and strengthen his power base by not only invading Iraq, but also illegitimately utilizing his presidential powers by claiming executive privilege. In that way, he has avoided giving to Congress and the American public the reasons for his actions, which many in Congress claim as unlawful and suspect.

Yes, the seeking of power at the expense of his electorate and those opposing his unwise policies has become the driving force behind much of what President George W. Bush thinks and does. The presidency of this self-appointed "decider" has deteriorated to such an extent that power and control have become ends in themselves, rather than a means to an end, which would be to do the people's business fairly and equitably.

The Importance of Accountability

Since the political system becomes corrupted when politicians seek power for the sake of it and try solely to please the special-interest groups that helped get them elected in the first place, the political system needs a firm accountability to the electorate. To guard against allowing such selfish and self-serving forces to dominate the political landscape, and therefore running rampant through the halls of Congress and the streets of American cities, we need to follow President Dwight D. Eisenhower's advice.

When he gave his farewell address from the Oval Office on January 17, 1961, Eisenhower discussed the state of the Union and the importance of maintaining a balance of power between the various branches of government. Implied was his belief that there is no place for extremism of any sort in political thought, discourse, and action. In his address, he said,

My fellow Americans:

> Three days from now, after half a century in the service of our country, I shall lay down the responsibilities of office as, in traditional and solemn ceremony, the authority of the Presidency is vested in my successor.

> This evening I come to you with a message of leave-taking and farewell, and to share a few final thoughts with you, my countrymen....

> Throughout America's adventure in free government, our basic purposes have been to keep the peace; to foster progress in human achievement, and to enhance liberty, dignity and integrity among people and among nations. To strive for less would be unworthy of a free and religious people. Any failure traceable to arrogance or our lack of comprehension or readiness to sacrifice would inflict upon us grievous hurt both at home and abroad.

> Progress toward these noble goals is persistently threatened by the conflict now engulfing the world.

It commands our whole attention, absorbs our very beings....

Crisis there will continue to be. In meeting them, whether foreign or domestic, great or small, there is a recurring temptation to feel that some spectacular and costly action becomes the miraculous solution to all current difficulties. A huge increase in newer elements of our defense; development of unrealistic programs to cure every ill in agriculture; a dramatic expansion in basic and applied research—these and many possibilities , each possibly promising in itself, may be suggested as the only way to the road we wish to travel.

But each proposal must be weighed in the light of a broader consideration: the need to maintain balance in and among national programs—balance between the private and the public economy, balance between cost and hoped for advantage—balance between the clearly necessary and the comfortably desirable; balance between our essential requirements as a nation and the duties imposed by the nation upon the individual; balance between action of the moment and the national welfare of the future. Good judgment seeks balance and progress; lack of it eventually finds imbalance and frustration.

Our government and citizens must strive to avoid any form of extremism. Whether it is a tightly controlled dictatorship or a democracy without some reasonable limits, extremism will not survive the test of time. Extremism doesn't promote harmony and working together, but rather, promotes disharmony and chaos. That's why terrorism will eventually fail as a state-sanctioned government.

An example of the greatest degree of extremism is illustrated in Nelson DeMille's book *Wild Fire*. It involves a right-wing plot to set off a nuclear device in two U.S. cities which would provoke our existing government to implement an existing plan called Wild Fire. That plan would automatically respond to the so-called nuclear terrorism in our country, with the intent of destroying the majority of people in the Middle East.

In DeMille's author's note, he says, "As for the secret government plan called Wild Fire, this is based on some information I've come across, mostly online, and can be taken as rumor, fact, pure fiction, or some blend thereof. I personally believe that some variation of Wild Fire (by another code name) actually exists, and if it doesn't, it should."

Frankly, I don't agree with DeMille when he says in his quote that a program such as Wild Fire should exist if it doesn't already.

How is killing the majority of Muslims in the Middle East going to create a greater sense of peace and tranquility on earth? That type of action will only incite the remaining Muslim nations to rise up against our country. How is it any different than Hitler's final solution to what he perceived as the Jewish problem?

What we must do as a nation is to root the terrorists out, isolate them, and bring them to justice. Just as we would deal with a disease or infection, the object is to destroy the illness, not kill the patient.

In order to accomplish that, we must stop using massive armies to fight terrorism, but rather, preemptively strike the terrorist cell in the effected country by using a highly trained small intelligence cadre who will eliminate that group of revolutionaries, so they will no longer be able to cause harm to our country or any other.

In our war on terrorism, we must begin to develop a massive program to cultivate, train, and nurture a relationship with people of Mideastern heritage to work with our government, as well as train others to speak Arabic and understand the various cultures of the region. Throughout the book, I have quoted a number of people who have intimate knowledge of the Middle East and Muslim cultures, yet our government does not seek their advice and counsel. What a marvelous untapped resource that has yet to be exploited.

The Permanence of Terrorism

With the advent of terrorism in this country and the plight of the needy, we need to change what's important to us as Americans. We need to stop being a country of consumers and start dealing with ideas and beliefs. Today, we don't need a concentration of our country's energies to help grease the wheels of industry so that the quality and amount of the goods and services continues to improve. Rather, we need to concentrate our energies outward, helping others in need, and in that way, help strengthen our country's moral fiber. If we do that, our nation's soul will be proudly placed front and center for all to witness and embrace.

Also, by doing that, we can unite as a country again—Republican, Democrat, and independent alike. Together with the family of nations, we can fight the terrorism scourge.

If this is not done, we cannot possibly succeed; if it *is* done, ultimately, we cannot possibly fail. I say "ultimately" because it will be a long, hard struggle before ours and the other nations of the world will succeed by containing terrorism. As a country, we must stop thinking in absolutes, certainties, and quick fixes. We must be willing to tolerate ambiguities. By that I mean we must stop thinking that if we do this and that, such and such will be bound to happen.

Because terrorism is anathema to us, and because we can't understand why these insurgents are willing to commit suicide to kill innocent people, and because so few of them can kill so many of us, the final outcome of containing terrorism will still be open to question until we get a better formula to stop this scourge from happening.

We are so accustomed to providing a solution to every problem that arises that we feel we can use the same formula in dealing with terrorism as we do in dealing with any other problem. However, terrorism is a battle of ideas that will eventually rule the day; no specific course of action will make terrorism disappear.

In fact, it is indeed possible that, from time to time, terrorism will appear to win the war. But this I can say with certainty: if that happens, that mind-set will only be temporary. England appeared to be down and out as she fought Nazi Germany, she held on, and with the help of other nations, the war was won.

Because our country is not used to sitting on their anxieties and tolerating a little monetary and emotional discomfort, we look for a quick fix. Well, there is no easy solution. Terrorism will continue to be part of our nation's backdrop from this point forward. We need to learn to live with it.

There is indeed strength in numbers. By coming together as a nation and meeting with other like-minded countries, we are bound to prevail. But for many, it will be a long and heartbreaking journey we are embarking upon—for many innocent lives will be lost along the way.

We are still in the early phases of this war on terrorism. It is our and our allies' collective integrities that will provide considerable comfort to each of us as our nation's ship of state continues to ride the stormy and threatening waters.

But in order for that to happen, we need to know what this country believes in. Much debate and discussion needs to be had by our president and elected representatives. Eventually, our president needs to address his American public and explain what we as a country believe in, and what he expects from Congress and all Americans. By doing that, our president will have defined America's integrity. That will provide all of us with a kind of national pillow that we can place each of our heads on when we become weary in our fight to preserve and protect what each of us and our nation believes in. No greater solace can be provided than that.

What is meaningful is what's written in people's hearts, not what is legislated. Our society needs to ask itself whether our presidential and congressional candidates are concerned with matters of the heart. If they are, and those kinds of issues are important to you, then you can support such a candidate with your vote.

Let's review what has happened to this country since the advent of terrorism on September 11, 2001.

After 9/11, we had the whole world behind us, which included many Muslim countries. Today, most nations of the world are against us. What happened? The Iraq war was the catalyst that turned everything around, so that other countries view us with dismay and anger. The venom and hatred other nations feel toward us is like food that has gone bad; it's unpalatable.

We are no longer considered a country to be emulated. We are hated and mistrusted by other nations. If we don't take off our rose-colored glasses and start looking at ourselves as we really are, our potency as a country will continue to diminish, and we will continue to be disrespected.

The rich history of our nation, though short by global comparison, has produced an economic and military might the likes of which the world has never seen. Our status as the world's preeminent superpower remains unchallenged. But for how long? How much erosion can our foundation bear before the structure is threatened?

Exercising Voting Power

We are at a crossroads in deciding how to wield such power—and indeed, in deciding exactly what our global responsibilities are. Presently, we have made a choice to unilaterally pursue our global interests and national security through the use of military force. The tangible costs, both in human life and treasure, have been abominable. The intangible costs manifest themselves in generating the undercurrents of national disunity, domestic anxiety, and international instability.

When are we going to learn that waging war does not solve anything? To put it simply, we have reached the point in history where war is no longer a viable option. With the weapons of mass destruction, we face the real possibility that we as a nation can be annihilated, or at least have our quality of life dramatically reduced to the point where living is no longer worthy of consideration. Why don't we expunge "war" from our vocabularies?

In place of the word "war," let's substitute the words "diplomacy" and "negotiation." I know it's easy to say, "Get real! The terrorists are out to destroy us, so what's there to negotiate?" Well, there are reasons to not adopt a belligerent, antagonistic, and winner-take-all mentality, since, for starters, all of our lives and the future of the world are at stake.

Sitting down and talking with our adversaries doesn't mean we have to sacrifice any of our principles in order to do business with them. The important thing to do is enter any discussion with an open mind. Up to this point in recent history, this is not something we were prone to do. Case in point: we are unwilling to talk with Iran about helping us reduce the terrorism in Iraq before that country agrees to the United Nations inspecting their nuclear facility. Since they're unwilling to allow inspections to occur, we assume they have something to hide. That may or may not be so. Even if it is true, it's still worthwhile to initiate talks. If we're going to assume the role of the leader of the free world, we'd better put our best foot forward and assume the role of a benign and benevolent manager, rather than an adversarial protagonist.

I know you may say, "Well, in the year 2007, we are now beginning to change our thinking and show a greater willingness to come to the table and discuss mutual issues and concerns with Syria and Iran, the likes of which has not happened in years past."

That's all well and good, but the point of this book is to help us avoid having to drag our government to the negotiating table kicking and screaming, or to look at diplomacy as a policy of last resort. This should be standard operating procedure when dealing with all nations, hostile or friendly alike.

Most Muslims are not radical terrorists. We must also remember that there are many Muslim dictators and rulers who do not subscribe to the terrorist's belief system and the radical Islamic interpretation of the Koran.

The recent choices our government has made have caused significant damage in all manner of issues related to human relationships, both domestic and international. We can, however, now choose to use our tools of talent, influence, and wisdom, along with our precariously held position as preeminent power, to repair the damage we have wrought—and in so doing, restore our national integrity.

This must be an All-American effort at the voting booth, in our halls of government, at our workplaces, and in our places of worship. We—yes, we the people—have allowed our national identity to be hijacked by a narrow ideology brought to power by masterful political maneuvering. When it is exposed for what it is, a sizeable portion of our people do not find this ideology to be representative of them.

As in any problem-solving strategy, the first step is to recognize that there is indeed a problem. The next step is to develop a plan. As concerned and responsible Americans, you need to demand that your representatives at all levels of government represent your interests and values. Your toolbox includes letters, e-mails, phone calls, and that big old sledgehammer known as contributions. You also need to stay informed by using the library, reading newspapers and magazines, and keeping up with the news on radio and television.

Americans are victims of our own complacency; corporations, special-interest groups, and cagey politicians have outpaced us in the political arena. We have become, as they say, "fat, dumb, and happy." Let's make the commitment to get off our duff and do our part to restore our system to a truly representative government, where all the people are represented. The rest will take care of itself.

Many people in this great country, as well as those around the world, realize that we need the will and support of each other if we are to survive in this war on terrorism. This includes not only our allies, but the peace-loving Islamic community as well—a tall order, considering the direction this country has been going since George W. Bush became president of the United States.

Our ship of state must turn around and return home. We must stop meddling in other countries' internal affairs. We must change our nation's priorities. We must stop trying to establish democracy in Islamic countries. We must start responding to the needs and concerns of all Americans, not just the special-interest groups and political base of whatever party is currently in power. We must reunite our divided states of America, so that we can all say how very blessed we are to be Americans.

If you want to turn the ship of state around, you have to strip it down from the huge supertanker it is today to a fast speedboat. As it is today, it is not capable of altering course quickly and easily, and in today's global economy, the ability to do that is paramount. Any country, and any corporation, that is unable to adapt and shift with ever-changing world situations is doomed to wither and die.

In Lincoln's day, news took time to arrive and allowed leaders time to formulate how to react to situations. Today, decisions must be made immediately, often with little solid intelligence. There is no time to ponder how to react, and we need leaders who carry with them in their heads enough knowledge of history and of the world that they can make almost instant decisions that will protect us all.

As has been true in the past, and will continue to be true in the future, there are individuals who have the character of Lincoln who are capable of leading us through an uncertain future in good order.

In order to find a president that reflects the principles and beliefs of our nation as Lincoln did, we must view our voting obligation in a new light. Instead of accepting politics as usual, we must expect politicians to tell us how things really are, rather than what they think we want to hear. When we as voters communicate through our actions and questions that we are looking for candidates who will level with us, even when it means telling us things that we don't necessarily agree with or want to hear, then politicians will be encouraged to communicate what we value, which is honesty and candor in a campaign. We must make it clear that we value straight talk, not a candidate who parses and schemes in order to get votes.

It's time for all of us to accept our responsibility as Americans. We must strive for a sense of community. We must foster integrity, humility, and critical thinking, both in ourselves and in our elected officials. We must reach out to other countries and cultures with open minds. We must focus on electing the right leaders, discussing the right issues, and acting for the right reasons.

If we do all of that, perhaps our giant will become both powerful and peaceful once again. If we do all of that, we will be able to again say, "I'm proud to be an American."

INDEX

A

accountability, 108, 158, 164–65, 181, 230–32. *See also* integrity
acting, 213
action
  by citizens, needed, 53–54, 189–90, 192, 194–95, 199–214
  lack of, 223–25
  by president, needed, 191, 207–8, 209, 212
Adams, John, 160
adaptability, 237
ADHD, 34–39, 57, 70
adversarial thinking, 118, 156–57
advisors, to president, 125–26, 174–75
affect, 210–11
Afghanistan, 45
African Americans, 14, 129–30
Al Qaeda, 16, 49
All the Best, George Bush (Bush, G.H.W.), 66
alternative energy, 223–25
ambassadorship, 225–26
Ambling Into History (Bruni), 36
"America Is Acting Mighty Arrogant" (Lyke, D.), 109
"America, the Beautiful" (song), 75–76
American flag, 85–87
"Animal House Summit" (Dowd), 36–37
anxiety, 99–100, 114
appearance, physical, 169, 171
appointees
  of Bush, 58–60, 71, 125–26
  generally, 228
  of Lincoln, 61
approval ratings
  of Bush, 49, 58, 121, 168
  of Congress, 49, 168
  as sign of divisiveness, xxiii
aristocracy, artificial, 67
Aristotle, 119

armed forces. *See* troops
arms race, 25–27
arrogance, 2–4, 53–54. *See also* self-interest
Articles of Confederation, 221–22
Aslam, Abid, 187
The Assassins' Gate (Packer), 59
Attention Deficit Hyperactivity Disorder (ADHD), 34–39, 57, 70
authority, respect for, 157–59

B

balance of power. *See* checks and balances
basic services, costs of, 12
bias, 115–16, 129–30, 191–93, 200–202. *See also* discrimination
The Bible, 200–202
Big Eight Economic Summit, 36–37
Bill of Rights, 180
Bin Laden, Osama, 16, 64, 168
Blair, Tony, 37
Borge, Victor, 192
Boston Tea Party, 184–85
Bradley, Omar N., 73
bridge to nowhere, 23–24
British East India Tea Company, 184–85
Brokaw, Tom, xviii
Brooks, David, 46–47
Bruni, Frank, 36
budgets. *See* government spending
Bureau of International Information, 164
burning, of American flag, 86–87
Bush, George H. W., 62, 63–64, 66–68
Bush, George W., 31–41, 43–54
  ADHD and, 34–39, 57, 70
  advisors, 125–26
  appointees, 58–60, 71, 125–26
  approval ratings, 49, 58, 121, 168
  behavior, 36–37, 90–91, 211

character, 10–11, 175, 229
and Cheney, 157
cognitive abilities, 65–66
communication skills, 31–35,
  37–40, 134
confidence, lack of, 62
as divider, 172
and G.H.W. Bush, 66–67
inaction of, 217–18
and Iraq war, 8–10, 45, 55, 210
and Lincoln, compared, 174,
  175–76
and 9/11, 43–44
privelege, effects of, 71
public opinion and, 122, 124–26
quoted, 73, 80
religion and, 62–65
and terrorism, 44–45

C
CAGW, 24
"A Call for Leadership", 96–97
campaign contributions, 94
capitalism, 27–29, 197–99, 226–28. *See
  also* corporations
Carter, Jimmy, 204–6
Central Intelligence Agency (CIA), 59
CEO salaries, 187–89
change
  recommendations for, 53–54, 189–
    90, 192, 194–95, 199–214
  voter pressure for, 158, 237
Chase, Salmon P., 148, 159–60
checks and balances, 45–46, 221,
  230–31
Cheney, Richard, 71, 157
China, 130–33, 168
church and state, separation of, 60–61,
  62–65, 202–3
citizens. *See also* civic duty; patriotism
  accountability and, 230
  basic rights, 191
  dialog among, 64
  empathy and, 211–14
  and government spending, 11–12

influence of, 8–9, 20
integrity, 97, 208–10
leadership qualities of, 226–28
mistakes, learning from, 14–15, 68,
  69
priorities, 12–14
qualities desired, 169
representation of, 9–11
responsibilities, 51, 53–54, 164–65,
  199–214
sacrifice by, xviii, 79–81
wealth and, 196–98
Citizens Against Government Waste
  (CAGW), 24
civic duty, 75–83, 93–103. *See also*
  citizens; common good; patriotism
  materialism, avoiding, 77–78
  need for, 170, 221–23, 236–38
  patriotism and, 78–83
  terrorism and, 97–101, 176–77
  voting as, 13–14, 51, 65, 126,
    154–55
  wealth and, 196
civil servants, 66–71
Civil War
  corporations and, 185
  deaths from, 83
  Lincoln and, 13, 147–48, 172–76,
    182, 210–11
class, 117–18
Clinton, William Jefferson, 68, 88–89
"Closing of a Nation" (Brooks), 46–47
coaching metaphor, 156–57
cognitive abilities. *See also*
  introspection; psychology
  ADHD and, 34–39, 57, 70
  critical thinking, 112, 202–3, 233,
    236–37
  passion and, 119
  skepticism, 110, 158
cognitive dissonance, 114
common good. *See also* civic duty
  communication and, 100–101
  humanism and, 202–3
  vs. materialism, 225, 232–33

money and, 189–90, 196–98
as national priority, 218–21
patriotism and, 80
politicians and, 91, 170–71
religion and, 200–202
vs. self-interest, 76, 101, 164–65,
190–93, 196–98, 221–25, 228–29
and terrorism containment, 45
values and, 149–50
voting and, 154–55
communication. *See also* language
with adversaries, 52, 235–36
among citizens, 64, 99–102
in combating divisiveness, 192–93
dissenting opinions, 57–60, 61,
131–32
emotional intimacy and, 147–49
extremism in, 104–6
free speech, 86
listening, 134
negotiation, 134, 235–36
nonverbal, 37–40
by politicians, 8–10, 31–35, 237–38
speed of, 237
by voters, 236–38
compassion, 212–14
competitiveness, 118, 156–57
complacency, 236–37
compromise, 20, 221–25
Confederation, Articles of, 221–22
conflict resolution, 130–33
Congress, 49, 168, 217–18
conservative label, 113–15
Constitution, 180, 183–84, 221–23
consumerism. *See* materialism
Continental Congress, 221–22
contrary thinking, 114
coping mechanisms, 99–100
"Corporate Biggies Prove You Can't
Buy Happiness" (Lyke, D.), 108
corporations, 108–9, 183–89, 194–95.
See also capitalism
corruption, 164–65, 185, 228–29
costs. *See also* government spending
food, 12

health care, 12, 168, 194–95
Iraq war, 12, 24, 229
military, 52, 72, 167
pork-barrel projects, 2, 21–24, 117,
229
"Counting Votes While the Bombs
Drop" (Moore), 125–26
crime, terrorism as, 17
critical thinking, 112, 202–3, 233,
236–37
criticism, 73. *See also* dissent
Cuban missile crisis, 69, 174
culture, Islamic. *See also* Muslims
and democracy, 19–20, 46–51
extremism in, 17–18
foreign policy and, 28–30

D

debt, 194
deception, 40
Declaration of Independence, 149, 180
declaration of war, 126–27, 163–64,
173
defense mechanisms, 127–28
defense spending, 24–27, 52
DeMille, Nelson, 231–32
democracy
American promotion of, 2–4
capitalism and, 27, 184–89, 226–28
defined, 183
development of, 47
and Islamic culture, 19–20, 46–51
principles of, 164
responsibilities of, 14–15
Democrats
author as, 107
behavior vs. rhetoric, 117
labeling and, 112–15
and Republicans, compared, 117,
213
successful, examples of, 69
voter choice and, 199
denial, 217–18
dialog
with adversaries, 52, 235–36

among citizens, 64, 99–102
dictators, 55–57
diplomacy, 134, 235–36
diplomatic protocol, 37–38
disadvantaged citizens, 2, 12, 91,
94–95
discrimination, 14, 129–30, 192. *See
also* bias
disenfranchised groups. *See*
disadvantaged citizens
dissent
as civic duty, 13–14, 51
flag burning, 86–87
integrity and, 157–59
dissenting opinions, 57–60, 61, 131–32
divisiveness
in American history, 221–25
and approval ratings, xxiii
Bush and, 172
communication and, 192–93
income and, 188
partisanship, 167, 192, 199
terrorism and, 176–77, 190–93
domestic issues, as national priority,
237
Douglass, Frederick, 175
Dowd, Maureen, 36–37
duty. *See* civic duty

E
E Pluribus Unum, 72, 220
earnings, 187–89, 229
Edwards, John, 40
ego and egocentrism, 127–28. *See also*
self-interest
Eisenhower, Dwight D., 67–69, 72,
230–31
electability, 169
elections, xxiii. *See also* voting
electorate. *See* citizens; voters
Ellsworth, Elmer, 210
Emancipation Proclamation, 161, 175,
176
emotional intimacy, 147–49, 210–11
emotions, 99–100, 105, 114, 225–26.

See also love
empathy, 132, 143, 145, 147, 211–14
empowerment, xv
energy policy, 223
engagement, of citizens. *See* civic duty
England, 184
entitlement, sense of, 145
equality, 128–33, 168, 183–90
Equatorial Guinea, 56
Erikson, Erik, 162–63
ethics. *See* integrity
executive privilege, 229
expertise
vs. loyalty, 57–60
regarding Middle East, lacking,
50–51, 59, 232
extemporaneous speaking, 32–35
extremism, 103–19. *See also* ideology
and American leadership, 60–61, 64
author and, 106–11
vs. balance, 230–32
combating, 118–19
defined, 103–6
human tendencies toward, 111–15
Islamic, 17–18, 52–54
vs. moderation, 115–18
Exxon Mobile Corporation, 187–88

F
fear, 99–100, 105
Federal Emergency Management
Agency (FEMA), xxvi
feelings. *See* emotions
FEMA, xxvi
"Fight the Roots of Terrorism" (Niva),
15–20
"Fighting Terrorism" (Lieven), 50
finances, national. *See* government
spending
Fireside Chats, 81–82
First Amendment, 86
flag, American, 85–87
Flag Protection acts, 86–87
Foggo, Kyle "Dusty", 59
food, costs of, 12

foreign oil. *See* oil
foreign policy. *See also* Middle East
  of Bush administration, 134, 168
  capitalism and, 27–29
  models for, 130–33, 136
  9/11 and, 44
  oil and, 56
  and promotion of democracy, 2–4
France, 20
Franklin, Benjamin, 72, 221
free speech, 86
Freud, Anna, 162
Frey, Eric, 3
Friedman, Thomas L., 3, 58–59
Fromm, Eric, 133
fuel efficiency, 223
fundamentalism, 203–7

G

Gandhi, Mahatma, 134, 203–4, 215
Gardner, John W., 103
gas rationing, 81
G-8 Summit, 36–37
General Motors, 186
Germany, 20
Gestalt principle, 176–77
giving, 143
Goldwater, Barry, 104–5, 206–7
Goss, Porter, 59
government accountability, 164–65,
  181, 230–32
government power. *See also* politics
  checks and balances, 45–46, 221,
    230–31
  citizens and, 7–9
  local control, 110, 116
  war and, 235
government spending
  appropriateness of, 11–12
  as capitalism, 27–29
  military and defense, 24–27, 52, 72,
    167
  morals and, 30
  pork-barrel, 2, 21–24, 117, 229
Greatest Generation, xviii–xix

greed, 189–90
Gulliver's Travels (Swift), 7–8

H

habituation, 141
Hamilton, Lee, 18
handicapped citizens. *See* underserved
  citizens
happiness, pursuit of, 142–45, 145–47
Hayes, Rutherford, 185–86
health care, 12, 168, 194–95
Hendrix, Jimi, 135
Herndon, William, 32
Herper, Matthew, 140–41
history
  lessons of, 14–15, 72–73
  sense of, 174, 176
honesty, 127–28, 160–62
Hugo, Victor, 146
humanism, 202–3
humility, 135, 145
humor, 32, 35
Hurricane Katrina, xxiii, xxvi, 95
Hussein, Saddam, 55
Huxley, Aldous, 119

I

icons
  flag, 85–87
  presidency, 88–91
ideals
  personal, 153–56
  of presidential behavior, 90–91
identity, 181–85, 196
ideology, 64, 132–33, 203–7. *See also*
  extremism
ImClone, 108
immigration, 168
impotent giant analogy, 1–5
income disparity, 187–89
independent thought, 23, 109–10
inequality, 128–33, 168, 183–90
influence, 72, 218
insurance industry, 194–95

insurgents. *See* terrorists
integrity, 151–65. *See also*
  accountability
    change and, 158
    of citizens, 97
    defense mechanisms and, 127–28
    vs. despair, 162–63
    as leadership quality, 67–71
    of Lincoln, 182
    loss of, xviii
    national, 163–64, 234
    of Nixon, 160–62
    personal, 108–9, 153–56, 208–10
    of politicians, 151–53, 154, 159–60
    power and, 228
    psychology of, 159–60, 162–63
    rebellion and, 157–59
    values and, 153
intelligence. *See* cognitive abilities;
  introspection
international relations. *See* foreign
  policy
intimacy. *See* emotional intimacy
intolerance
  for ambiguity, 134
  in social relationships, 46, 48, 118–
    19, 203–8, 231–32
intrinsic factors, 146
introspection
  by citizens, 146, 158, 213–14
  by politicians, xvii, 65–66, 175, 182
Iran, 26, 235–36
Iraq, 46–51, 225–26. *See also* Iraq war
Iraq Study Group, 18
Iraq war
  Bush and, 8–10, 45, 55, 210
  civic duty and, xviii, 79–81
  as civil war, 48, 121
  communication regarding, 8–10
  costs, 12, 24, 229
  deaths from, 121, 168
  declaration of, 126–27
  9/11 and, 173–76
  public opinion and, 124
  reasons for, 15–20, 30

significance of, 217, 234
  and terrorism, 98–99
  win at all cost mentality, 156–57
Islamic culture. *See also* Muslims
  and democracy, 19–20, 46–51
  extremism in, 17–18
  foreign policy and, 28–30
Israel, 18

J

Japan, 163–64
Jefferson, Thomas, 62, 67
Johnson, Christine, 96–97
Johnson, Lyndon Baines, 89, 103,
  104–6, 157

K

Katrina, Hurricane, xxiii, xxvi, 95
Kennedy, John F., 67–68, 69, 101, 174
Kennedy, Robert, 174
Kerry, John, 126
Khan, Adam, 128
King, Martin Luther, 96
Korean conflict, 68

L

labeling, 104, 111–13, 116
land, 185
language. *See also* communication
  bias in, 116
  extremism and, 104
  labeling and, 111–13
  vs. rhetoric, 40, 104, 117, 152, 154,
    192, 237–38
  unconscious, 64, 67, 71
leadership qualities, 55–73
  of Bush, 122
  and church/state separation, 62–65
  cognitive abilities and, 65–66
  in combating terrorism, 51–54
  confidence, 61–62
  consistency, 55–57
  discipline, 71–72
  diversity, fostering, 61

guidance, attention to, 72–73
honesty, 160–62
integrity, 67–71
lack of, 176–77
of Lincoln, 144, 152
moderation, 60–61
national interests, dedication to,
66–67
needed, 96–97, 167–77, 216–25
negotiation, 136
patriotism, 81–82
presidential behavior and, 90–91
role models and, 115
team mentality and, 57–60
of voters, 226–28, 236–38
legislation, stalled, 223–25
LeMay, Curtis, 69
liberal label, 113–15
Lieven, Anatol, 50
Lilliputians, citizens as, 7–8
Limbaugh, Rush, 115
Lincoln, Abraham
advisors of, 174–75
appointees of, 61
and Bush, compared, 174, 175–76
character, xvii, 147, 161, 181–82,
210, 212
and Civil War, 13, 147–48, 172–76,
182, 210–11
communication skills, 31–32, 39–40
and Declaration of Independence,
149–50
and dissenting opinions, 87
integrity, 127–28, 209
leadership qualities, 61–62, 144,
168–69
as modern president, 167–77
morals of, 204
presidential qualities, 133–34,
146–47
priorities of, 83
and public opinion, 121, 123–24
quoted, 173, 185, 209
as storyteller, 148–49
as unifier, 170

Lincoln on Leadership (Phillips), 31–32,
144, 146–47, 152
listening, 134
local control, 110, 116
Loewenstein, George, 141
Lombardi, Vince, 156
losing, 156–57
love, 128–33, 133–34, 146, 149–50
loyalty, vs. expertise, 57–60
Lyke, Doug, 107–11
Lyke, H. John
background of, 129–30
on extremism, 106–11
on religion, 207–8
Lyke, Ned, 111

M
Madison, James, 26–27
Manhattan Project, 224
Marfan syndrome, 169
"Martha Stewart Should Speak Up"
(Lyke, D.), 108
materialism
combating, 189
vs. common good, 77–78, 225,
232–33
corporate power and, 183–90
happiness and, 143–44
and values, 140–42
McCain, John, 49, 22
media
extremism and, 104
labeling and, 113–15
press conferences, 125
talk-shows, 104, 192
medical care, 12, 168, 194–95
medications, 194–95
Merkel, Angela, 37–38
Merry, Robert W., 19–20, 28–29, 217
middle class, 168
Middle East
democracy in, 19
expertise regarding, lacking, 50–51,
59, 232
Islamic culture, 17–18, 19–20,

28–30, 46–51
stability in, 18
Wild Fire plan in, 231–32
military. *See also* Iraq war; security; troops
draft, 79
spending, 52, 72, 167
mistakes, learning from, 14–15, 68, 69, 72–73
moderate label, 113–15
moderation, vs. extremism, 115–18
money. *See also* capitalism; materialism
and common good, 189–90, 196–98
and values, 140–42, 143–44
"Money Won't Buy You Happiness" (Herper), 140–41
Moore, James C., 125–26
morals
corporate behavior and, 108–9
fundamentalism and, 203–7
government spending and, 30
presidential, 88–89, 204
Muslims. *See also* Islamic culture
attitudes toward, 231–32
extremist, 52–54
moderate, 51, 53
vs. terrorists, 16, 236

N

narcissism. *See* self-interest
nation building, 47
national priorities, 179–98
citizen feedback on, 13–14, 23–24
common good as, 14–15, 190–93, 218–20
corporate power and, 183–89
domestic issues, 237
health care, 194–95
integrity, 234
leadership and, 66–67, 167–68
vs. local control, 110, 116
materialism, combating, 189
peripheral issues to, 179, 219, 237
success, defining, 195–96

taxes, 193–94
terrorism, 12, 15–20, 176–77
negotiation, 134, 235–36
9/11. *See also* terrorism
Commission, 43–44
effects of, 197–98, 234
and Iraq war, 15–20, 173–76
and patriotism, 78–83
response to, 43–44
Niva, Steven, 15–20
Nixon, Richard, 68, 88–89, 140, 160–62
nonverbal communication, 37–40
North Korea, 26, 168
nuclear war, 69
nuclear weapons. *See* weapons of mass destruction

O

Obama, Barack, 211
Obiang Nguema, Teodoro, 56
oil
capitalism and, 27
foreign policy and, 56
policy-making and, 223–25
refineries, 223–24
war and, 19
open-mindedness. *See* tolerance
other-centeredness. *See* common good
Our Endangered Values (Carter), 204–6

P

Packer, George, 59
Palestine, 18
parenting, 66–67, 70–71, 111, 145–47
partisanship, 167, 192, 199, 225–26.
See also Democrats; party affiliation; Republicans
party affiliation, 110, 112–15, 117–18
passion, vs. reason, 119
patriotism, 78–83, 87, 129–30. *See also* civic duty
peace
conditions for, xvii, 18–19, 232

personal, 146
  quotes regarding, 72, 73, 135
  relationship therapy and, 131
peripheral issues, 179, 219, 237
personal liberties, 180
personality traits, 145, 159–60. *See also*
  cognitive abilities; psychology
Phillips, Donald II, 31–32, 144, 146–
  47, 152
pleasure principle, 222
polarization, 96
political appointees
  of Bush, 58–60, 71, 125–26
  generally, 228
  of Lincoln, 61
political funding, 2, 94
politicians
  character of, 151–53, 211–14
  common good and, 170–71
  communication by, 8–10, 31–35,
    237–38
  emotional intimacy and, 210–11
  funding of, 94
  inaction of, 218
  priorities, misplaced, 94–95
  responsibilities of, 221–23
  as role models, 181
  self-interest of, xv–xvi
  vs. statesmen, xiv, 227–28
politics. *See also* government power;
  presidents
  extremism in, 103–19
  influences on, 218
  integrity and, 228–29
  labeling in, 112–15
  and land, 185
  money and, 226–28
  and religion, 200–202
  straight talk in, 237–38
  superficiality in, 169, 171–72
poor citizens. *See* underserved citizens
pork-barrel spending, 2, 21–24, 117,
  229
"The Post-Post Cold War"
  (Friedman), 3

Powell, Colin, 9, 48
preemptive war, 17, 126–27, 173–74
prejudice, 115–16
presidency
  as icon, 88–91
  public opinion and, 121–37
  successful, examples of, 68–69
presidents, 167–77. *See also* leadership
  qualities; *individual names*
  behavior of, 36–37, 39–40, 191
  character traits, desirable, 88–91,
    147, 176–77
  as civil servants, 66–67
  leadership of, needed, 216–25
  mistakes, learning from, 72–73
  personal history, effects of, 67–68,
    70, 71
  responsibilities of, 66–67, 172
  and voter leadership, 226–28
press conferences, 125
prestige, 229
pride, national, 10–11, 129–30, 136,
  225–26
privilege
  effects of, 67, 71, 117, 189–90
  executive, 229
projection, 135
protest
  as civic duty, 13–14, 51
  flag burning, 86–87
  integrity and, 157–59
protocol, 37–38
Psychological Self-Help (Tucker-Ladd),
  141, 143
psychology. *See also* cognitive abilities
  developmental stages, psychosocial,
    162–63
  of identity, 181–85
  of integrity, 159–60, 162–63
  psychotherapy, 70, 101, 107
psychosocial stages of development,
  162–63
public, American. *See* citizens
public opinion, 121–37. *See also*
  approval ratings

Bush and, 122, 124–26
and declaration of war, 126–27
Lincoln and, 121, 123–24
negative, 134–37
physical appearance and, 169, 171
public speaking, 32–35
public virtue. *See* common good

Q
Al Qaeda, 16, 49
quick fixes, 233–34

R
racism, 129–30
Raymond, Lee, 187–88
Reagan, Ronald, 73, 89–90
reason, vs. passion, 119
rebellion, 157–59
refineries, 223–24
reflection. *See* introspection
Reich, Robert, 184
relationship therapy, 130–33
religion
    author on, 207–8
    bias and, 200–202
    Bush and, 62–65
    fundamentalism, 203–7
    Islamic culture, 17–18, 19–20,
        28–30, 46–51
    Muslims, 16, 51, 52–54, 231–32,
        236
    separation of church and state,
        60–61, 62–65, 202–3
    vs. spirituality, 203
Republicans
    author as, 107
    behavior vs. rhetoric, 117
    and Democrats, compared, 213
    labeling and, 112–15
    successful, examples of, 68–69
    voter choice and, 199
Revolutionary War, xiv, 8–9, 13, 78,
    184–85, 222
rhetoric

vs. action, 40, 152, 154
vs. straight talk, 237–38
of talk shows, 104, 192
Rice, Condoleezza, 56
role models, 111, 115, 181, 208
Rome, 224
Roosevelt, Franklin Delano
    character, 67–68
    on common good, 177
    communication skills, 40, 81–82
    policies, 8, 224
    public opinion and, 124
Roosevelt, Theodore, 73, 221
Rove, Karl, 119, 125–26
Rumsfeld, Donald, 71

S
sacrifice, 79–81
salaries
    of CEOs, 187–89
    of politicians, 229
Sands of Empire (Merry), 19–20,
    28–29, 217
"Saying No to Bush's Yes Men"
    (Friedman), 58–59
scandals, 154–55
Scowcroft, Brent, 62
seal, of United States, 220
Second World War. *See* World War II
security, 25, 26, 44–45. *See also*
    terrorism
selective avoidance, 114
selective perception, 115
self-aggrandizement. *See* self-interest
self-examination. *See* introspection
Self-Help Stuff That Works (Khan), 128
self-interest
    vs. common good, 76, 164–65, 190–
        93, 196–98, 221–25, 228–29
    of corporations, 183–89
    moving beyond, 101–2, 143–44,
        149–50, 164–65
    national, 2–4, 27, 45
    personal, xv, 77–78, 80
    pleasure principle and, 222

of politicians, 218–20
presidency and, 209–10
values and, 145
September 11 attacks. *See also*
  terrorism
  Commission on, 43–44
  effects of, 197–98, 234
  and Iraq war, 15–20, 173–76
  and patriotism, 78–83
  response to, 43–44
sexual misconduct, 88
shame, 225–26
skepticism, 110, 158
slavery, 14, 130, 159–60, 182
Snow, Tony, 122
Social Security, 168
soldiers. *See* troops
sovereignty, 9
spirituality, vs. religion, 203
Stanton, Edwin McMasters, 148
state, and church, separation of, 60–61,
  62–65, 202–3
state control, 110
statesmen, vs. politicians, xiv, 227–28
stereotypes. *See* bias
Stewart, Martha, 108
story telling, 32, 148–49
straight talk, vs. rhetoric, 237–38
Sullivan, Harry Stack, 191, 195
summits
  of G-8 nations, 36–37
  regarding terrorism, needed, 53
superficiality, 169, 171–72
Supreme Court, actions of, 86–87
surge, troop, 48–49
symbols
  flag, 85–87
  presidency, 88–91
Syria, 236

T

talk-shows, 104, 192
tax cuts, 11
taxes, 81, 184–85, 193–94
Tea Party, Boston, 184–85

teamwork, 57–60
tennis players, 156
term limits, 218–19
terrorism. *See also* 9/11
  as call to civic duty, 79–81, 176–77
  combating, 232
  and common good, 190–91, 219–
    20, 225
  containment vs. defeat of, 44–45,
    53, 54, 97–98, 232–33
  as crime, 17
  extremism and, 17–18
  Iraq war and, 98–99, 225–26
  labeling and, 116
  and national priorities, 12–14,
    95–101
  negotiation and, 135–37
  preparedness for, 93
  response to, 15–20, 176–77
  security and, 25, 26, 44–45
  strategies against, 50–54, 83,
    118–19
  unity and, xvi–xvii
terrorists, vs. Muslims, 16
theocracy, 19
tolerance. *See also* extremism
  for ambiguity, 134
  in social relationships, 46, 48, 118–
    19, 203–7, 207–8, 231–32
troops. *See also* military
  in Civil War, 83
  in Iraq, 48–49, 225–26
  in Revolutionary war, xiv, 222
  sacrifices of, 79
  in Vietnam, 157
  in WWII, 8
Truman, Harry S., 67–68, 172
trust, 9
Tucker-Ladd, Clayton E., 141, 143
two-party system, 222–25. *See also*
  partisanship

U

unconscious
  actions, 64, 67, 71

mind, 101
underserved citizens, 2, 12, 91, 94–95
unity. *See also* common good
    civic duty and, 79
    vs. divisiveness, 96, 172
    as national priority, 170–72, 182,
      190–93, 219–22
    terrorism and, xvi–xvii, 233
U.S. Department of State Bureau of
    International Information, 164
"U.S.: Pay Gap Widens Between
    CEOs and Workers" (Aslam), 187

V
values, 139–50
    emotional intimacy, 147–49
    happiness, pursuit of, 142–45
    and integrity, 153
    love and, 149–50
    money and, 140–42
    9/11 and, 198
    parenting and, 145–47
    religious, 200–202
Vietnam War, 86, 157
vigilance, 80
"A Visit to the Bridge to Nowhere"
    (Wallechinsky), 23–24
volunteerism, 149–50
voters, qualities desired, 162, 213–14.
    See also citizens
voting
    as civic duty, 51, 65, 126, 154–55
    power of, 199–214, 236–38
    religion and, 208

W
Waite, Richard R., 107
Wallechinsky, David, 23–24
war. *See also individual wars*
    alternatives to, 19–20
    causes of, 13
    vs. crime, 17
    declarations of, 126–27, 163–64,
      173

    nuclear, 69
    oil and, 19
    power and, 235
    preemptive, 17, 126–27, 173–74
    quotes regarding, 26–27, 72–73
    unjustified, xviii
Washington, George, 67–68, 223
Washington Post, 56
waste, in government spending, 2,
    21–24, 117, 229
Watergate, 88
wealth
    and inequality, 183–90
    power of, 196–98
weapons of mass destruction, 14–15,
    19, 25, 52, 69, 235
Webster, Daniel, 222
whole, and parts, 176–77
Wild Fire, 231–32
Wild Fire (DeMille), 231–32
Williams, Serena, 156
Williams, Venus, 156
Wilson, Charles Erwin, 186
"With Friends Like These"
    (*Washington Post* editorial staff), 56
women
    and integrity, 109
    in workplace, 79
"Women Know When It's Moral to
    Buck the Team" (Lyke, D.), 109
word salads, 33–35
World Values Study, 46
World War II
    civic duty and, xiv, xviii, 78–79,
      80–82, 224
    declaration of, 163–64
    lessons from, 163–64
    public opinion and, 124
    support for, 8–9